DAVID STEPHEN CALONNE

William Saroyan

MY REAL WORK IS BEING

FOREWORD BY DICKRAN KOUYMJIAN

THE UNIVERSITY OF NORTH CAROLINA PRESS

CHAPEL HILL AND LONDON

© 1983 The University of North Carolina Press
All rights reserved
Manufactured in the United States of America

Library of Congress Cataloging in Publication Data

Calonne, David Stephen, 1953–
William Saroyan, my real work is being.

Bibliography: p.
Includes index.
1. Saroyan, William, 1908–1981—Criticism and
interpretation. I. Title.
PS3537. A826Z6   1983   818'.5209   83-1184
ISBN 0-8078-1565-9

Photograph by Paul Kalinian, Fresno, California

For my parents,
Pierre and Mariam Calonne,
And for Gloria

CONTENTS

Foreword by Dickran Kouymjian
ix

Acknowledgments
xiii

Introduction
3

ONE
A Trapeze to God, or to Nothing
12

TWO
I Want to Live While I Am Alive
28

THREE
Exiled in America: The Armenian Quest
47

FOUR
The Child Is Father of the Man
58

FIVE
World and Theater
71

SIX
The Human Comedy
98

SEVEN
Allegories for the Stage
117

EIGHT
The Men of Your People Are Fathers
131

NINE
The Way of Memory
142

Notes
151

Bibliography
171

Index
179

Foreword

DICKRAN KOUYMJIAN

William Saroyan (31 August 1908–18 May 1981) has had less sustained critical attention than any other major American writer of the century. Why? Despite his early bravado and the conspicuous handlebar mustache of later years, he was a private man, "an introvert with the good sense to act like an extrovert." He was unpredictable both in punctuality and attitude when it came to interviews, as one of the leitmotivs of his autobiographical interlude, *Not Dying*, so humorously describes. He never encouraged a Saroyan cult. Artificial publicity was the kind of fraudulence he could not abide, hence his disdain for press agents, media personalities, producers, promoters, and the "gang" of parasites who were secondary to the actual creation of a work of art.

Saroyan's disinterest in media success probably explains in part his casual attitude even toward those who wished to promote him properly. He was not optimistic that critics would penetrate his meanings. For him the writing itself, together with his frequent explanations of it, should have been sufficient. Reviewers too often failed to understand both the formal structure of his works, especially the plays, and their wondrous nature. The introduction to his improvisatory play *Sam the Highest Jumper of Them All or the London Comedy* is characteristic of this state of affairs. It contains a "Letter to Fifteen Drama Critics," all of whom panned the premiere production in 1960: "I say Sam is a good play. I am sorry you say it isn't. One of us is obviously mistaken. Knowing the paltry little I know, I cannot believe it is me."

Paradoxically, given his attitude toward reviewers, Saroyan was careful to save, label, and order everything he wrote so that future

scholars and critics might redress the past's not always benign neglect. The last twenty years of Saroyan's life—the Paris-Fresno years
—reflect the ambiguity of the situation. He set out simultaneously
to organize his early life and papers; to reflect ever more deeply on
the past, while carefully documenting, at times by the hour, every
event of his present; and to continue to write every day. His success
in these areas was uneven. He was given the time neither to super-
vise the arranging of his archives nor to examine fully the making of
his own past. To the very end, though, more fully than we can now
imagine, he produced a constant, at times near compulsive, flow of
energized literature.

The quantity of unpublished material left by him surpasses the
massive bibliography of his already published works. Included are
scores of plays, numerous novels and memoirs, stories, poems, essays, thousands of letters, nearly fifty years of journals, diaries,
dream books, personal memoranda, and more than a thousand paintings and drawings. For convenience and inventory, these materials
are now gathered at the Bancroft Library in Berkeley. The half dozen
studies now in progress or in press, including this one, are based
perforce on the published works, the few unpublished manuscripts
in public and private collections, personal knowledge, and interviews with those who knew the man. Not until Saroyan's will is
probated will investigators have access to the unknown Saroyan.

David Calonne's *William Saroyan: My Real Work Is Being* is the
first study to present the entirety of known Saroyan as an integrated
whole. Calonne's choice of title, part of a quotation from the last
published work, *Obituaries*, is indicative of his approach: a close
examination of the writing itself. There is little speculation in the
volume. No theories to be tested. No dubious psychological or
pseudo-psychoanalytic suppositions to improvise with. Grasping
the universal character of Saroyan's thought, Calonne has been able
to construct a sound and all-encompassing *apparatus criticus*, one
with which we can reexamine an artist who was more than just an
eccentric, "crazy" Armenian-American writer whose moment of
glory passed with the forties.

Personal details are only called up for broad strokes: a fatherless
California childhood, success on Broadway, marriage, family, and

divorce, semi-exile in Paris. Instead of dwelling on biographical details, Calonne searches for the inner coherence of every work, whether story, play, novel, or memoir. By revealing gradually the integrity and meaning of each, he fashions a general method for perceiving those ideas which inspired Saroyan and drove him to express that acquired wisdom in clear, usually humorous, and always poetical language.

In relating the author's style and temperament to those writers he was either influenced by—Whitman, Sherwood Anderson, Shaw—or had affinities with—Thomas Wolfe, Henry Miller, Samuel Beckett—Calonne provides the criterion by which Saroyan's place in twentieth-century literature can be judged. Clearly the poor critical reception (as opposed to warm audience acceptance) accorded many of Saroyan's theatrical works after the initial successes of *My Heart's in the Highlands* and *The Time of Your Life* (which won a Pulitzer Prize) was due primarily to the unrecognized avant-garde character of their themes and the method employed to stage them. Saroyan was among the first Americans to become comfortable with surrealism. And a decade before the works of Ionesco, Adamov, and Beckett, he was already writing powerful "absurd" plays. Later, Saroyan was to be closely attracted to Beckett and the theater of the absurd because his own techniques and dramatic vision, too sophisticated and complex for Broadway in the 1940s, became the substance of serious theater in the 1950s.

In spare, elegant prose, singularly free of excessive adulation or sentimentality, Calonne has given us a meditation on Saroyan firmly anchored in the works themselves. With this study, proper assessment of Saroyan's literary worth can be said to have begun. In time Calonne's analysis may be modified here or refocused there; for the moment it consistently rings true. The book's adroit and convincing philosophical framework should serve as a catalyst for new studies on particular facets of Saroyan's writing. Henceforth, it will be difficult to discuss Saroyan without reference to this work. Though earlier writers have considered many of the points Calonne insists upon, none has synthesized them into a coherent system.

How unfortunate that such a clear vision of Saroyan was not produced decades ago. How sad Saroyan couldn't have read it.

ACKNOWLEDGMENTS

Many people have helped me in the gestation of this work over the past four years. Jerome Bump first encouraged me to write a study of Saroyan and helped immeasurably at every step. Alan Friedman, Anthony Hilfer, Christopher Middleton, and David Wevill have all offered penetrating comments and ideas. Gloria Gannaway read and discussed these pages with me, offering wonderful insights from the beginning. Dickran Kouymjian read the manuscript for the University of North Carolina Press and has generously shared his massive knowledge of Saroyan as writer and man with me. My brother, Ariel Calonne, has always been a stimulating interlocutor, and we have had many happy philosophical talks. To my parents, Pierre and Mariam Calonne, and my late grandparents, Vagharshak and Flora Galoostian, I owe a deep debt of gratitude, because it is their enthusiasm and love for literature, for art, for music, for beauty, which made this book possible.

I also thank the staffs of the Fresno County Free Library, the library of California State University at Fresno, and the Humanities Research Center, Austin, Texas, for assisting me in my work. And, finally, to the used and rare-book shops of San Francisco, Fresno, and Austin—many thanks for your help in finding books for me.

WILLIAM SAROYAN

INTRODUCTION

William Saroyan's career began in 1934 with the publication of *The Daring Young Man on the Flying Trapeze*. From that time on, he wrote prolifically, producing a steady stream of short stories, plays, novels, memoirs, and essays. During the thirties and forties, Saroyan reached the peak of his fame; by the mid-fifties his reputation had declined substantially. Peter Collier has attributed this critical devaluation to the fact that "the generation of academic critics had now come to power who were overseeing the development of the kind of dense, cerebral literature which justified their profession."[1] Absent from Saroyan's work were the rich symbolic and ironic textures so highly prized by the New Critics. He was not an allusive, learned writer in the manner of T. S. Eliot; he was not interested in exploring the intricate psychological labyrinths that Henry James was so fond of; he was not a brilliant, medieval, mystic scholastic with a passion for complexity like James Joyce. Furthermore, Saroyan's often flippant and antiacademic tone was not calculated to endear him to the professors.

Another complaint commonly voiced by critics was Saroyan's tendency toward "escapism." For example, Philip Rahv found Saroyan's role as lover of mankind irritating; he wrote that in *The Human Comedy* Saroyan insisted "evil is unreal," although the world is obviously mired in pain and tragedy.[2] Linked to this charge of escapism was the fact that Saroyan was not fashionably political; he supported no "ism" and was therefore accused of lacking a social conscience. This attitude put him out of favor with the proletarian writers of the thirties, who were anxious to enlist him in their cause. Yet Saroyan would take no political stand other than that affirming the brotherhood of man; he recognized no authorities, no leaders, no programs to save the world.[3] For Saroyan, no political plan of action could be successful, for the revolution had to take place within the human heart.

Many critics, then, have often dismissed Saroyan for not being what they wanted him to be, rather than consider his virtues and faults on the writer's own terms. Of these views, perhaps the most outrageous is the charge that he was a simple-minded, sentimental romantic whose naive optimism did not reflect the terrible realities of the age. Saroyan's affirmations are not unearned; his bridge of faith is carefully and consciously built over a turbulent ocean of doubt and despair. The angst of the twentieth century pervades his work; we can see his brooding depression not only in the later work but in an early play, *The Time of Your Life*. Saroyan's lonely and pathetic characters sense the oncoming fury of World War II, and the knowledge that life is poised precariously at the rim of disaster haunts their dialogue. This darker, despairing, existential side of Saroyan's work has been almost completely ignored by commentators.

The alienation and melancholy that characterize much of Saroyan's work are, of course, typical of twentieth-century literature. Yet Saroyan is a special case, for the feeling of rootlessness which pervades his imagination finds an important source in the historical reality of the Armenian people. In 1896, twelve years before Saroyan's birth, 200,000 Armenians were massacred by the Turks. In 1915, the Turks deported the Armenian population of 2,500,000 to Syria and Mesopotamia; more than a million and a half Armenians were killed during this process.[4]

This suffering was not a new experience for the Armenians, however; their history is a nightmare of bloodshed and oppression. At one time or another during its long history, Armenia was ruled by Arabs, Mongols, Persians, and, most recently, Turks. The Ottoman Empire conquered most of Armenia during the sixteenth century, and Turkish nationalism and realpolitik finally culminated in the genocide of 1915. The Armenian diaspora began in earnest; of those who escaped deportation, many fled to Russia and to the United States.

Armenak and Takoohi Saroyan were among the thousands who

came to America during the first wave of the massacres. Their fourth child, William, was born in 1908 in Fresno, California. William was the only American Saroyan; his two sisters were born in Bitlis, and his brother in Erzeroum, Armenia.

In California's San Joaquin Valley, Saroyan's parents found a region similar to their native land. The San Joaquin was the land of the grape; the fertile earth was covered with vineyards, producing an abundant supply of wine and raisins. There were apricots, figs, pomegranates, persimmons, lemons, grapefruits, oranges, peaches, walnut trees, and olive groves. Here the Armenians prepared all the foods they had known in their homeland: rice pilaf, *dolma* (grape leaves filled with rice and meat), the omnipresent *madzoun* (yoghurt), and shish kebab.

The winters were mild and the summers very hot. Here the dark-skinned, dark-haired Armenians spoke the musical language of their homeland. They remained faithful to ancient traditions: to their lovely, melismatic music, to folk dancing, to the Armenian Apostolic church. Although Armenians would establish communities in other parts of America, California attracted the greatest number because it was the ideal region for a predominantly agricultural people.

In America, however, the problems of the Armenians were not yet over. Although California was idyllic and splendid, the racial conflicts that had driven the Armenians to their newfound land continued. In the autobiographical *Here Comes, There Goes, You Know Who*, Saroyan remarked: "The Armenians were considered inferior, they were pushed around, they were hated, and I was an Armenian. I refused to forget it then, and I refuse to forget it now, but not because being an Armenian had, or has, any particular significance."[5]

Here Saroyan typically discounts the importance of race, yet the fact remains that the Armenians were not really absorbed into the fabric of American life. They remained alienated, often yearning to return to their native land. They were isolated within their own communities, out of step with mainstream American culture. It is no accident, then, that Saroyan's work conveys a powerful sense of not being at home in the world.

If the Armenian people were symbolically homeless in their

American exile, Saroyan himself, after the age of three, was literally homeless. The death of his father in 1911 surely contributed to his lifelong obsession with death and estrangement. Saroyan's mother was forced to place him in an Oakland orphanage, and it is evident from his autobiographical writings that his childhood was often profoundly unhappy. Midway through his career, Saroyan wondered: "Well, first of all, just where was my home? Was it in Fresno, where I was born? Was it in San José, where my father died? Was it in Oakland, where I spent four very important years? . . . Home was in myself, and I wasn't there, that's all. I was far from home."[6]

This deep sense of self-division was with him from the beginning. It was the poverty (in every sense of the word) of his early life which drove him to art, to literature, and to the quest for meaning: "I took to writing at an early age to escape from meaninglessness, uselessness, unimportance, insignificance, poverty, enslavement, ill health, despair, madness, and all manner of other unattractive, natural, and inevitable things. I have managed to conceal my madness fairly effectively."[7]

Saroyan returns obsessively throughout his career to this theme of "madness," to a consideration of the possible reasons for the intensity of his sorrow and psychic dislocation. He begins to reveal a kind of "race-melancholy" which underlies the Armenian temperament. In the late story "The Assyrian," he explores the dark side of his sensibility under the guise of an Assyrian hero, Paul Scott: "The longer he'd lived the more he'd become acquainted with the Assyrian side, the old side, the tired side, the impatient and wise side, the side he had never suspected existed in himself until he was thirteen and had begun to be a man."[8] Another foreign alter ego, the Arab in *The Time of Your Life*, repeats to himself: "No foundation. All the way down the line"—at once expressing the pain of the alien, the exile, and Saroyan's own sense of cosmic disorder and spiritual vacuity.[9] The "old side" of Saroyan's self is the old Armenian soul oppressed through the ages, wise with the wisdom of suffering, and tired from the long search for home.

Saroyan also identifies this madness with illness, which is "an event of the soul more than of the body." He tells us, "I have been more or less ill all my life," a statement remarkable for both its extremism and its honesty.[10] In *Days of Life and Death and Escape to the Moon*, a late memoir, he draws various aspects of his own self-analysis together in reexamining the past: "Most of the time illnesses of one sort or another came to me regularly, all the year around. I can't believe it is all from the sorrow in my nature, in my family, in my race, but I know some of it is."[11] Saroyan is thus aware that his psychology is a composite of his Armenian heritage, the effects of his family life, and some innate quality inherent in his own personality.

It should be clear from these comments that, for Saroyan, the world is not inhabitable as it is: it therefore must be remade through art. In *The Necessary Angel: Essays on Reality and the Imagination*, Wallace Stevens considers "the idea of nobility as a characteristic of the imagination." He concludes that nobility "is a violence from within that protects us from a violence without. It is the imagination pressing back against the pressure of reality. It seems, in the last analysis, to have something to do with our self-preservation; and that, no doubt, is why the expression of it, the sound of its words, helps us to live our lives."[12] Saroyan, like Stevens, is not at home in the world as it is; but he is very much at home in his own imaginative recreation of it in his work. There may not be "real" homes and families like the one depicted in Saroyan's play *The Beautiful People*, but that is beside the point. As Stevens points out, the artist must *create* nobility, must press back against the world's chaos to create a livable sphere of existence. The function of the artist is to resolve, through the imagination, the conflicts of his own life as well as the eternal oppositions of human existence.

For Saroyan, art is a way toward health, toward reconciliation, toward psychic regeneration. He once observed that he needed to write "because I hate to believe I'm sick or half-dead; because I want to get better; because writing is my therapy."[13] Deeply aware of the fragmentation and spiritual anarchy of life in the modern world, he exhibits a driving impulse toward joy, self-realization, and psychic integration. He has remarked that

> the imperative requirement of our time is to restore faith to the mass and integrity to the individual. The integration of man is

> still far from realized. In a single age this integration can be
> immeasurably improved, but it is impossible and useless to
> seek to imagine its full achievement. Integration will begin to
> occur when the individual is uninhibited, impersonal, simul-
> taneously natural and cultured, without hate, without fear, and
> rich in spiritual grace.[14]

Achieving this state of balance is by definition a continuing struggle, for the self is located in a world of ceaseless change, flux, and
instability. Yet for Saroyan, it is the quest for self-realization which
gives life its ultimate purpose and meaning.

Saroyan's work, then, records the attempt to integrate the divided
self. Affirmation and despair, comedy and tragedy, inner harmony
and inner fragmentation, order and chaos, art and "reality," home
and exile, life and death—all these polarities exist in a state of
dynamic tension; they represent what Saroyan has called the "gay
and melancholy flux" of experience. In his last work, *Obituaries*, he
wrote: "My work is writing, but my real work is being."[15] Thus his
work as an artist is the activity of writing; but his more profound
task as a human being is to live life fully. Art's function is simultaneously to expose the fragmentation of our experience and to reveal
the possibility of true "being." With Matthew Arnold, Saroyan believes the greatest triumph of life is making contact with our "only
true, deep-buried selves."[16]

This deep yearning for unity, for profound communion with soul
and universe, is a primary theme of American literature from Whitman and Thoreau to Jack Kerouac and Henry Miller. The celebratory
impulse in Saroyan's writing can be traced directly back to Whitman's singing of self in *Leaves of Grass*; his affirmation of the inner
journey finds its roots in Thoreau's transcendentalism. Saroyan
seeks the experience of being; he wants to go straight to the core of
things—energetically, immediately, passionately. He is, in Philip
Rahv's conception, a "redskin." Stephen Axelrod has pointed out
that Rahv believed

> American literature composes itself into a debate between
> "palefaces" and "redskins." The "palefaces" (Henry James, T. S.
> Eliot, and Allen Tate would belong to this party) produce a

patrician art which is intellectual, symbolic, cosmopolitan, disciplined, cultured. The "redskins" (Walt Whitman and William Carlos Williams would tend to belong here) produce a plebeian art which is emotional, naturalistic, nativist, energetic, in some sense *un*cultured. . . . All such formulations attest to a basic bifurcation in American literature between writers who experience primarily with the head and those who experience primarily with the blood.[17]

These remarks define exactly Saroyan's literary identity. He wants to feel the world directly, intuitively—like D. H. Lawrence, "with the blood." His emotional impulses are fundamentally rooted in the Romantic tradition: he affirms the possibilities of the self to achieve realization through the powers of love, imagination, and creativity.

Saroyan's work is thus a great deal more complex and multivalent than many commentators have acknowledged. His writing is a blend of the affirmative, mystical, and rambunctious qualities of the American romantic sensibility and the profound sadness which finds its matrix in the tragic history of the Armenian people. On the one hand, he is thoroughly American in his persistent expansiveness, verve, and spontaneity. His writing is autobiographical, the dominant mode employed by such representative American authors as Whitman, Thomas Wolfe, and Henry Miller. Yet he is also the Armenian with his heart in the highlands, grieving for his lost homeland, speaking for those lost in an alien culture. He praises and broods, moves outward toward the world in extrovert fashion and holds closely inward to himself the loneliness of the poet.

Precisely this sense of man's essential aloneness links Saroyan's work directly to the main currents of modern philosophical thought and to the major modernist writers; he has acknowledged his deep love for the work of both Samuel Beckett and Eugene Ionesco.[18] One of the few observers to have discerned this important aspect of Saroyan's work is Edward Hoagland, who has pointed out that Saroyan is "brother at once to Thomas Mann and to the author of *Krapp's Last Tape*."[19] The existential strain in Saroyan has been noted by Thelma Shinn, who remarked that his work may be seen as the record of the search for meaning within the self.[20] Shinn's article is important, for it begins to explore Saroyan's existentialism and romanticism as complementary aspects of the quest for true being. The difficulty of this search has also been emphasized by William Fisher, who argued that in mid-career Saroyan's "novels and plays became strange battlegrounds where belief struggled with skepticism."[21] These articles are among the few which have been devoted to a serious consideration of Saroyan's place in modern literature. Hence, among major American authors, his writing has not yet received the responsible critical attention it merits.

Saroyan himself was fully aware early in his career that he was being unjustly neglected, as is apparent from his reaction to the critical reception of the plays.

> As it happened first with my short stories, my plays appeared so suddenly and continued to come so swiftly that no one was quite prepared to fully meet and appreciate them, so that so far neither the short stories nor the plays have found critical understanding worthy of them. If the critics have failed, I have not. I have both written and criticized my plays, and so far the importance I have given them, as they have appeared, has been supported by theatrical history. If the critics have not yet agreed with me on the value of my work, it is still to be proved that I am not the writer I say I am. I shall some day startle those who now regard me as nothing more than a show-off, but I shall not startle myself.[22]

Unfortunately, this situation has changed little after forty years. When Saroyan was appreciated, it was often for the wrong reasons. Furthermore, what he has said here of his short stories and plays proved to be true of the novels and autobiographical writings as well.

Saroyan's central concern as an artist has been the unfolding of humanity's deepest spiritual aspirations; typically, his work focuses directly on the individual struggling to live life with grace and meaning. I propose specifically to explore in depth this search for authentic being as portrayed in works that reveal Saroyan's persistent thematic concerns. In short story, play, novel, and memoir we repeatedly find a cluster of themes which power his vision: the relation of art to reality, love and loneliness, the exile in search of home, the world of childhood and the family, and the autobiographical quest. The dramatic conflict in each of Saroyan's best works is the same: characters confront an essential chaos in the world (or within the self) which divides their being and impels them toward the search for identity. In his first play, *My Heart's in the Highlands*, the boy Johnny Alexander says at the end, "I'm not mentioning any names, Pa, but something's wrong somewhere."[23] Yet for Saroyan there is also something right somewhere, and it is this dialectical tension between despair and joy which gives his work its strength and lasting worth.

CHAPTER 1

A Trapeze to God, or to Nothing

Saroyan's prolific career can be divided into five phases. From 1934 to 1939 he wrote short stories; from 1939 to 1943 his energies were directed toward playwriting; the years 1943–51 saw the appearance of his first two novels (*The Human Comedy* and *The Adventures of Wesley Jackson*), as well as plays and short fiction; between 1951 and 1964 Saroyan published a series of novels dealing with marriage and the family; and finally, from 1964 until his death in 1981, Saroyan devoted himself primarily to the exploration of his past through a steady output of autobiographical writings.

It is through the short story genre, then, that Saroyan made his initial impact as a writer. During this first creative period, Saroyan published eight volumes: *The Daring Young Man on the Flying Trapeze and Other Stories* (1934), *Inhale and Exhale* (1936), *Three Times Three* (1936), *Little Children* (1937), *Love, Here Is My Hat* (1938), *The Trouble with Tigers* (1938), and *Peace, It's Wonderful* (1939); *My Name Is Aram*, a story-cycle, appeared in 1940.[1] Saroyan has estimated that during these years he wrote "five hundred short stories, or a mean average of one hundred per annum."[2] It is with this genre that Saroyan is most clearly associated in the minds of many readers.

These early collections project a wide variety of thematic concerns, yet they are united in their portrayal of an America *entre deux guerres*. Saroyan's first books powerfully reflect the painful realities of the Depression, which shook the United States in the thirties. The young writer without a job in "The Daring Young Man on the Flying

Trapeze" goes to be interviewed for a position and finds that "already there were two dozen young men in the place."[3] The story "International Harvester" from *Inhale and Exhale* also gives a bleak vision of impending economic collapse: "Shamefully to the depths fallen: America. In Wall Street they talk as if the end of this country is within sight."[4]

It has often been remarked that much of the success of Saroyan's early work was due to the fact that his readers saw their troubled lives vividly portrayed in them—these were stories of the times. Yet for all the agony depicted, there are also great hope and vigorously defiant good spirits. It might seem strange that this period of history could birth anything but despair. As Maxwell Geismar has remarked, though, "the depression of the 1930s, apparently so destructive and so despairing, was actually a time of regeneration" for the major writers of the period. Furthermore, "the American writer had gained moral stature, a sense of his own cultural connection, a series of new meanings and new values for his work."[5] The crisis these writers were experiencing was, of course, more than merely economic. A deep cultural schism had rocked Europe since Nietzsche's apocalyptic prophecies and affected such American writers as Henry Miller, whose *Tropic of Cancer* appeared in the same year as Saroyan's first book. In Miller we also see the joy of breaking through, the sweet agony of rebirth, the "rosy crucifixion" that accompanies all gains in "moral stature." At the abyss one can weep; yet to sing requires the same amount of exertion.

Saroyan's case as a writer was not unique. He was part of a whole new wave of American authors of the thirties who sought "new meanings and new values" and who differed markedly from the generation that preceded them. For the writers of the thirties, the anguish and poverty of America's depression years were not unknown experiences. Alfred Kazin has remarked that

the "new" writers looked as if they had been born to trouble—
as in fact they had been, for they were usually the products of
city streets, factories and farms. More than the age of the
ideologue, of the literary revolutionary and the "proletarian"

novelist, roles usually created within the Communist movement, the Thirties in literature were the age of the plebes—of
writers from the working class, the lower class, the immigrant
class, the non-literate class, from Western farms and mills—
those whose struggle was to survive. When you thought of the
typical writers of the Twenties, you thought of rebels from
"good" families—Dos Passos, Hemingway, Fitzgerald, Cummings, Wilson, Cowley. What was new about the writers of the
Thirties was not so much their angry militancy, which many
shared, as their background; writers now came from anywhere.[6]

This analysis fits Saroyan exactly. The son of immigrant Armenians
who spent his youth selling newspapers, working in a telegraph
office, pruning grapevines, and roaming the streets of Fresno, he had
been "born to trouble," to poverty, to an orphan's life. Like Steinbeck, Saroyan made literature out of the experience of being down
and out. Having known emptiness and deprivation in life, he sought
to create plenitude and health in his work.

It is precisely Saroyan's affirmative voice which appealed to readers in Depression America. He unabashedly set out to praise the
brotherhood of man during a catastrophic period of deep social and
spiritual anxiety. As the decade moved inexorably toward the horror
of World War II, Saroyan continued to speak out for the unity of
humanity: he was opposed only to those who affirmed nationalism
and separatism. In the dedication to *Peace, It's Wonderful*, he wrote
that the book is "against all men who, deliberately or unconsciously,
with guilt or in innocence, out of nobility or stupidity, with regret or
not with regret, are imposing death on the present world of helpless
human beings."[7] At the beginning of his career, Saroyan established
a defiant stance against all the forces of darkness which sought to
crush the freedom of the individual, to prevent the search for authentic selfhood.

The threat to the individual posed by rising worldwide militarism
and by the Depression's agony is reflected in Saroyan's first book,
The Daring Young Man on the Flying Trapeze.[8] These twenty-six
stories depict the quest for self-realization which would pervade his
entire work. Throughout the collection we observe characters in-

volved in the struggle for deeper awareness in a world which often stifles their true, inner selves. For many of Saroyan's characters, life is often a difficult balancing act in which the conflicting claims of a harsh outer reality and one's desire for inner wholeness must be reconciled.

Saroyan's choice of a trapeze artist as the defining symbol of this search for balance is thus powerfully suggestive. The "daring young man" of the title story is a twenty-two-year-old writer who is slowly dying of starvation. As he muses to himself, the philosophical implications of Saroyan's title become clear: *Through the air on the flying trapeze, his mind hummed. Amusing it was, astoundingly funny. A trapeze to God, or to nothing, a flying trapeze to some sort of eternity; he prayed objectively for strength to make the flight with grace"* (p. 21). Far from being a slight and merely entertaining song, "The Daring Young Man on the Flying Trapeze" suggests to the story's hero the perilous nature of humanity's search for meaning and the essential tenuousness of life itself. Here we also see Saroyan's familiar pairing of positive and negative: "a trapeze to God, or to nothing," the continual oscillation between faith and despair which occurs throughout his work. The young writer is indeed involved in a life-and-death struggle; in order to survive the difficulty of the times, he must become the ultimate trapeze artist— he must learn "to make the flight with grace."

This desire to fly, to achieve a sense of graceful balance, is apparent in the story's opening paragraph. The rush of a single, stream-of-consciousness, nonstop sentence conveys the complex simultaneity of the young writer's vision of the world.

> Horizontally wakeful amid universal widths, practising laughter and mirth, satire, the end of all, of Rome and yes of Babylon, clenched teeth, remembrance, much warmth volcanic, the streets of Paris, the plains of Jericho, much gliding as of reptile in abstraction, a gallery of watercolors, the sea and the fish with eyes, symphony, a table in the corner of the Eiffel Tower, jazz at the opera house, alarm clock and the tap-dancing of doom, conversation with a tree, the river Nile, Cadillac coupe to Kansas, the roar of Dostoyevsky, and the dark sun. (P. 17)

The effort here is to get as much of the feel of life into language as possible. This is Saroyan the poet, the lyric celebrator, the rhapsodist. He becomes in this passage a cataloger like Whitman, attempting to show the oneness of all things through multiplicity. We perceive all the disparate elements of the universe fused into wholeness; there is an integration, a simultaneity of places, objects, and beings which were formerly separated by space and time.

The influence of surrealism is also apparent in the juxtaposition and lamination of conventionally unrelated data: "jazz at the opera house, alarm clock and the tap-dancing of doom, conversation with a tree." Perhaps the delirium induced by hunger has contributed to the writer's ability to identify himself with the cosmos; he is everywhere at once and at once everything and feels reverence for the sanctity of each object perceived by his consciousness. He places each cluster of concepts "horizontally," side by side: the ancient world (Rome, Babylon) next to the contemporary (Paris, Cadillac coupe to Kansas); "high-brow" culture (symphony, Dostoyevsky) next to "low-brow" culture (jazz); affirmation (practicing laughter and mirth) next to despair (tap-dancing of doom). In so doing, the writer celebrates the amorphous shape of reality and revels in the dense, paradoxical texture of human experience: he absorbs the universe into himself and sends it out again as life-giving art.

Yet this lyrical evocation of the lovely particularity and connection of things, filtered through the imagination of a gifted artist, is balanced by troubling intrusions: "Karl Franz, black Titanic, Mr. Chaplin weeping, Stalin, Hitler, a multitude of Jews, tomorrow is Monday, no dancing in the streets" (p. 18). The writer enters the streets of San Francisco, finds a penny, thinks of the books he has yet to read, and in his hunger begins to sense the approach of death: "He accepted the thought of dying without pity for himself or for man, believing that he would at least sleep another night" (p. 21). He then goes to employment agencies and department stores where he is informed that there are no jobs to be had. At the YMCA he composes an "Application for Permission to Live," ironically registering his antipathy for a society which in its increasing lunacy has placed death above life. Owing to the fetid atmosphere of the place and his growing hunger, he begins to grow faint. Going to the library to read Proust, he again feels that life is slipping away and returns to his room.

Saroyan handles the death of the daring young man with great subtlety and restraint: "Then swiftly, neatly, with the grace of the young man on the trapeze, he was gone from his body. For an eternal moment he was all things at once: the bird, the fish, the rodent, the reptile, and man. An ocean of print undulated endlessly and darkly before him. The city burned. The herded crowd rioted. The earth circled away, and knowing that he did so, he turned his lost face to the empty sky and became dreamless, unalive, perfect" (p. 25). These last lines are carefully muted, and seem to embrace death as a friend. We see the language of the story's opening paragraph repeated, thus symbolizing a consummation, a coming together of the disparate fragments of life into a new unity. What begins as a poetic invocation of life's possibilities in its overwhelming abundance becomes at the end a kind of hymn to death.

Our understanding of the "graceful flight" the writer has been striving to make is also expanded as the trapeze-artist metaphor returns in a new context: the trapeze symbolizes the delicate transit from life into death, the essential unity of life and death. The last words, "dreamless, unalive, perfect," carefully avoid including "death," thus suggesting that the demise of the story's hero should not be taken with tragic solemnity. Rather, we are left at the end feeling that a necessary reconciliation has taken place, a completion, a kind of "perfection."

It is curious that this first story deals with the death of a young writer, for it is as though Saroyan exorcised here a part of his own personality, allowed a part of his self to die so that he might go on living as an artist. That there is a powerful link between the daring young man and the author himself is clear from the San Francisco setting, where Saroyan began his own career against great odds. The literary self-consciousness of the artist also reflects Saroyan's deep love for books and his effort to establish an original voice. There are references in the story to Dostoevsky, T. S. Eliot, de Maupassant, Twain, Shakespeare, and Flaubert.[9] Of course the story is meant as a portrait of a well-read dying author; however, literary name-dropping continues throughout the collection.

In "Seventy Thousand Assyrians," Anderson, Mencken, Hemingway, and Sinclair Lewis are among the writers mentioned. These are some of the figures any aspiring young American author would be most aware of during the thirties, and it becomes clear as the book progresses that the daring young writer is most often William Saroyan himself, striving to make a place for his own literary gifts among the famous of his generation.

The Daring Young Man on the Flying Trapeze is a book with an "I" on nearly every page, and it is evident from the preface to the first edition that Saroyan harbored few doubts concerning his talent or aesthetic principles. His brash flippancy can be seen in the remarks about the inhibiting power of tradition and the "rules" of story-writing on the beginning author: "Forget Edgar Allan Poe and O. Henry and write the kind of stories you feel like writing. Forget everybody who ever wrote anything" (p. 10). According to Saroyan, the weight of the past prevented spontaneity in new writers. In the original preface, he pointed out that "American expression has one basic defect. It lacks freedom. It doesn't move along easily. This first book was intended to introduce a little freedom into whatever future American expression might seek in the short story form. . . . Ease is what I wanted to introduce" (p. xiii). Saroyan's desire is to break into new paths of literary expression, to reject the stultifying strictures of tradition in favor of open and energetic forms.[10]

The need to deny tradition and influence is common among writers, particularly at the beginning of their careers. Yet Saroyan's first book was profoundly affected by the work of other writers, Sherwood Anderson's in particular.[11] Malcolm Cowley has written that Anderson was a "writer's writer, the only story teller of his generation who left his mark on the style and vision of the generation that followed. Hemingway, Faulkner, Wolfe, Steinbeck, Caldwell, Saroyan, Henry Miller . . . each of these owes an unmistakable debt to Anderson, and their names might stand for dozens of others."[12] Indeed, the "style and vision" of Anderson's *Winesburg, Ohio* are readily discernible in many of the stories of *The Daring Young Man on the Flying Trapeze.*

Anderson's famous story-cycle supplied Saroyan with a precedent for exploring the search for identity as well as a style which exhibited the very virtues of "ease and freedom" which he so highly valued. In the story "Sophistication," Anderson had described the painful struggle of George Willard into manhood in simple, clear sentences.

> George Willard, the Ohio Village boy, was fast growing into manhood and new thoughts had been coming into his mind. All that day, amid the jam of people at the Fair, he had gone about feeling lonely. He was about to leave Winesburg to go away to some city where he hoped to get work on a city newspaper and he felt grown up. The mood that had taken possession of him was a thing known to men and unknown to boys. He felt old and a little tired. Memories awoke in him. To his mind his new sense of maturity set him apart, made of him a half-tragic figure. He wanted someone to understand the feeling that had taken possession of him after his mother's death.
> There is a time in the life of every boy when he for the first time takes the backward view of life. Perhaps that is the moment when he crosses the line into manhood.[13]

The powerful influence of Anderson on Saroyan's literary sensibility can be seen in the story "And Man."

> With the beginning of spring that year came the faint and fragmentary beginning of this thought, burning in my mind with the sound of fire eating substance, sweeping through my blood with the impatience and impetuosity of a deluge. Before the beginning of this thought I had been nothing more than a small and sullen boy, moving through the moments of my life with anger and fear and bitterness and doubt, wanting desperately to know the meaning and never quite being able to do so. But now in November I was as large physically as a man, larger, for that matter, than most men. It was as if I had leaped suddenly from the form of myself as a boy to the vaster form of myself as a man, and to the vaster meaning of myself as something specific and alive. (P. 92)

It is clear from a comparison of these two passages that Saroyan had been deeply affected by Anderson's prose rhythms and themes.

Although the "ease" of expression in both passages is obvious, Saroyan tends to move away from Anderson's bare, reportorial syntax toward a more lyrical and intense phrasing: "the sound of fire eating substance, sweeping through my blood with the impatience and impetuosity of a deluge." Thematically, both stories take place in late fall, and both concentrate on a moment of awareness in the lives of boys who self-consciously look back at their own process of growth.

This intense focusing on a single instant of illumination when a character suddenly perceives the hidden reaches of reality, becomes aware of things as they are, links Saroyan most profoundly to Anderson's work. In the passage above, this perception occurs as an opposition—boy/man—which is typical of Saroyan's dichotomous vision of experience. But more important, as Roger Asselineau has remarked, both stories contain "a poetic epiphany in the course of which we are suddenly brought into contact with the inexpressible mystery of life."[14]

We find another such epiphanic moment of experience during which time seems frozen in "The Earth, Day, Night, Self." Here Saroyan presents a young man contemplating his pregnant girlfriend and the child that is slowly growing within her.

> He saw the earth growing in her through him, the universe
> falling into the boundaries of the form of man, the face, the
> eyes, solidity, motion, articulation, then awareness, then quiet
> talk, quiet communion, himself again, and yet another, to
> proceed through time, one day, one night, the earth, and the
> energy of man, himself. . . . He began to laugh softly, touching
> the girl where it was growing, feeling fine. (P. 177)

These fissures in time during which characters experience true being through relation to Other and to the cosmos, when the despair or fullness of their lives is revealed to them, occur throughout *The Daring Young Man on the Flying Trapeze.*

In Saroyan's book, as in *Winesburg, Ohio,* many of the characters feel despair more often than wholeness. Like the "grotesques" of Anderson's small town, they are, as James D. Hart has remarked, "puzzled, groping, baffled, and possess no vision of order or channel for directing their energies against the frustrations of contemporary existence."[15] In Saroyan's Fresno, California, we meet many people like those who live in Winesburg. For example, in the story "Seventeen," the young man Sam Wolinsky "wanted to do something. A feeling of violence was in him, and he was thinking of himself as something enormous in the world. He felt drunk with strength that had accumulated from the first moment of his life to the moment he was now living, and he felt almost insane because of the strength" (p. 141). Sam is an adolescent trapped and overwhelmed by the powers of sexuality which are assailing him. He searches for a means by which to express his innermost self and meets only defeat and frustration. Like many adolescents and adults depicted in Saroyan's work, Sam is seeking not only the satisfaction of his lust but also a deep transformative experience through communion with another human being. He is seeking love, and also something ineffable, which is perhaps not available in human existence.

If Anderson was the writer who provided Saroyan with an epiphanic narrative method, Walt Whitman supplied a model of transcendence and bravura. In the "essay-story" "Myself upon the Earth," Saroyan writes: "Every life is a contradiction, a new truth, a new miracle, and even frauds are interesting. I am not a philosopher and I do not believe in philosophies; the word itself I look upon with suspicion. I believe in the right of man to contradict himself." (p. 54).[16] The thought as well as the language here is from Whitman's *Leaves of Grass*: "Do I contradict myself? / Very well then I contradict myself, / (I am large, I contain multitudes)".[17] For Saroyan, as for Whitman, the contradictions of experience must be embraced; life's paradoxes cannot be overcome by forcing them into air-tight "systems" or philosophies. The inner self must be allowed to grow free—unfettered by the false twistings and "proofs" of logical constructs.

In "Myself upon the Earth" we can hear echoes of Thoreau's voice as well as Whitman's: "I do not believe in transportation, in going places with the body, and I would like to know where anyone has ever gone. Have you ever left yourself?" (p. 53). Here is the limitless realm of humanity's interior being; for Saroyan, as for Thoreau, the most important voyaging is not accomplished in the external, "real" world. Rather, the deepest purpose of life lies in inner exploration. Furthermore, in "And Man" Saroyan writes: "The real growth was going on inside, not simply within the boundaries of my physical form, but outward through the mind and through the imagination to the real largeness of consciousness, of knowing and feeling and re-membering" (p. 93). It is precisely this expansion of consciousness which Saroyan's characters seek as they quest continually for the springs of their true selves.

The lyrical, expansive, and affirmative voices in *The Daring Young Man on the Flying Trapeze* are undifferentiated: they sound the same in every story, threading through their unrest like a melody of faith, like the sturdy bass in a chorale-prelude. The varied essay-stories of the book are integrated by the dominating presence of this assured voice saying that all shall be well, that all manner of things shall be well. We hear it again in "Common Prayer."

> The plains, Lord, and all the silences of mind, lost corridors, pillars, the places where we walked, the faces we saw, and the singing of little children. But most of all hieroglyphics, the holiness, the figure in stone, the simple line, our language, the articulated curve of, let us say, leaf and dream and smile, the fall of hand, touch of limbs, love of universes, no fear of death and some longing. Yea, and the light, our sun, Lord, and the sun of unknown men, the mornings lost in time of giants and pigmies everywhere, a man named Bach, a man named Cezanne, and the others with lost names, the multitudes now come together as one. (P. 265)

Here again is the Whitmanesque cataloging noted in the title story, as well as echoes from Thomas Wolfe's *Look Homeward, Angel*. It is clear from these "cosmic" passages that Saroyan had begun evolv-ing a language that strove to capture moments of expanded con-sciousness. Like William Blake, he wants to cleanse the doors of perception, so that everything might appear to man as it is: infinite. The self then becomes aware of the unity of all created things—"the multitudes now come together as one."

Saroyan consistently employs the medium of prose-poetry to convey this sense of universal unity. The passage above utilizes the poetic techniques of assonance and alliteration; it is highly paratactic, metaphorical, evocative, lyrical.[18] Language becomes a kind of net with which the writer seeks to catch the ineffable; he seeks to render in poetic terms his vision of the mystery at the heart of existence. For Saroyan, language, the act of writing itself, assumes a central importance, for it is the vehicle through which the transcendent becomes accessible to consciousness. He envisions artistic activity as a primary mode through which the self can achieve balance—a point of view more fully explored in his third book, *Three Times Three*.

Saroyan's conception of the artist and his place in society also finds expression in *The Daring Young Man*. Of the twenty-six stories in the book, nine have writers as narrators or central characters.[19] The writer in many of these stories is an outsider who is preoccupied with the "impractical" world of literature. In the gently humorous "The Shepherd's Daughter," the narrator's grandmother tells him: "You are supposed to be a writer, and I suppose you are. You certainly smoke enough cigarettes to be anything, and the whole house is full of the smoke, but you must learn to make solid things, things that can be used, that can be seen and touched" (pp. 267–68). Paul of "Among the Lost" is out of place reading F. R. Leavis's *New Bearings in English Poetry* in a San Francisco gambling joint. "Big Valley Vineyard" is an autobiographical sketch of an author in Fresno, who shuttles back and forth between the vineyards and the world of books; he is practically "living in the fiction room of the public library" (p. 124). A fellow vineyard worker tells him: "You people who read books . . . ah, I cannot be like you. How do you do it?" (p. 129). But there is no trace of effeteness in these stories; these are not ivory-tower writers who look down upon nonintellectuals. Although they are essentially occupied with the discovery of their interior worlds, with things that cannot "be seen and touched," they do not see life and art as irreconcilable opposites.

On the contrary, these authors often exhibit a deep contempt for artifice, for the lie of "refined expression" and "literature." In "Myself upon the Earth," the narrator tells us:

I am a story-teller, and I have but a single story—man. I want to tell this simple story in my own way, forgetting the rules of rhetoric, the tricks of composition. I have something to say and I do not wish to speak like Balzac. I am not an artist; I do not really believe in civilization. I am not at all enthusiastic about progress. When a great bridge is built I do not cheer, and when airplanes cross the Atlantic I do not think, "What a marvelous age this is!" I am not interested in the destiny of nations, and history bores me. (P. 53)

This mood of healthy American defiance can also be found in Henry Miller's *Tropic of Cancer*: "A year ago, six months ago, I thought that I was an artist. I no longer think about it, I *am*. Everything that was literature has fallen from me."[20] Here we find the same disdain for "civilization"; for Miller, as for the writers in *The Daring Young Man*, to live the literary life is to be occupied with the individual quest for significance—a quest which ultimately has nothing to do with the false excitement of daily events or the "objective facts" of history.

A fierce opposition to conventional values, and not an elitism based on intellectual achievement, sets these artists apart from society. They live in a world which does not highly prize the search for being, a quest which is finally the motivating power behind all artistic creation. They are spiritual anarchists whose nonconformity celebrates the potentials of the individual human spirit.[21] As we have seen, the daring young man dies because of his inability to find employment in a society whose collapse is due precisely to its exclusively materialistic values: he has failed to complete his "Application for Permission to Live" in a socially satisfactory fashion. His alienation finds its roots in the continual frustration of the efforts of the self to find a center in an increasingly hostile world. The writers we meet in Saroyan's work often insist on their right to tell the story of man; yet they are also often tragically estranged from themselves and the world—they are homeless.

Writers, however, are not the only people in Saroyan's work afflicted by the pain of homelessness. The author's experience as the son of Armenian immigrants sensitized him at an early age to the plight of the displaced person in America; indeed, the problems of the foreigner in a strange land became one of his major themes. In "Seventy Thousand Assyrians," for example, a young writer meets an Assyrian barber named Theodore Badal, who tells him there are only "seventy thousand Assyrians in the world, and the Arabs are still killing us. They killed seventy of us in a little uprising last month. There was a small paragraph in the paper. Seventy more of us destroyed. We'll be wiped out before long" (p. 39). Assyria was once a great civilization, but now it appears that the entire race will be destroyed. The narrator says that "these remarks were very painful to me, an Armenian. I had always felt badly about my own people being destroyed" (p. 38). An explicit comparison is drawn between the situation of Badal and the narrator's own feelings of alienation as an Armenian. Armenia was also a country with a glorious past, and its people were decimated by the Turks in the early part of this century.[22]

In Saroyan's later writing there would be many more Theodore Badals, men lost in a new land yearning after the past and a home. Yet Saroyan is not content to take refuge in hatred and separatism. "Seventy Thousand Assyrians" is written "in tribute to Iowa, to Japan, to Assyria, to Armenia, to the race of man everywhere, to the dignity of that race, the brotherhood of things alive" (p. 40). Here he affirms the theme that would dominate all his subsequent work.

> If I have any desire at all, it is to show the brotherhood of man. This is a big statement and it sounds a little precious. Generally a man is ashamed to make such a statement. He is afraid sophisticated people will laugh at him. But I don't mind. I'm asking sophisticated people to laugh. That is what sophistication is for. I do not believe in races. I do not believe in governments. I see life as one life at one time, so many millions simultaneously, all over the earth. Babies who have not yet been taught to speak any language are the only race of the earth, the race of man: all the rest is pretense, what we call civilization, hatred, fear, desire for strength. . . . But a baby is a baby. And the way they cry, there you have the brotherhood of man, babies crying. We grow up and we learn the words of a language

and we see the universe through the language we know, we do
not see it through all languages or through no language at all,
through silence, for example, and we isolate ourselves in the
language we know. Over here we isolate ourselves in English, or
American as Mencken calls it. All the eternal things, in our
words. If I want to do anything, I want to speak a more universal
language. The heart of man, the unwritten part of man, that
which is eternal and common to all races. (Pp. 31–32)

Saroyan's sympathy is with the estranged of every race; he rejects
nationalism and continually reiterates the hope for a united world.
His concern for the situation of the Armenian immigrant is not
motivated by chauvinism; rather the uprooted of every race become
in his imagination symbols of the alienated condition of modern
man.

The estranged, indeed, are blessed; their suffering denotes a spiritual purity absent in more self-satisfied and "fortunate" people. It is
no accident that Saroyan, like Beckett, most deeply loves the estranged, the oppressed, the poor, the downtrodden, the misfits, the
tramps. From the starving daring young man to the impoverished
Macauley family in *The Human Comedy*, Saroyan's "common" yet
supremely "uncommon" people possess an inner magnificence, a
grave beauty which holds secret the tragic, eternal, and unwritten
language of the heart. In his work, the meek shall indeed inherit the
earth; it is only for the cruel and power-hungry that he holds a fierce
and abiding contempt. They are dead to life's most sacred and tender
mystery: the universal connectedness of all living things.

In many of his works, it is children who are most in tune with this
mystery. In *The Daring Young Man* the terrible story of how visionary innocence is perverted can be seen in "War." Here two boys,
Prussian Karl and Joseph, who is of Slavic descent, have a fist fight
which mirrors in its "ignorance and immaturity" the same process
by which nations "seek to dominate or destroy one another" (p.
242). The hope for brotherhood is shattered as the boys imitate the
hatreds and fears of the "adult" world. The child's peaceable kingdom has opened its gates to a lunatic, adult intruder: war.

As we have seen, the twenty-six stories of *The Daring Young Man*

present in microcosm the major themes that recur throughout Saroyan's work. It is a book full of energy and longing; although it is
influenced by earlier American writers, it reveals an authentically
original literary personality. With time, Saroyan would outgrow this
self-conscious literariness. In the books that followed during his
first creative phase, he would continue to refine his thought and
technique to accommodate new insights. The themes considered in
this first chapter would surface repeatedly: the impulse uniting
these concerns is the search for unification, for home, for a graceful
trapeze flight to God—or to nothing.

CHAPTER 2

I Want to Live While I Am Alive

In the collections Saroyan published between 1936 and 1940, the struggle for affirmation of life continues. For Saroyan, it is clear, living itself is the highest value; he violently opposes any system, belief, or authority which seeks to thwart the unfolding of the individual's inner self. He depicts a modern world which is mired in illusion, which has forgotten the spiritual dimension of experience. In *The Trouble with Tigers* he describes humanity as "this mangled tribe, this still unborn God"; thus the deepest potentials inherent in life have yet to be realized by many people.[1] The essential divinity of humanity is still tragically submerged, and the function of the artist is to reveal this hidden inner realm. To ignore this divine impulse within is to destroy one's potential for achieving authentic selfhood and psychological maturity.

In the six volumes that appeared after *The Daring Young Man*, this central idea is revealed in a variety of thematic formulations. Although it would be a distortion to identify each book with the exposition of a single theme, certain general patterns may be discerned. In the seventy-one stories of *Inhale and Exhale*, Saroyan offers a comprehensive treatment of all the concerns discussed in chapter 1, with the addition of pieces written during his travels to Europe and Russia. *Three Times Three* illustrates Saroyan's deepening concern with the place of art in modern life; *Little Children* focuses on the world of childhood, while *Love, Here Is My Hat* presents characters seeking wholeness through relationships. Finally, both *The Trouble with Tigers* and *Peace, It's Wonderful* reflect the approach of World War II. In each story collection, Saroyan again directs his attention to the chaos of a turbulent world.

Perhaps the most significant aspect of Saroyan's growth as a writer during this period was his exploration of art and its relationship to the process of becoming one's true self. He returns repeatedly to the role of the artist in contemporary society, developing and refining his ideas in a number of different contexts. One of his most powerful portraits of the artistic sensibility came out of personal experience— his meeting with Jean Sibelius in July 1935. In "Finlandia," from *Inhale and Exhale*, Saroyan contemplates the composer and the genius of his music.

> All I wanted was music. No dialectics. Just the simple old-fashioned fury of one man alone, fighting it out alone, wrestling with God, or with the whole confounded universe, throwing himself into silence and time, and after sweating away seven pounds of substance, coming out of the small room with something detached, of itself, alive, timeless, crazy, magnificent, delirious, blasphemous, pious, furious, kindly, not the man, not all men, but a thing by itself, incredibly complete, an incision of silence and emptiness, and then sound and the shapes of things without substance. Music. A symphony.[2]

The experience of great music was to become an integral part of Saroyan's life as a writer, and it is in "Finlandia" that he first explored its aesthetic dimensions. He remarked in *Razzle-Dazzle* that "I am a writer who is a composer. You will see music in all of my writing—the form and quality of music in all of it."[3] For him, as for Rilke, "Gesang ist Dasein"—singing is being.

In "Finlandia," the artist is depicted creating in isolation, "wrestling with God," achieving the order which is a symphonic work. The composer has created "something detached, of itself, alive, timeless"—a new reality whose harmonious structure makes the disintegrated self whole. Through the composition of music, Sibelius has made contact with a metatemporal realm, with an eternal energy which exists continuously in the present.[4] The narrator/Saroyan feels "closer in spirit to him [Sibelius] than any writer" because the composer moves in a dimension beyond words, beyond the mind's linear, "logical," idea-bound limitations. Sibelius lives in being and recreates it immediately in sound, an experience which the writer can only approximate through language.[5] Yet the creation of music is described as a furious agon, a process analogous to giving birth. The artist struggles relentlessly with chaos, "throwing himself into silence and time," and finally emerges triumphant after imprinting meaning upon the emptiness of the universe. Sibelius is involved in a titanic "contest with non-existence," a struggle which engages all of his energy and genius.[6]

"Finlandia" is important in Saroyan's development, for it is here that he begins to evolve a coherent aesthetic philosophy; as his career progressed, it became evident that art was central to his quest for meaning and personal wholeness. As he pointed out in the preface to *The Hungerers*: "The human form itself is a broken form. It shouldn't be. It is a miraculous form. Art always has a better chance of having whole and unbroken form than the living have, but the only reason art seeks to achieve this unbroken form is to encourage its achievement in the living. Art is for the living, whether they come into contact with it or not."[7] Saroyan denies "art for art's sake"; he believes art exists to aid humanity in its continuing process of self-discovery and growth. Art has a practical raison d'etre, and he therefore has no interest in pure aestheticism.

Saroyan pointed out later in his career that man's "hope is for meaning, which is everything: and he achieves meaning, inventing it or discovering it, through art."[8] For him, as for Nietzsche, art is the highest metaphysical activity of man. It gives us a feeling of connection to power, meaning, truth, holiness—to the deepest hidden reaches of life's mystery. The meaninglessness of the "real world" and the disorder of experience are precisely what he seeks to overcome, indeed to redeem, through art.

In the story "The World and the Theatre," for example, a ten-year-old boy has begun to grow disgusted with the unrelieved pain of the Depression, a time when "there was no work in the packing-houses and everybody was out of work and in need of money and all kinds of people were too proud to go down to the city and get some free groceries and maybe a little money and these people were all starving to death" (p. 19). Rather than endure passively the agonies that surround him, the boy discovers the world of vaudeville: "To hell with the outside, I said. To hell with the streets and all the things I see there. It was warm in the theatre and the stage was flooded with light. The scene was a city block, but it wasn't like any city block I had ever seen. It was like a city on another earth, all bright and fine, full of light, a good place to be and live" (p. 23).

This is the occurrence of the great divide: the realization by the child that art and life, reality and imagination, "inside and out-side," are twin, contiguous realms of experience—the world and the theater. The vision of the theater as a fragile, enclosed space protect-ing the vulnerable temporarily from the unrest outside is a concep-tion of the place of art which, as we shall see in chapter 5, pervades Saroyan's dramatic philosophy. For the unnamed boy of this story, the theater is an entrance into an imaginative world which supplies momentarily an affirmative picture of life's unrealized possibilities. Just as Sibelius's music made possible a vision of "the shapes of things without substance," so the theater has opened the boy's imagination to a world "full of light."

In his next book, *Three Times Three*, Saroyan continued to ex-plore the role of the artist in a difficult time.[9] The story "Baby" is divided into fifteen sections; each gives a brief lyrical sketch of some aspect of the American experience. In section three, Saroyan again divides existence into two realms: "The surface life and the inward one, the inward one waiting patiently for another century. It will come. Horror cannot exist forever. The inward life will lift its broken body out of the nightmare and breathe" (pp. 104–5). The nightmare here is both the Depression and the oncoming fury of World War II, and we meet again the lost of *The Daring Young Man*: "The street of America is a long street, and the lost who walk along this street are many" (p. 103).

In section eight, the narrator launches into autobiography, and it becomes clear that again we are hearing the voice of Saroyan him-self—the young artist who wants to change the world, who wants to see the resurrection of an America now lashed by the tempest of economic and spiritual collapse: "I will show them God in them-selves, I said. I will teach them to remember. I will talk to them in the language of revelation" (p. 112). Saroyan identifies the expansive energy of America with his own youthful aspirations as a writer; both are full of unrealized potential, a groping earnestness, and burdened with an awareness that the old world is in its death throes.

The function of the artist in "Baby" is revelatory; he must show a reverence for the miraculous nature of life which pushes outward toward new birth even in the darkest time: "I want to know about these things. Life in all things. Insects, rodents, reptiles, fish, beasts, man. Do you realize how pure a gem is the living eye? The germ, the germ. I want to understand the germ, the seed, the energy, the egg, the beginning, the timeless and imperishable force of being. Big Joe, the great American country boy, seeking God in the glory of the female body. O baby maybe" (p. 113).

The voice of the poet urging his hearers on to greater self-knowledge can be heard in this passage, and also in section 12: "I think we must begin again to see. I think we must learn again to look. An apple is an apple, but for the love of God look at an apple before you eat it and you will have become a man alive and for a moment a man who cannot die" (p. 121). To be fully alive is to cultivate a Zen-like attentiveness to the experience of the moment; to be an artist is to learn the art of living, to revel magnificently in "the imperishable force of being."

There is also in "Baby" a new, free, syncopated rhythm, a rhythm which was to catch the ear of later American writers.

> Sang baby. O maybe. Sang motors and wheels till Saturday
> night in America, and a hundred thousand jazz orchestras sang
> *So come sit by my side if you love me,* and the sad-eyed, weary-
> lipped Mexican girl silenced Manhattan uproar with soft,
> velvet-petaled singing of darkness and death, O heart there is
> no end to the river's flowing. Sang locomotive north through
> snow to Albany and west to Chicago, O baby maybe. (P. 124)

We hear the freedom of music in this passage, with its alternating onrushing excitement and brief, staccato, elemental sentences. The alliterative use of "s" is also apparent when it is read out loud. This rhapsodic urgency is, as we have seen, a central aspect of Saroyan's literary style. It is the language of being, attempting to catch in its quick energetic movement some of the texture, mystery, and flux of experience. It is the obsession of the artist to "get to the probable truth about man, nature, and art, straight through everything to the very core of *one's own* being."[10]

Saroyan's desire to achieve unification of the warring opposites of self and world through his paratactic style illustrates his typically Romantic attitude concerning the place of language in the transformation of consciousness. For him, it was impossible to express the fluctuating rhythms of selfhood in the typical language of his day. The Heraclitean flux of being cannot be transfixed; thus it is essential to invent a malleable and fluid style which renders the immediacy of life as experienced in the timeless moment.

As we see in "Baby," the artist must express the fluid self in fluid forms. For Saroyan, "a writer is great insofar as he is simultaneously artful and artless, a swift-moving inhabitant of both the inevitable and visible world and the uncreated but creatable, uncharted, invisible, fluid, limitless but nevertheless real other world."[11] This is a precise description of the twin realms outlined in "Baby": the "surface life and the inward life." Although the world the artist depicts is "uncharted" and "invisible," it is nevertheless available to consciousness and must be poetically, lyrically invoked through rhythmic, musical language.

It should be clear, then, why Saroyan became a literary godfather to the Beat Generation, and specifically to Jack Kerouac and his fellow writers.[12] In this early prose, Saroyan was a true innovator, spawning a fresh new style—a fusion of jazz, Whitman, the quick tempi of American life, popular songs, and the oral tradition of Armenian literature. It is precisely this *oral*, musical dimension of Saroyan's prose-poetry, along with its emphasis on immediate, passionate experience, which appealed so powerfully to the Beats: his words are meant to be *heard*. It has been pointed out by Lawrence Lipton that Beat literature "is the spoken word committed to writing. It is oral in structure. . . . The printed poem is not the poem. It is only the 'score' of the poem, just as in music the score is not the music. It has to be *played back*."[13] Literature for both Saroyan and the Beats should be as immediate, visceral, improvisatory, and spontaneous as the experience of hearing great music. It must be realized, like life itself, in *performance*; then it will *breathe*.

"Baby" is noteworthy both for its stylistic innovations and for its search for the "inward life." Other pieces included in *Three Times Three* also emphasize that the writer's task is to help both himself and his public attain inner wholeness: "Maybe art is a correction of errors, within the artist, in the world, in man, in the universe."[14] But most important, Saroyan here begins to organize his insights concerning the artistic experience into an organic whole. In "Life and Letters" he considers the relation of "real" time to time as we perceive it when we read a work of literature.

> In letters time is not the same thing that it is in life, not the same thing that it is in the universe, time in letters is not daybreak, day, noon, afternoon, evening, and night. In letters time is altogether an inexplicable and magnificent thing, and in so small a thing as a mere short story time can become so tremendous an intensification of experience that the reader, God bless him and keep his eyes unastigmatic, will have lived more richly, more greatly, more swiftly, more meaningfully, and more magnificently than he could ever have had the wit or daring or madness to live in the light of day, in the world. (P. 93)

In the world of literature, our awareness of time is mysteriously altered; "real" time is transcended and our experience is intensified through the artful compressions of the short story form. The successful work of art captures a sense of timelessness, and it is evident here that Saroyan again conceives of literature as an expander of consciousness in the Romantic mode. As we have seen in "Finlandia," he sees art as opening the mind to a more significant realm of awareness, onto a "place of reality" where the self is free joyously to exfoliate.[15] The description of time in short stories applies equally well to his other work—especially, as we shall see, to such plays as *The Time of Your Life*.

Also emphasized is the idea that life for the artist is a continuing process of inner exploration; it is "an inward progression of an inward time, an inward growth of an inward world or universe, an inward purification of the inward identity, and an inward strengthening of the inward body" (p. 94). In reading a great work of art, therefore, our own "inward lives begin to accelerate" in the same way as does the writer's. The writer triumphs over time by creating "the growth of immortality in another" (p. 96). The reader's experience of time is not only "intensified" but also "accelerated" as he makes contact with the same world the writer inhabited at the moment of composition.

"Quarter, Half, Three-Quarter, and Whole Notes" continues Saroyan's discussion of literature and the nature of the creative personality in a series of brief sentences and paragraphs. The isolation of the artist is accepted as a prerequisite for successful inner journeyings: "There is only one way to write a story and only one way to write one sentence and that is to be pious and simple and inwardly isolated; above all things inwardly isolated. When you move through the mob you must move through it alone; otherwise there is a chance that your vision will be blurred" (p. 137).

Samuel Beckett, with whom Saroyan shares many spiritual and philosophical concerns, has also written about the solitude of the artist in his study *Proust*: "For the artist, who does not deal in surfaces, the rejection of friendship is not only reasonable, but a necessity. Because the only possible spiritual development is in the sense of depth. The artistic tendency is not expansive, but a contraction. And art is the apotheosis of solitude."[16] Saroyan's "inward isolation" is Beckett's "solitude"; it is a solitude in which the artist cultivates an inner strength and resolution of purpose—a strength which may be dissipated through an exclusive immersion in social life.[17]

The creation of integral works of art can come about only when the self has achieved a measure of balance and integration. In "Quarter, Half, Three-Quarter, and Whole Notes," Saroyan uncovers the primary link between life and art.

> It is essential for anyone alive to establish a personal method
> of living and to impose personal limitations: one must possess
> one's identity fully and vigorously and steadily, if one hopes
> to dominate time rather than be dominated by it. The year
> is empty because the moment was empty, and the moment
> *need* not be empty. There must be no evasion. Evasion occurs
> when one performs acts not pertinent to the ultimate object of

one's activity in life, which is to achieve personal wholeness, and to give the material world reality and order. A story (or any other work of art) does not occur when one does the actual writing: it began to occur when one began to live consciously and piously. The writing, which is the least of it, follows inevitably. (P. 137)

Achieving "personal wholeness" through writing is directly connected to the level of authenticity the artist has attained. The impulse to live "consciously" and fully again links Saroyan to Whitman, whose poetry charts the continuing process of the self's quest for unity: the world is complete for the man who is himself complete. In addition, to live successfully in time and not be burdened by it one must "possess one's identity fully." In life, then, one transcends time through being in control of the self; in art, time is overcome through the magic of literary construction and technique.

A final piece dealing with the artistic process is to be found in *Peace, It's Wonderful*. In "The Sweet Singer of Omsk," Saroyan writes another autobiographical story (he mentions himself by name) about his daimon: "I admit it. I am possessed. Most of the time not violently so. But often enough. Not haunted, mind you. The presence is not an evil one. It is often angry and bitter and furious, but most of the time it is warm and friendly and amiable and gentle and courteous, and at times a little gallant, even. It is a good presence, and in varying degrees it is with me always."[18] Saroyan tells us that "very often I do not know what I write, what I say. I simply write, something perhaps more significant than I know, which falls in place by itself, rather strangely" (p. 156).

The "presence" is of course the Muse, and Saroyan echoes the Romantic conception of the artist as a kind of instrument through which the energy and fire of divine creativity are expressed. The artist is essentially passive during this process. Stravinsky has said that "I am the vessel through which *Le Sacre du Printemps* passed," and it is clear Saroyan feels similarly about his writing. André Gide's remark that "the true artist is always half-unconscious of himself, when he is producing" also comes to mind: at their most inspired, artists are aware that their work is being done for them—by the

Muse, the unconscious, the daimon, "the presence." Hence Saroyan writes: "I have always suspected that what I am doing is not the work of one man" (p. 159). The speed with which some of Saroyan's best works were written (*The Time of Your Life* was finished in six days) supports the notion that "the presence" played a central role in his artistic creation.

The stories so far considered thus contain a coherent exposition of Saroyan's developing aesthetic philosophy. Great art is a process by which the individual can achieve true being: it is a way into expanded states of consciousness. As has been shown, he discounts "outer travelling" for "the more places you reach the more you understand that there is no geographical destination for man."[19] Rather, "home" can best be reached in "the world of one man at a time: the inner, the boundless, the ungeographical world of wakeful dream."[20] It is precisely this "ungeographical world" which many of Saroyan's characters so ardently seek, and from which they are so terribly alienated.

Although Saroyan's advocacy of this inner world is powerful and for the most part convincing, art's absolutions ultimately have little impact on the ceaseless struggles of everyday life. Although art, as we have seen, offers an opportunity for inner wholeness to some of Saroyan's characters—through the music of Sibelius, the pleasures of the theater, or the ecstasy of literature—just as many are cut off, alienated from the true, vital sources of spiritual sustenance. The irony is that the transcendence that they seek often seems accessible only through language, through the splendors and therapeutic qualities of Saroyan's poetic prose. The search for love and wholeness in the "real world" is often frustrating and unfulfilling—the yearning remains unappeased.

"At Sundown" from *Inhale and Exhale*, for example, is another Andersonian story of youth's longing for love and understanding: "And I remember dimly this strange longing I once had which soon became tragic, quietly in the heart where all great tragedies occur" (p. 349). The incurable loneliness of the human heart is illustrated in many of Saroyan's early stories; his characters must learn to accept the fact that breaking through completely to another human being is an illusory dream. The search for communication leads them to an even deeper awareness of their own essential organic apartness as the grandeur and intensity of romantic expectation are deflated by reality.

> Day sank beneath night, and darkness increased. We stood by the water, shivering, and not knowing which way to go. Slowly, we returned to the street, to life on earth, to the city, and we entered one of the beach restaurants. Sitting across the table from Myra, seeing in her eyes the death of this longing, and in it the death of my own longing, I knew that it was ended, and that in a year or two Myra would marry some young fellow with a good job and be his wife, like any other girl, and swallowing hot coffee, I knew also that the first thing in the morning I would buy myself a new suit and a new hat, and forget the whole thing, and stay alive as long as possible, puny and weak and mortal. (P. 356)

The movement here is from the hoped-for immortality of love to an acceptance of mortality, from the myth of absolute oneness to the daily particularity of a new suit, from the ungeographic to the geographic realm.

The quest for love is closely associated in Saroyan's imagination with the search for home, for a place of rest and calm. Being human means exhausting one's self in the effort to reach home, to be more than "puny and weak and mortal." In "The Trains" from *Love, Here Is My Hat*, we return to the concept of travel as a metaphor for the journeyings of the human spirit as it seeks serenity. Joe Silvera, a twenty-four-year-old painter, has returned to his hometown of Fresno after an absence of seven years. Yet he does not *feel* at home, and he spends hours looking out the window, watching the trains come and go.

> He would watch for the appearance, far in the south, of the crack passenger trains from Los Angeles. And listen for their cry of arrival: the whistle desolating and full of human anguish, like the ungodly anguish of the heart after possessing flesh and losing spirit; and the last minute haste, the roar, the fire and smoke; and then, almost meaninglessly, sadly, the slow stop,

the tentative pause, the swift-ending moment of rest; and then
the going again, unlike the movement of the spirit, the train
going from city to city, place to place, climate to climate, configuration to configuration. Unlike the going of the spirit,
which traveled ungeographically, seeking absurdly magnificent
destinations: all places, the core of life, the essence of all mortality, eternity, God. And, he thought bitterly, seeking everything else, in one big bright package.[21]

The human heart is continuously dissatisfied, restless, seeking ultimate consummation. It is not content to arrive at geographical
places in time and space; it seeks not the superficial, but the very
mystery of existence.

Joe Silvera realizes, with Thomas Wolfe, that you can't go home
again. Indeed, he begins to wonder whether home is merely a word
signifying nothing, whether his spirit wants a magic which exists
outside human existence.

The magic was not in the world. It was in a dimension made out
of the longings of the inhabitants of the world: and that's where
home was too. If home were a place, then he was home. But it
was not a place: it was a synchronization of a multitude of
subtle and constantly changing substances and rhythms and
perceptions and values in a number of people together, as a
family; or in two people, as himself, and the lost girl, for instance; or himself and a friend, like old Otto Bennra in Vienna.
    Maybe it was; maybe it wasn't too. He didn't know. Maybe it
was another of the mirages the heart was constantly creating.
He was afraid it was a mirage; and he was afraid home was
movement for the body, travel; and he was sorry this might be
so. (Pp. 13–14)

This is paradigmatic of the psychological quandary in which many
of Saroyan's characters find themselves. Joe Silvera is tantalized by a
magnificence he senses beneath the appearances of everyday life and
deeply hopes his dreams are not illusory.

During his fourth month back home, Joe has an opportunity to
determine whether or not his desires are to be realized. He spends a

quiet Sunday morning watching the trains come and go, eats break-
fast, and goes to a bar to drink beer. He becomes inebriated and goes
to Court House Park, where he approaches an attractive young
woman. He invites her to dinner, and after eating they return to his
rooms, where he shows her his paintings. When they awake in the
morning, Joe knows it is she who will decide his future; she will
help him make the decision whether he should remain in Fresno or
leave the city.

As they look silently out the window at the trains arriving at the
depot, he holds her next to him, "inwardly frantic about her reaction to this common event, which to him had become uncommonly
significant and touching. If she said nothing, if she did no more than
turn to him with any sort of satisfactory glance, he would take her
in his arms, and know that he would stay, and he hoped desperately
that communion would be established between himself and the
girl" (p. 19). Her only response to this highly charged emotional
situation is: "The trains certainly make a lot of noise, don't they?"
(p. 19). Joe begins to laugh and hurries the girl home. Her insensi-
tivity to his fragile and intense inner world and lack of understanding of the "ungeographical" motions that the human heart suffers
leave no doubt in Joe's mind that there is nothing for him at "home,"
for he cannot find love.

The quest for self-integration through love is often frustrating, for,
as Yeats put it, "Love has pitched his mansion in the place of ex-
crement." In "War and Peace" we meet Sammy, a twenty-year-old
San Fransciscan whose pained introversion is rooted in a violent
sexuality. He is helplessly attracted to women and afraid of their
power over him. Like Sam Wolinsky of "Seventeen," Sammy is
wracked by animal need and channels his lust into a love for reading. Sammy's mother worries about his intense self-involvement,
and the young man resents her wanting him to be a "good boy. He'd
like to tell her he stank from being a good boy" (p. 110). Sammy is
plagued by the feeling that he is ugly, a "small evil-looking animal
which breathes and wants glory" (p. 113). He leaves the house for
the evening and considers visiting a brothel, but, unlike Sam Wolinsky, he holds back, realizing that "he could always buy with money
the one thing of life which has its beauty and magnificence in being

given" (p. 114). He returns home and immerses himself in Tolstoy's *War and Peace*, returning to the unhappy womb of his mother's house and to the escape of literature.

Neither Joe Silvera nor Sammy, however, is a special case: they are humanity in microcosm, for they "want what everybody wants and never gets." They desire, as we are told in "The Poor Heart," "the enormity and abundance that isn't ever steadily part of this life" (pp. 116, 121). The human heart with its infinite longings and unappeasable appetite for wholeness cannot be satisfied by the things of the material world, and its yearning for a deeper reality is often frustrated. The last story in *Love, Here Is My Hat*, "Am I Your World?" ends with the sobering words: "It's kind of funny the way a man can stay alive when everything but his body is dead; when everything but comedy is dead and buried, when the whole world is a cemetery" (p. 145). Saroyan's characters *do* stay alive, however. If many are "so inwardly violent and bewildered, so marvelously lonely," it is because they are poets of feeling whose real inner life depends on the sweet shudder of response felt from another human heart.[22]

This desire of Saroyan's characters to establish communion with themselves and others exemplifies the phrase that serves as the title for this chapter: I want to live while I am alive.[23] They want life above all things, and the real struggle is not only interpersonal; rather, they are up against the spiritual aridity of their age. *Peace, It's Wonderful* contains one of Saroyan's most powerful statements on estrangement in the modern world, "Noonday Dark Enfolding Texas." Traveling through El Paso by train, the narrator experiences a wasteland, a landscape devoid of meaning and hope: "It was a dead city, it was part of a dead world, a dead age, a universe dying, aching with loneliness, gasping for breath. That is the thought that frightens you. That makes you want life the worst way" (p. 133). The world is yearning for a new birth, a new consciousness, a new way of being; the omnipresence of death and decay makes the narrator's commitment to authentic living all the stronger.

The story ends darkly with a vision of humanity reminiscent of T. S. Eliot's "hollow men."

> I went down to the street and began walking through the beau-
> tiful, ugly, dying city. The girls were like the girls of all places,
> only different. They were Texas, but different from ever before.
> They were Texas in the sudden darkness of noonday; enfolded
> in the dark; sealed in the far away dream. One of them was the
> one I was seeking, and knew she was, so that, even in that
> desolation, there was meaning at last to write home about.
> Afterwards, on the train, going away from Texas, rolling out of
> the dream, I listened to the men in the smoker roaring with the
> lonely laughter of the living, and suddenly I began to cry, roar-
> ing with laughter, because I knew we were all dead, didn't know
> it, and therefore couldn't do anything about it. (Pp. 133–34)

This death-in-life is the ultimate estrangement, the terror of the
human soul trapped in static isolation. The real tragedy is that these
men (and the narrator includes himself among them) do not realize
that they are dead, that their inner selves are suffocating.

For Saroyan, this lack of self-knowledge and absence of authentic
communication between human beings leads to the ultimate estrangement: the insanity of political and social upheaval, the idiocy
of war. Warnings of impending catastrophe can be found in his earliest work; for example, *Inhale and Exhale* contains an autobiographical sketch, "The Little Dog Laughed to See Such Sport," which
he wrote in London in 1935.

> So before the war starts (and everybody alive, from the cab
> driver to the Professor of Economics, at Columbia, will tell you
> the war will soon start), I want to tell the world that I am not
> interested. I am completely bored with the war. It has nothing
> to do with me. I have no quarrel of such a ridiculous nature,
> although I have quarrels enough. I want nothing of it. I refuse to
> accept its reality. Kill yourselves all you like. Do it artfully,
> with the finest guns and gases invented. (P. 414)

Saroyan was forced finally to "accept the war's reality," although
he attempted in books like *The Human Comedy* and *The Adventures of Wesley Jackson* to soften its horror. It was extremely difficult for him to acknowledge that death had triumphed over life,

that there was a spirit of evil in the world, that his dreams of universal brotherhood had been shattered. The character and mood of his writing changed following the war; he found it more problematical to sustain a poetic and lyrical attitude toward life's possibilities. Just as World War I literally sickened D. H. Lawrence, Saroyan was also finally unable to assert that the war had nothing to do with him.[24]

War is the triumph of a mob consciousness which levels distinctions between people and fails to recognize the sanctity of individual life. In *Three Times Three*, the failure of the masses to achieve self-realization is discussed. In the introductory note to "Public Speech," Saroyan writes:

> I sincerely wish I could believe with the Communists that
> there is hope for the masses, but I cannot. I honestly believe
> there is hope for man, for one man at a time, and I honestly be-
> lieve that, with all the encumbrances of the world, all the vi-
> ciousness, all the deceit and cruelty, man's only hope of sal-
> vation is himself; he is his salvation. God is. . . . The masses
> aren't ready, I'm afraid, for the shock of genuine knowing, and
> not spiritually equipped to face the inward tragedy which oc-
> curs with genuine knowing. I don't think the Communists
> are either. (Pp. 69–70)

In the text of the piece, the speaker tells his audience that "all who live are born out of flesh, and living is private" (p. 81). Again it is humanity's inner world which Saroyan seeks to celebrate and protect from the encroachment of any system, capitalist or communistic, which denies individual freedom: "I hate all who seek to complicate that which parades the earth in barefoot simplicity: the living of the inhabitants of the earth" (p. 83).

Although Saroyan points out that the majority of humanity is not prepared for true self-knowledge, this should not be construed as an elitist remark. By "genuine knowing," Saroyan means the achievement of authentic being—and by this definition, few of any age can be counted as successful. Yet this stage of development also brings with it an "inward tragedy"—perhaps the knowledge that the quest for balance is a lonely and difficult one. To really grow as a person requires great struggle and anguish; but to remain as one is—static, undeveloped, dead—requires no effort. Political solutions to the problems of inner growth are fraudulent because the struggle for "genuine knowing" is ultimately a private, individual, interior quest.

According to Saroyan, it is precisely this fearful consciousness insisting on the mythologies of nationalism and governments which is responsible for the world's chaos. His anarchic, life-affirming passion reaches a rhetorical climax in "The People, Yes and Then Again No" from *The Trouble with Tigers*: "This is your world and it is my world, and it is not real estate, and not nations, and not governments; it is this accidental place of mortality; it is this pause in time and space. It is this chance to breathe, to walk, to see, to eat, to sleep, to love, to laugh. It is not financial statistics. It belongs to this mangled tribe, this still unborn God, man" (p. 164). The noblest and best qualities of people are yet to appear; but they will emerge as humanity grows out of psychological and spiritual infancy. If this tribe is "mangled," it yet has a chance to become whole.

Later in his career, Saroyan wrote: "When I speak of the human race I speak of the *concealed* human race, the *still* concealed human race, which is trying to come out from under, as it has been trying for a million years or more."[25] The struggle of life is man's struggle to express the limitless potential that lies buried within the individual soul. Life is not a matter of quantifiable data, of "statistics"; there is no algebra of the spirit. Rather, life is a vast mystery which should be revered and celebrated. Because people do not realize this, the human race is yet unborn, still in the womb of evolutionary development.

Humanity's potential for peace and brotherhood and life's awful stark actualities are contrasted in Saroyan's writings of the period. In four of the pieces of *The Trouble with Tigers*, we sense the oncoming tide of death. In "O.K. Baby, This Is the World," the Fascists make their approach to Madrid; "Everything" discusses the war in China; Mussolini's armies invading Abyssinia form the background of "Citizens of the Third Grade." In "The Tiger," Saroyan states the controlling theme of the book: "The room cold and the moment clear and cold and tragic. The presence. The word, unwritten. The tiger, unseen. Brother, I mean death. The red headline across the emptiness of time" (p. 8).

The war's impact on life in America can also be seen in three stories from *Peace, It's Wonderful*. In "The Greatest Country in the World," a Czechoslovakian and his fourteen-year-old son quarrel when the boy suggests that Germany will overcome his father's homeland through its superior military capabilities. "The War in Spain" depicts a naive eighteen year old convinced of the romance of combat who leaves to become a soldier. And in "The Best and Worst People and Things of 1938," two men in a bar discuss the tragic state of the world. One nominates Hitler as "Heel Number One of the Year" (p. 146). The ultimate mood these stories convey is aptly and concisely expressed by the Scandinavian longshoreman of "The Monumental Arena": "There is a mistake in some place of our life" (p. 75).

Yet the final story in the book, "The Journey and the Dream," refrains from despair or nihilism and ends in a kind of prayer urging pity and hope. The narrator of the story has been gambling and drinking all night, and in the morning, he tells us that

> when I walked into the street I was laughing because it was so good to be in the world, so excellent to be a part of the chaos and unrest and agony and magnificence of this place of man, the world, so comic and tragic to be alive during the moment of its change, the sea, and the sea's sky, and London, and London's noise and fury, and the cockney's lamentation, the King's palace, the ballet at Covent Garden, and outside Covent Garden the real ballet, and France, and the fields of France, and Paris, and the streets of Paris, and the stations, and the trains, and the faces, and the eyes, and the grief, and Austria, and Poland, and Russia, and Finland, and Sweden, and Norway, and the world, man stumbling mournfully after God in the wilderness, the street musicians of Edinburgh crying out for God in the songs of America, dancing after Him down the steep streets, the tragic dream stalking everywhere through day and night, so

that when I walked into the street, I was laughing and begging God to pity them, love them, protect them, the king and the beggar alike. (P. 177)

Here is Saroyan's typical fusion of laughter and tragedy, of tears and ecstasy. Man is hungering after spiritual illumination, "stumbling mournfully after God in the wilderness," still estranged from himself and the world. Yet the narrator is also laughing, laughing through loneliness, pain, grief. Finally he hugs the world's chaos to his soul and achieves the joy of acceptance.

CHAPTER 3

Exiled in America: The Armenian Quest

If life placed obstacles in the path of those Americans seeking to realize themselves, the difficulties were especially great for the Armenians whom Saroyan made an important feature of his imaginative world. The thousands of exiles who made their way to America during the early part of this century were fleeing "the pain and the grief of our torn land"—the massacre of more than a million and a half of their countrymen during the years 1896–1915.[1] The life of Armenians in the United States would supply Saroyan with one of his central themes: the estrangement of the foreigner in a new world. Furthermore, in his imagination the displaced person would become symbolic of the alienated condition of humanity in the contemporary world.

Saroyan's attitude toward his own Armenian-American identity at first glance seems paradoxical. On one level he is constantly assuring the reader that as a human being he transcends all racial boundaries; yet the fact that he is an Armenian is continually put before us.[2] He obsessively casts back into his past to examine the roots of his Armenian identity. In three stories from *Inhale and Exhale*, Saroyan explores the "Armenian question" as well as his own divided condition as an Armenian-American. In a story dealing with his youth in Fresno, "Antranik of Armenia," he tells of learning about the Armenian general who fought the Turks during the massacres.

> I didn't learn to speak Armenian until my grandmother came to our house and every morning sang about Antranik the soldier

until I knew he was an Armenian, a mountain peasant on a
black horse who with only a handful of men was fighting the
enemy. That was in 1915, the year of physical pain and spiritual
disintegration for the people of my country, and the people of
the world, but I was seven and I didn't know. From my own
meaningless grief I could imagine something was wrong in the
world, but I didn't know what. My grandmother sang in a way
that made me begin to find out, singing mournfully and with
great anger, in a strong voice, while she worked in the house.
(P. 257)

Toward the end of the story, the narrator begins to ponder the fate
of the Armenian people, as well as his own double identity.

To hell with it, I said. It's all over. We can begin to forget
Armenia now. Antranik is dead. The nation is lost. The strong
nations of the world are jumping with new problems. To hell
with the whole God damn mess, I said. I'm no Armenian. I'm an
American.
Well, the truth is I am both and neither. I love Armenia and I
love America and I belong to both, but I am only this: an inhabitant of the earth, and so are you, whoever you are. (P. 263)

Although fiercely aware of his Armenian roots and American loyal-
ties, the narrator is finally "both and neither"—he remains an "inhabitant of the earth." Thus Saroyan's concern with his Armenian
ancestry ultimately affirms brotherhood and reminds us of the
threats against it.

"The Armenian and the Armenian" is a travel sketch in which
Saroyan again presents both his love for his cultural traditions and a
one-earth philosophy: "There are only Armenians, and these in-
habit the earth, not Armenia, since there is no Armenia, gentlemen,
there is no America and there is no England, and no France, and no
Italy, there is only the earth, gentlemen" (p. 437). The piece ends
with a defiant flourish, showing Saroyan's indignation at the plight
of his ancestral homeland.

Go ahead, destroy this race. Let us say that it is again 1915.
There is war in the world. Destroy Armenia. See if you can do

it. Send them from their homes into the desert. Let them have neither bread nor water. Burn their houses and their churches. See if they will not live again. See if they will not laugh again. See if the race will not live again when two of them meet in a beer parlor, twenty years after, and laugh, and speak in their tongue. Go ahead, see if you can do anything about it. See if you can stop them from mocking the big ideas of the world, you sons of bitches, a couple of Armenians talking in the world, go ahead and try to destroy them. (P. 438)

Here is the characteristic Saroyan disdain for all ideological pretense, and his plea expands outward from the Armenians to include a shout of defiance in behalf of oppressed people everywhere.

Another powerful meeting between two Armenians is portrayed in "The Death of Children." When the boy-narrator meets Gourken, who comes from Van, Armenia, he feels a mystical sense of kinship with him: "And there was another who came quietly like a shadow, and he became my brother, whom I loved even more than I love my brother Krikor" (p. 140). The boys speak in Armenian with one another and become deep friends. Gourken attends school for a few years, and then one day the narrator's mother tells him: "Do you know that little boy, Gourken, who came from the old country? He is dead. And she showed me a photograph of him that had been printed in the *Asbarez* and she read the account of his life, and it was then that, standing in our house, I could feel a form of my life turning inward with this boy to return to memory, and it was then that I stood without a brother and felt the living death in me" (pp. 141–42).

The boy Gourken becomes symbolic of the death of the entire Armenian nation and its hopes for an independent life. The story takes place during Saroyan's boyhood, when he was seven or eight— hence during the height (1915) of the genocide. With the death of Gourken, something also dies within the narrator. A part of his own identity dies with the boy; an atavistic sense of ancient racial connections is suddenly awakened in him by Gourken, only to be swiftly extinguished by his early death.

Saroyan's growing awareness that the Armenian sensibility could provide a rich source of literary inspiration is reflected in "The Living and the Dead" from *Three Times Three*. He explores Armenian alienation not as an isolated phenomenon but as symptomatic of universal estrangement. Political activity, "love," and the escape of alcohol are all presented as false solutions to the problems that afflict the modern world. At the opening of the story, the narrator, Mike, is visited by his friend Pete, who attempts to enlist him in the left-wing cause; but Mike tells him that "under Communism . . . you'll be exactly the way you are now" (p. 40). Again Saroyan insists that the revolution must take place within the human spirit—the desire to change conditions only from the outside is doomed to failure. The tone in this first section is light and playful, however, setting the mood for the entrance of Mike's grandmother.

We recognize this grandmother from her earlier incarnation in "The Shepherd's Daughter." Both grandmothers are full of stories of life in Armenia and each looks askance at her grandson's immersion in books and the literary life: "Then my grandmother came into the room and stared bitterly at everything, grumbling to herself and lifting a book off the table, opening it, studying the strange print and closing it with an angry and impatient bang, as if nothing in the world could be more ridiculous than a book" (pp. 41–42). Both women are full of exuberant energy and exhibit a fierce independence of spirit. They presage the eccentric, humorous, and gentle Armenians who would populate the pages of *My Name Is Aram*.

Mike loves his grandmother deeply, regarding her as the greatest woman he has ever known. She begins to tell him of her murdered husband Melik, and contrasts his flamboyant energy with Mike's penchant for afternoon naps and reading: "For the love of God, said my grandmother, my husband Melik was a man who rode a black horse through the hills and forests all day and half the night, drinking and singing. When the townspeople saw him coming they would run and hide. The wild Kourds of the desert trembled in his presence. I am ashamed of you, she said, lolling around among these silly books" (p. 43).

Mike's grandfather was a wild nonconformist who lived life intensely and with great passion. For Saroyan, the Armenians possess personality, vividness, colorfulness, individuality—life. Many are, like Melik, *characters* who define themselves by a mad and exalted love of life.

In remembering her dead husband, Mike's grandmother grows lonely for her past life in Armenia. As the two play the card game *scambile*, she slowly descends into a mood of sorrowful remembrance: "Our tongue, she shouted, is a tongue of bitterness. We have tasted much of death and our tongue is heavy with hatred and anger" (p. 46). The grandmother's broken English, mannerisms, and tales are vividly rendered as we plunge into her world of sad memories. She is Mike's link to his Armenian heritage, and her melancholy fuses with his as the story progresses to its somber conclusion.

In the third section, Mike leaves his house for a bar—the Barrel House on Third Street in San Francisco. The section begins with his speculations on man's quest for "inward grace, inherent freedom of form, inherent truthfulness of being" (p. 52). To achieve being itself, that lovely gracefulness which all creatures except man "naturally possess" is extremely arduous

> because of the multitude of encumbrances halting the body and spirit of man on all sides: the heavy and tortuous ideas of civilization, the entanglement of the actual world in which we are born and from which we seem never to be able to emerge, and, above all things, our imprisonment in the million errors of the past, some noble, some half-glorious, some half-godly, but most of them vicious and weak and sorrowful.
>
> We know we are caught in this tragic entanglement, and all that we do is full of the unholiness of this heritage of errors, and all that we do is painful and difficult, even unto mere being, mere breathing, mere growing, and our suffering is eternally intensified by impatience, dissatisfaction, and that dreadful hope which is all but maddening in that its fulfillment seems unlikely, our hope for liberation, for sudden innocent and unencumbered reality, sudden and unending naturalness of movement, sudden godliness. (P. 52)

Man is trapped in a reality which prevents the leap into a redemptive unity, into the full divinity of being itself. On his way to town, Mike thinks that "the whole world, caught in time and space, seemed to me an absurdity, an insanity." Seeing a child crying at a window, he reflects on "the children of the world eternally at the window, weeping at the strangeness of this place" (p. 53).

The combined force of his grandmother's melancholy (which he says is his own "natural state") and the pain and suffering he sees around him finally drives Mike to alcohol. Yet drunkenness, "of all evasions, is the most ignoble, since one escapes to nowhere, or at any rate to a universe even more disorderly, if more magnificent, than our own, and then returns with sickened senses and a stunned spirit to the place only recently forsaken" (p. 53).[3]

Yet at the same time, alcohol has in it the truth of divine madness, and we are meant to think of Mike's grandfather Melik when the drunkard is described as "the most absurd of the individualists, the ultimate egoist, who rises and falls in no domain other than that of his own senses, though drunkards have been, and will long be, most nearly the children of God, most truthfully worshippers of the universal" (p. 53). We remember that Melik was just such a seeker after the Godhead in his Dionysian revels over the hills of Armenia. Furthermore, as he left the house, his grandmother had shouted after Mike, "Get a little drunk. Don't be so serious," thus reinforcing the implied connection between Mike and his legendary grandfather (p. 51).

Arriving at the Barrel House, Mike gets inebriated on "rotten whiskey," talks with Nick the waiter, and telephones a girl named Paula who refuses to see him because she is marrying a lawyer. Mike then goes to the Communist meeting which he had told Pete he might attend, and in the last drunken paragraph the story's various themes are brought together.

> I'm drunk, I said, and Paula's getting married to a lawyer, and Pete wants to save the world, and my grandmother is homesick for Armenia, and Nick's wife is going to have another baby, and listen, comrades, if I don't go easy climbing these stairs I'll fall down and bust my head, comrades. What good will it do when everybody has bread, comrades, what good will it do when everybody has cake, comrades, what good will it do when everybody has everything, comrades, everything isn't enough, comrades, and the living aren't alive, brothers, the living are

dead, brothers, even the living are not alive, brothers, and you
can't ever do anything about that. (P. 62)

The unappeasable hunger of the human heart can never be satisfied,
and desire will forever outreach fulfillment. Mike's inebriation has
allowed a sudden moment of illumination: as in "Noonday Dark
Enfolding Texas," the living and the dead are one.

"The Living and the Dead" is important in Saroyan's canon because it links the plight of the Armenian to a wide set of thematic
concerns. Mike's Armenian grandmother is lost in the new world,
trapped within her unhappy memories. Yet in the context of the
story as a whole, her estrangement is not seen as a solely personal
problem: it is the universal condition of humanity. Mike is painfully
aware that the political solutions offered by Pete are illusory, for
even when "everybody has bread," man's profoundest spiritual ques-
tionings remain unanswered.

Saroyan felt, however, that he was unsuccessful in combining the
story's various themes into an organic whole. Although he liked
parts of "The Living and the Dead," he thought that "with a little
luck, it might have been a great story."[4] In *The Boys in the Back
Room*, Edmund Wilson wrote that although the piece "miscarries,"
it is "one of the best things Saroyan has done."[5] Wilson points out
that it is a mistake for him to "neglect his craft," and that the faults
in his work are due to an unwillingness to devote himself to the hard
labor of revision. For "The Living and the Dead" to have achieved its
potential, he "would have had to take the whole thing more seriously and to work it out with care; and he knows that he can get
away with an almost infinite number of less pretentious pieces
without having their second-rateness complained of."[6]

As we have seen in *The Daring Young Man*, Saroyan wanted to
bring freedom and ease into American writing. Yet with ease also
comes self-indulgence, and his impulse to publish his work without
adequate revision has been often criticized. In view of scattered
comments throughout his work it is clear that this attitude toward
publication is not based on a lack of the self-critical faculty. Rather
it stems from a belief that life is imperfect, and hence art should not
exclude the rough-hewn or less-than-perfect.

This is a stance Saroyan shares with such "redskins" as Whitman,

Miller, and D. H. Lawrence, whose work is riddled with "clumsiness." To accept the work you must accept the man—excrescences and all. Saroyan has written: "I have always been amused by miscellaneous people who have believed that such and such a work of mine had something, whereas another work hadn't. If I wrote it, I said, it had what all the rest of what I had written had—it had my livingness. . . . Life and art are not separate. If they are, if they could be, art is a fraud, however wonderful."[7] Theoretically, Saroyan may believe this is true of his work as a whole; yet in specific instances, as we have seen with "The Living and the Dead," he is fully aware when his performance does not meet expectations.

A more in-depth portrayal of the Armenian-American experience is to be found in "Countryman, How Do You Like America?" from *Little Children*. Here we meet "Sarkis who came to America from the village of Gultik, in Armenia, in 1908 when he was not yet thirty years of age" (p. 191). He goes to Lynn, Massachusetts, works in a shoe factory, but suffers from loneliness. An Armenian priest convinces him to meet a girl he knows, and in a scene at once humorous and poignant, they become acquainted. She turns out to be unattractive, and Sarkis will not be convinced by the priest that he will grow to love her. At this point, a fellow Armenian arrives from California and sings the state's praises, telling Sarkis that it is just like their homeland, with "sunshine, vines, meadows, olive trees, fig trees, brooks, cows" (p. 196).

Sarkis then goes to California's San Joaquin Valley and works in a vineyard—but here too he finds difficulty communicating. His co-workers are not able to understand his conversation; he is lost, isolated, adrift in the new and strange culture of America. When Arshag Dombalian, also from Gultik, comes to the coffeehouse where Sarkis spends his Sundays and asks him how he likes America, Sarkis's response is typical of many of Saroyan's displaced immigrants: "What shall I say? Go; come; and with men known and unknown turn trays. That is all. Go, come; go, come; known, unknown; and turn trays" (p. 198).

This broken, telegraphic, and expressive English is the language we hear the Arab speak in a play Saroyan wrote two years later, *The Time of Your Life*: "No foundation. All the way down the line.

What. What-not. Nothing. I go walk and look at sky."[8] The spare
speech of both Sarkis and the Arab powerfully conveys their sense of
futility. Whether they come or go, meet people or remain alone,
remain unemployed or turn trays in vineyards, is immaterial—
everything they do is equally meaningless for there is "no foundation" to their existence.

At this point, the story shifts to a new focus—Sarkis marries and
becomes a successful farmer. He has children; one son becomes a
farmer and the other graduates from Berkeley—both his sons and
daughters speak and write English. Sarkis's children will be Americans; they have grown up naturally accepting their place in the new
world and the technological changes that are occurring. As Sarkis
muses to himself:

> It was all marvelous. The change he had seen in life and in the
> world, right before his very eyes. The telephone. The automo-
> bile. The tractor. Carpet-sweepers. Vacuum cleaners. Washing-
> machines. Electric refrigerators. The radio. His sons and daugh-
> ters speaking English, writing English, learning many things. It
> was a great age, a great time.
>
> Still, it was sad. He did not know. In Gultik it was fine too.
> One knew the man one spoke to. Arab, Arab; Kurd, Kurd; Turk,
> Turk; one knew. One knew the face, the eye, the nose, the very
> smell. It was home. One talked and knew who one was talking
> to; but in America what was it? He could never forget what it
> was in America. (P. 200)

Sarkis is still very much a member of the old generation; his heart
is in the highlands of Armenia and will never leave there. The story
ends with Sarkis "mournfully" sharing his sorrow with some fellow
Armenians, repeating his litany of lostness: "What do I know? Go,
come; and with men known and unknown turn trays" (p. 200). He is
still a sad man, uprooted and confused by the American experience.

With "Countryman, How Do You Like America?" Saroyan begins
to explore the developing gap between the Armenian immigrants
and their American-born children. As Henry Seidel Canby has observed, the "pioneer generation of the native born of foreign stock"
adjust themselves to life in America with great ease.[9] The older gen-

eration, however, remains firmly connected to the past; they continue to speak their native language and preserve intact the ancestral traditions of Armenia. Saroyan's exploration of the relationship between the two generations continues throughout his career—especially, as we shall see, in *My Name Is Aram*.

An illuminating contrast to Sarkis's melancholy experience in California's San Joaquin Valley can be found in a story from *Peace, It's Wonderful*: "The Warm, Quiet Valley of Home." While Sarkis regarded Armenia as "home," here the second-generation Armenian-American narrator feels deeply connected to the land of his birth: "It was September again and it was very pleasant. It was very hot, but it was very pleasant too. This was my valley, where I had been born. This earth and sky was home. This temperature was. My cousin was. The way he talked was. The memories he knew were part of it. The people he remembered" (p. 60). The valley is depicted here as a bright, sunny world which is full of sweetness and light. The narrator and this cousin are fortunate, for they can indeed go home again; they can reestablish their roots in the land, feel the oneness of self and nature, speak to dear relatives.

The two go for a drive in the country, drink beer, and, most important, make contact with their Armenian ancestors through a ritual firing of guns.

> We saluted many Armenian soldiers and scholars and writers and priests. We saluted many great men who were dead.
>
> We made a lot of noise in the hills, but it was all right because there was nobody around.
>
> When we got back to the car the beer was not quite as cold as it had been in the morning, but it was cool and good to drink.
>
> We drank the beer, my cousin cranked the car, we got in and drove out of the hills into the warm, quiet, lovely valley that was our home in the world. (P. 62)

The feeling of peace and contentment depicted here is in stark contrast to the perpetual unrest and loneliness that stirred in the immigrant Sarkis's heart. The San Joaquin is home for the two men; they experience the balance of being through their love of the land where they grew up and by nurturing a respectful relationship with the deep sources of their racial inheritance.

As we have seen, Saroyan depicts the Armenians caught in the struggle for happiness in an alien culture. Although many suffer from intense grief and loneliness, his eccentric foreigners exhibit a passionate vitality and exuberance—Grandfather Melik's "mad" nonconformism comes to mind. In later works, such as *My Name Is Aram*, his gay and melancholy Armenians continue to seek both a physical and metaphysical "home." Their fierce yearning would come to symbolize the desire of all his "maladjusted" characters for some sustaining faith and beauty.

CHAPTER 4

The Child Is Father of the Man

Saroyan's work is full of children; they make an appearance in virtually every major book and are among his best-drawn characters. He deeply loved the world of childhood and repeatedly sought to recreate it in his writing. Unlike many adults, children know how to *be*; they live fully and creatively in the timeless moment. It is their un-self-conscious faith in the miraculous nature of experience which he celebrates.

> Kids are the best company of all of course, but they grow up, and even before they do you can't spend much time with them because it bores them. They are in fact the only aristocracy of the human race, and after them come those who fail or refuse to wholly relinquish the aristocracy they acquired at birth; that is, the better poets and scientists and other creatively alive people, for the one thing all childhood has in common, as everyone by now knows, is creativeness. And the one thing all adulthood has in common is literalness: the great block to any real achievement of growth. Thus, the so-called adult is for the most part a case of blocked growth, of failure to live all of life at once, from birth to death.[1]

As we have seen, the aspect of modern experience which most troubles Saroyan is precisely this inability of humanity creatively to transform itself, to live life fully and joyously. Throughout his work, the adults who are most successful at achieving self-knowledge are those who retain the vitality, sense of wonder, and faith that is associated with childhood.

Saroyan's own young life in the San Joaquin Valley and its capital city, Fresno, is the subject of many of his childhood stories. A thoroughly autobiographical writer, he is never more so than when singing the brilliant and tragic memories of his California boyhood. The "I" in virtually all these stories is the author himself, at once telling and transforming his own experience in the act of writing.

As early as the stories of *Inhale and Exhale*, he had hewn out a fresh, clean, pure language to render the mind of a child. In "Five Ripe Pears," he tells of a six-year-old boy's theft from a neighbor's orchard: "I saw the pears before they were pears. I saw the bare tree twigs. I saw the leaves and the blossoms, and I kept seeing the pears until they were ready. I *made* them. The ripe ones belonged to me" (p. 16). It is significant that this tale is *remembered* by the adult narrator; the tone combines the voice of the adult in the present act of recollection with the voice of his six-year-old self of the past: "The trees grew in a yard protected by a spike fence, but some of the branches grew beyond the fence. I was six, but a logician. A fence, I reasoned, can protect only that which it encloses" (p. 13). The quick wit and flippant style show the mature humor of an adult, while the purity of perception is rendered in the language of a child, a technique which Saroyan would use later in *My Name Is Aram*.

The boy is then punished by his school principal: the perennial Saroyan tale of the imaginative, "creatively alive" and nonconforming child put in his place by the "authorities." For Saroyan, childhood is by no means wholly a time of innocent sweetness and light; many of his young characters exhibit a maturity and toughness far beyond their years. This is due in part to the fact that their viewpoints are often conveyed through adult narrators; yet it is also attributable to the harsh and painful realities of the author's own boyhood.

An orphaned street kid, he learned the ways of the world early. In "Resurrection of a Life," also from *Inhale and Exhale*, the narrator tells of his boyhood when he sold newspapers, spent time in theaters ("the theatre stood in the city like another universe," p. 5), and visited the San Joaquin Baking Company to smell the freshly baked bread: "But always he returned to the city, back again to the place of man, the street, the structure, the door and window, the hall, the roof and floor, back again to the corners of dark secrecy, where they were dribbling out their lives, back again to the movement of mobs, to beds and chairs and stoves, away from the tree, away from the meadow and the brook" (p. 7).

If the San Joaquin Valley was a place of spiritual peace and psychic connection, the city is described as a place of chaos, decay, and death. As the story continues, the boy yells the headlines of 1917: "*Ten thousand Huns killed, ten thousand*" (p. 8). With experience comes a loss of faith and the feeling that God is absent from the world. "No, he could not believe. He had seen for himself. It was there, in the city, all the godlessness, the eyes of the whores, the men at cards, the sleeping fat man, and the mad headlines, it was all there, unbelief, ungodliness, everywhere, all the world forgetting. How could he believe?" (p. 10).

The experience of doubt and despair comes early to many of Saroyan's characters, as it did to the author himself. As we have seen in the introduction, it was precisely the "ungodliness" of the outside world which drove him to the quest for faith and beauty through writing. The question asked in the above passage was one which he must have asked himself often during the poverty-stricken, lonely, and fatherless days of his childhood: "How could he believe?" The painful transition from faith to doubt and crisis to "maturity" is a journey which young Homer Macauley will also make in *The Human Comedy*; he too asks the hard questions of existence and suffers the agonies attendant upon soul-making.

Childhood is thus not only a time of creative ebullience and energy; it is also a time of spiritual testing, psychological disequilibrium, and uncertainty. The moment the permeable membrane of imaginative freedom is violated by the constraints of the "real world," the child must begin to move toward a new interpretation of experience. To be troubled is to grow: Saroyan at once celebrates the pristine innocence of childhood and affirms the natural rhythms of existence which necessarily push the young soul into spiritual crises. Children as well as adults live their lives within the gay and melancholy flux; if they possess sufficient inner strength, they are able to retain the Wordsworthian "aristocracy they acquired at birth."

Saroyan's children often show lovely and deep poetic qualities; yet they are most unsavory when they behave most like adults. In "Citizens of the Third Grade" from *The Trouble with Tigers*, he explores the process by which adult fears and hatreds are imitated by children. Adults are often "little children," dwarfed psychologically and emotionally, who pass on failure to their offspring. In this story, Tom Lucca is an Italian boy in Miss Gavit's class; he has been inculcated with a fierce nationalism. In the same class are the black twins Cain and Abel Jefferson, who are resentful of Tom's Fascist sympathies and his support of Mussolini's military adventurism in Ethiopia. Miss Gavit becomes a kind of arbiter between the warring factions, and although she realizes that Tom's attitude is potentially dangerous, she evinces prejudice herself: "Tom Lucca was impossible. He had no idea how dangerous his nervous and joyous behavior was getting to be. It was beginning to irritate Miss Gavit herself who, if anything, was in favor of having the ten million Ethiopians of Abyssinia under Italian care, which would do them much less harm than good and probably furnish some of the high government officials with shoes and perhaps European garments" (pp. 145–46). The narrator's irony is clear—Miss Gavit betrays the delusions of the white race which believes wholeheartedly in its "civilized" superiority over other cultures. Indeed, she is a rather naive twenty-seven-year-old teacher who "couldn't quite understand the continuous mess of the world" (p. 147).

Yet Miss Gavit shows real sensitivity to her students, and she realizes that although Tom Lucca exhibits a tough exterior to the world, he has a tender heart. He often shows kindness in his love for a friend's baby, and he generously gives his lunch to a boy whose father is unemployed. But when Miss Gavit keeps Tom after school one day to warn him about his behavior, he defends his pro-Fascist position with savage pride. Finally, the inevitable occurs, as the black twins and the Italians fight each other. Miss Gavit is shocked and thinks, "This is terrible; they've got no right to make these little boys fight this way. What did they want to invent guns for in the first place?" (p. 154).

Miss Gavit is appalled that neither Cain Jefferson nor the Italian Willy Trentino offers to apologize and become friends. She cries and is overcome with a sense of universal tragedy: "They killed those boys, they killed them, and she knew they were killing everybody everywhere" (p. 157). The ceremony of innocence is drowned, as the evil anonymous "they" of the world destroy the beautiful possibilities inherent in youth. The children, sadly, have become adults, and the movement from innocence to experience has terrible consequences.

In all the stories considered here, the complex inner lives of children are powerfully evoked. Children are human beings for Saroyan, not just symbolic representatives of some ideally beautiful world. As such, they are as vulnerable to the errors of adulthood as they are capable of achieving its ecstasies. His interest lies predominantly in the relationship between the child and adult worlds, in their symbiotic character. It is for this reason that it is difficult to determine for which age group this type of writing is "intended." He seeks to destroy in these instances the distinction between "children's" and "adult" literature: they are stories which are equally intelligible and appealing to both classes of reader.[2]

Saroyan's final work of his first creative phase, *My Name Is Aram*, is a "children's book" which is in the libraries of many adult readers. With *The Human Comedy* and *The Time of Your Life*, it is among his most widely known books. Here he combines the theme of childhood with his continuing interest in the Armenian immigrant in the United States. In the prefatory note to *My Name Is Aram*, he wrote that about half of the fourteen stories appeared originally in the *Atlantic Monthly* and that it was Edward J. O'Brien who encouraged him to "write more about the Armenians."[3] Here Saroyan openly acknowledged the San Joaquin Valley and the life of its Armenians as an important source of literary inspiration.

According to Saroyan, his experiences as a boy in the valley supplied "an abundance of material by nature so rich in the elements of comedy as to require little or no labor to select and chronicle." The act of writing was almost an act of transcription, for "the writer simply wrote the words while his spirit enjoyed their meaning" (p. viii). In connecting to the mother lode of his past, to the fables and family storytellers of his youth who "put me to roaring with laughter," he had found the subject matter of *My Name Is Aram*.[4] Saroyan's own original, joyful sense of humor was fecundated by the fables of his youth—a feel for life's ironies pervades his memories of an Armenian-American boyhood, 1915–25.

As was often the case in his earlier treatment of childhood, the stories of *My Name Is Aram* are *remembered*. The adult Aram Garoghlanian recalls the memories of youth, as we see in the book's opening piece, "The Summer of the Beautiful White Horse": "One day back there in the good old days when I was nine and the world was full of every imaginable kind of magnificence, and life was still a delightful and mysterious dream, my cousin Mourad, who was considered crazy by everybody except me, came to my house at four in the morning and woke me by tapping on the window of my room" (p. 3). This is a lyrical evocation of the past, when life was yet uncomplicated and the children's windows onto the world were unclouded by the sorrow of experience. Aram and his cousin take a horse belonging to the farmer John Byro, "an Assyrian who, out of loneliness, had learned to speak Armenian" (p. 12). He yearns for his homeland, as does Aram's colorful Uncle Khosrove, who repeats at every opportunity a favorite phrase, "pay no attention to it." The two boys ride the horse (which Mourad named "My Heart"), and when they meet Byro, he says that, although the horse certainly looks as though it is his, he would not accuse the boys of honest families of stealing. The story's charm and humor set the tone for the entire book, as we enter the world of memory, of sad, gentle, and eccentric uncles, of boys' adventures.

These adventures are unified through Aram's central role as narrator and hero. Aram, like Tom Sawyer, is highly imaginative and thoroughly individualistic. His spirit is in essential opposition to all forms of authority. What James Cox has said of Twain's "world of boyhood" applies equally well to Aram's experience in the San Joaquin Valley, for he too lives in a realm "where play, make-believe, and adventure are the living realities defining the false pieties and

platitudes which constitute the dull pleasure of the adult world."[5]
Aram's activities celebrate the triumph of freedom over restraint, of
the intense over the quotidien. School, the church, the arbitrary
rules of repressed adults—Aram and his friends are bemused at the
odd notions of the institutional world.

As with Twain's child heroes, many of Aram's unhappiest times
are related to his unwillingness to be "educated." He is in constant
conflict with school authorities. "A Nice Old-Fashioned Romance,
with Love Lyrics and Everything" shows Aram being punished by
the principal for writing love poems to his teacher on the black-
board, although his cousin Arak had been the actual offender. In
"The Circus," Aram and his friend Joey Renna are truant so they
might go to the circus, and both boys are mildly strapped. And in
"One of Our Future Poets, You Might Say," Aram demonstrates his
uniqueness to the board of education by inhaling and exhaling for
six minutes. He will be a poet in the future, an iconoclast—not a
statesman or a captain of industry, as his teachers would have it.

Aram is also unwilling to accept the pious sentimentality of or-
ganized religion, as we see in "The Presbyterian Choir Singers."
Aram tells us that he was "growing a little skeptical, as it were, of
the whole conventional religious pattern, and was eager, by hook or
by crook, to reach an understanding of my own, and to come to
terms with Omnipotence in my own way" (p. 129). Like Tom Sawyer, who when instructed to memorize his Bible lesson "chose part
of the Sermon on the Mount, because he could find no verses that
were shorter," Aram lives the religion of Life.[6] He has no need for
the letter because he already lives completely in the spirit.

Aram is a coherent and integrated self from the beginning of the
book, and his character remains essentially static. We do not see
him undergo the painful purgative experiences that catalyze Homer
Macauley's spiritual transformation. This fact has importance in
relation to the structure of the book, for although the various stories
describe Aram's life between the ages of eight and fifteen, they do
not follow his growth in a linear, chronological fashion. In the first
story, "The Summer of the Beautiful White Horse," he is nine years
old; "The Pomegranate Trees" depicts events occurring when the
narrator was between eleven and fifteen years old; yet the fourth

story, "One of Our Future Poets, You Might Say," returns to Aram when he is "eight going on nine or at the most nine going on ten, and good-natured" (p. 59). It is clear that Saroyan is not interested in giving us a strict chronological narrative of Aram's life. Because he does not change significantly, it is possible for Saroyan to take up his narrative at any point in time. *My Name Is Aram* is not a Bildungsroman, but rather a series of vignettes, of remembered scenes, of episodes which are connected stylistically and thematically.

One of the major themes linking the various stories together is Saroyan's emphasis on the "misfits" who have kept their inner purity and childlike innocence intact. They are not merely the mediocre instruments of society's institutions—the teachers and preachers Aram so vehemently scorns. Rather, it is with these isolated eccentrics and iconoclasts that Aram is able to achieve true communication.

In "The Three Swimmers and the Grocer from Yale," for example, Aram and two friends go swimming during a rainstorm and get caught in the river mud. As they walk home, they meet a strange grocer who in his nonconformity is considered "crazy" by Aram's friends. His colorful expressions ("Well, I'll be cut off a vine and eaten grape by grape by a girl in her teens" [p. 157]) and unbridled enthusiasm seem odd to them. But when the boys return a month later and the old man has been replaced by a "normal" grocer, they realize they have lost a true friend. They see that the kindness ("he gave away more than he sold" [p. 164]) and love which emanated from him seemed "crazy" because these are such rare commodities in the adult world. Aram muses at the end of the story: "He sure was some man. Twenty years later, I decided he had been a poet and had run that grocery store in that little run-down village just for the casual poetry in it instead of the paltry cash" (p. 165). The grocer "was an old man who seemed funny and young," and because he affirms the poetic in existence over the materialistic, he is Aram's spiritual blood brother (p. 155).

In "Locomotive 38, the Ojibway," Aram meets another outsider—a young Indian from the Ojibway tribe. He is extremely wealthy and buys a new Packard automobile, employing Aram as his chauffeur. The Indian's wild impulsiveness and vitality have made the conventional citizens of the town come to believe he is a lunatic. Aram naturally takes to him immediately; the Indian sits in the backseat of the Packard as Aram drives around the valley in search of places to fish and hunt.

> I drove that big Packard for this Ojibway Indian, Locomotive 38, as long as he stayed in town, which was all summer. He stayed at the hotel all the time. I tried to get him to learn to drive, but he said it was out of the question. I drove that Packard all over the San Joaquin Valley that summer, with the Indian in the back, chewing eight or nine sticks of gum. He told me to drive anywhere I cared to go, so it was either to some place where I could fish, or some place where I could hunt. He claimed I didn't know anything about fishing or hunting, but he was glad to see me trying. As long as I knew him he never laughed, except once. That was the time I shot at a jack-rabbit with a 12-gauge shotgun that had a terrible kick, and killed a crow. He tried to tell me all the time that that was my average. To shoot at a jack-rabbit and kill a crow. (Pp. 182–83)

Finally the Indian returns to Oklahoma with his brother, and Aram again ends the story by rejecting the idea that the Indian was crazy. In this adventurous and eminently "impractical" Indian, Aram finds another spiritual comrade—another defier of the constraints of the"real world." Neither of these "foreigners" conforms; the Indian and the Armenian-American are joyful colleagues in the imagination.

Aram's ebullient meetings with these eccentric adult friends are structurally balanced by the presence of the other misfits of the book: the Armenian immigrants. Interlaced with the happy stories of boyhood are portraits of Aram's relatives who yearn for Armenia, launch impractical business schemes, and immerse themselves in the world of the spirit. Although they live in the material world, many members of the Garoghlanian family long for an intense spiritual fulfillment, for a deeper dimension of meaning and significance. Like Aram and his friends, the Armenians are also caught in a world whose rules they reject; they often suffer for refusing to play society's game. They are poets whose hearts hear an unheard and lovely music sounding far away.

We meet such a poet in Uncle Melik of "The Pomegranate Trees." Aram tells us at the opening of the story that "Melik was just about the worst farmer that ever lived. He was too imaginative and poetic for his own good. What he wanted was beauty" (p. 35). When Melik attempts unsuccessfully to plant pomegranate trees in the desert, we feel a poignant stab of compassion for the tender-hearted, sweet-souled, "impractical" aliens who are Saroyan's beautiful people.

Melik's failure to make the trees bloom in the desert is symbolic of the alienation and homelessness that afflicts many of Saroyan's immigrants. The Arab Khalil of "The Poor and Burning Arab" also experiences deep despair. He finally dies, an "orphan in an alien world, six thousand miles from home" (p. 207). Like Melik, who cannot make the desert fecund with the fruit of his dreams, the Arab is unable to feel at home in the San Joaquin Valley.

Although the experiences of both Melik and the Arab are profoundly disappointing, we also see the mad and humorous aspects of Aram's family, thus relating the theme of "craziness" directly to his own relatives.[7] The Garoghlanian clan is full of "fools" like Uncle Jorgi of "The Journey to Hanford," who quietly dreams, plays the zither, and refuses to take a job. In the same story, the grandfather exhibits a comical and harmless fury, and his deliberate, idiosyncratic, yet precise English is uproarious. Uncle Gyko of "The Fifty Yard Dash" spends his time studying Oriental philosophy and practicing yoga, and Aram describes him lovingly.

> My uncle was getting all his dope free from the theosophy-philosophy-astrology-and-miscellaneous shelf at the Public Library. He believed, however, that he was getting it straight from God. Before he took up Yoga he had been one of the boys around town and a good drinker of *rakhi*, but after the light began to come to him he gave up drinking. He said he was drinking liquor finer than *rakhi* or anything else.
> What's that? I asked him.
> Aram, he said, eat ease weasdom. (P. 73)

Aram's deep affinity for his many uncles is immediately apparent. They are admirable because they follow their own inner lights against all opposition and are occupied with the search for "weasdom."

Yet Aram is not a completely naive observer of his relatives. The style and tone of the above passage betray a certain ironic detachment, a witty, colloquial hipness of perception. His uncle gets "all his dope free"—an expression implying that Gyko's wisdom might be slightly fraudulent. The phrase "getting it straight from God" also carries a suggestion of amusement at his uncle's sense of moral superiority. Finally, the fact that Gyko used to be "one of the boys" but is now enraptured by spiritual truth suggests that his conversion may be short-lived. Indeed, at the end of the story, Aram tells us:

> When my uncle Gyko came to visit me he was no longer hollow-cheeked. It seems he had finished his fast, which had been a long one—forty days or so; and nights too, I believe. He had stopped meditating, too, because he had practically exhausted the subject. He was again one of the boys around town, drinking, staying up all hours, and following the women.
>
> I tell you, Aram, he said, we are a great family. We can do *anything.* (P. 79)

Again, "it seems he had finished his fast" translates into "of course he had finished his fast"; "forty days or so; and nights too," followed by the offhand "I believe," betrays a wry amusement; Gyko's abandonment of meditation has occurred "because he had practically exhausted the subject"; this too elicits from Aram an ironic smile, for the phrase suggests that the subject has actually exhausted Gyko.

As the book progresses, we see that although Aram loves and understands his Armenian relatives, he is somehow distinct, different, a spectator. While many of the older generation are trapped, living their lives in yearning and quiet desperation, Aram's youthful energy and optimism define him as a member of the new generation. When Aram says to the Indian in "Locomotive 38, the Ojibway," "I'm no American," the Indian responds: "I know, the Indian said. You're an Armenian. I remember. I asked you and you told me. You're an Armenian born in America. You're fourteen years old and already you know you'll be able to drive an automobile the minute you get into one. You're a typical American, although your complexion, like my own, is dark" (p. 172). It is an eerie moment when

Aram is told by an Indian (another alienated outcast who is tolerated by white society, in this case because he is wealthy) that he does not really know himself. Although Aram may think of himself as an Armenian, he is essentially different from his ancestors—he is an American.

The contrast between the two generations can also be seen in "The Poor and Burning Arab." Khalil is the friend of Aram's Uncle Khosrove, and the two men come to visit Aram's house. The Arab rarely speaks, and when he does, it is "in a voice that seemed to come not so much from himself as from the old country" (p. 196). The two sad immigrants communicate through a kind of silent telegraphy of the soul, and Aram's mother asks him to leave so they can be alone. Aram sits in the dining room looking at a copy of the *Saturday Evening Post*, which he "knew by heart—especially the pictures: Jello, very architectural; automobiles, with high-toned people standing around; flashlights flashing into dark places; tables set with bowls of soup steaming; young men in fancy ready-made suits and coats; and all sorts of other pictures" (p. 201).

Symbolically, this is the most important scene in the book: Aram reading advertisements in a mass-circulation American magazine, as his foreign uncle and friend commiserate over their despairing lives. Present and past, youth and age, America and homeland, wealth and poverty—all are starkly contrasted in a single tableau. Aram is fascinated by the images of American popular culture; near the end of the story, Khosrove says that Aram "is an American. He was born here," thus showing that his relatives are also aware of his status as a member of the new generation (p. 206).

This passage also illustrates another prevalent stylistic feature of *My Name Is Aram*: poetic implication through understatement. Saroyan does not *tell* the reader that Aram is different; rather he suggests through symbolic images the developing gulf between the two generations. Words only point toward that which cannot be said, toward transcendental meanings implicit in everyday experience. When the silent communication between the two men continues, Aram is prompted to ask his mother what good words are since people seem to be able to talk without them. She responds: "Not very good, most of the time. Most of the time they're only good to keep back what you really want to say, or something you don't want known" (p. 204).

Indeed, as we have seen in the above passages, Saroyan uses a spare, economical, and silent language to describe Aram's world. Bonamy Dobrée has pointed out that in *My Name Is Aram* "the art is most definitely one of subtraction, of shearing away the trimmings; it becomes an art of inarticulateness, where the silences say more than the words."[8] Saroyan's desire to evolve such an art had been with him from the beginning; in 1936 he advised: "Do not write with words, write without words, write with silence."[9] Throughout Aram's adventures, Saroyan is after clarity: a precise yet suggestive lyricism which captures the quick movements of the spirit.

Through his agile prose and vibrant characterizations, Saroyan succeeds in balancing the positive and negative elements of *My Name Is Aram*. Aram's youthful vigor, keen imagination, and openness to experience temper the reader's response to the unhappiness of many of his relatives. In the book's final piece, "A Word to Scoffers," we are given Saroyan's philosophy of faith when Aram meets a missionary at the bus depot who tells him to believe everything. Yet as we have seen, from the beginning Aram's message had been affirmative and his attitude does not need changing. The book leaves us feeling we have entered an autonomous world of the imagination, a world momentarily caught before it makes the swift and inevitable transition into memory.

CHAPTER 5

World and Theater

When Saroyan turned seriously to the writing of drama in 1939, he continued his search for self-realization in the modern world. In plays such as *My Heart's in the Highlands* and *The Time of Your Life*, he sought to depict the deepest spiritual need of contemporary humanity—the desire to discover a way to live life meaningfully. The implicit question posed by his plays is: "How might we best live in order to fulfill our most profound potential as human beings?" In play after play, he attempted to reveal the world as a place of mysterious beauty and pain in which the individual struggles for psychological integration. The process of achieving wholeness is rarely easy for his questing characters; as we shall see, the plays gain their dramatic impetus from the continual tension between the possibilities of fulfilled selfhood and the actual suffering and disharmony of the world.

Between 1939 and 1943, Saroyan published and produced his most famous plays. Works such as *My Heart's in the Highlands*, *The Beautiful People*, and *Across the Board on Tomorrow Morning* were well received by many critics and audiences; *The Time of Your Life* was awarded the Pulitzer Prize as the best play of the 1939–40 season (which he refused on the grounds that the wealthy should not patronize art).

Although championed by critics like George Jean Nathan, Saroyan had a strained relationship with the theatrical world from the beginning. From the time his first play appeared on Broadway, critics found his work "surrealistic," "sentimental," and difficult to un-

derstand. His creation of a fragile, fluid, dramatic universe full of
strange, lonely, confused, and gentle people startled theatergoers
accustomed to conventional plot and characterization. His instinc-
tive, original, and highly innovative sense of dramatic form was lost
on many audiences. These plays were a confounding amalgam of
vaudeville, absurdism, sentiment, spontaneity, reverie, humor, despair, philosophical speculation, and whimsy; they seemed the un-
disciplined outpourings of a neophyte intent upon ignoring dramatic
convention and tradition. Many observers were both puzzled and
doubtful about his artistic aims and purposes.

The inability of early commentators fully to come to terms with
his dramatic practice can be traced to their failure to acknowledge
the significance of the concept of "play" (and, as we shall see later in
this chapter, of vaudeville), the philosophical relation between
imagination and reality, and the relation of both of these aspects to
Saroyan's central theme of self-integration. The plays are actually
far from being haphazard in conception or technique. Underlying
their structure is a coherent aesthetic philosophy which the author
had evolved over the years and elaborated in various essays, in autobiographical writings, and, most important, in his dramatic prefaces.

His penchant for utilizing the preface as a mode of artistic explanation can be traced to the influence of George Bernard Shaw,
whose iconoclastic defiance appealed powerfully to Saroyan.[1] Like
Shaw, he sought in his plays to uncover true sources of value, to
redeem the world's terrible chaos through the "play" of art. He also
believed with Shaw that the purpose of the playwright is both *do-
cere* and *delectare*: to teach *and* to entertain and delight. In an essay
entitled "The Two Theaters," Saroyan discusses the relationship of
the "real world" to the world of the theater, pointing out that "the
play of reality," of daily world events,

> is too big, too complicated, too endless, too contradictory,
> formless, meaningless, crazy, brutal, and lovely, and everything
> else, to be entertaining to a human being.
>
> So what? So we have the other theater and the other play. Our
> theater. Our play. Which brings me down to earth. I have always
> loved this theater because I have always liked order and I have

always liked looking closely and listening carefully and finding
out, and that is what the theater is. That is what any art is.
Most of all, though, I have liked *the play*. That is, the granted
unreality, as when children say *Play like*.[2]

The modern world is too complicated and chaotic to possess the
meaning and significance the artist seeks, for among human beings
"there is little artful living."[3] As we have seen earlier, art for Saroyan, as for Nietzsche, exists so that we will not perish from the
truth—the truth of the world's painful contradictions. Art, the writing of plays, makes a harmony where before there was a dissonance.
Art achieves this triumph through the "play," the "granted *unreality*" of the human imagination.

In his stimulating essay "On Reality," Saroyan concludes that
the reason the world has become such a melancholy place is that
"there's been no real imagination." Freshness and spontaneity have
disappeared, and the art of our time has been "shabby and pointless
and clinical."[4] When the imagination is restored to its primacy, however, reality is recreated, made endurable; its labor and pain are
transformed into play and delight. As he had written in the preface
to *Three Times Three*, "the activities of man on earth by nature
were meant to be activities of play, of ease and improvisation. Genius is play, and man's capacity for achieving genius is infinite, and
man may achieve genius only through play."[5]

It is precisely this emphasis on "play" which distinguishes Saroyan's dramatic work and which most confounded his early audiences.
Yet this concept is actually very much a part of the American literary tradition. We are again reminded of Whitman's "I loaf and invite
my soul" and his exaltation of the limitless potentialities of a life
lived with improvisatory ease and spontaneity. Saroyan's contemporary Henry Miller has also explored the relationship between art
and play: "Through art, then, one finally established contact with
reality: that is the great discovery. Here all is play and invention;
there is no solid foothold from which to launch the projectiles which
will pierce the miasma of folly, ignorance and greed. The world has
not to be put in order: the world *is* order incarnate."[6]

For Miller, as for Saroyan, the dull, daily routine of work "is the very opposite of creation, which is play, and which just because it has no *raison d'être* other than itself is the supreme motivating power in life."[7] Through the play of art the self makes contact with the deepest realities of life. Drama is an entrance, a magic opening into another world, and the theater is the place where the miraculous transformation of chaotic reality into form and imagination occurs.

It is this relationship between reality, imagination, and the search for true being that Saroyan's plays seek to explore. As we have seen, the artist is motivated to create by a fierce inability to accept reality as it is, and by the early forties the radicalism of Saroyan's own philosophical position became apparent.

> Nobody other than myself seems to understand that the world is not real. That in reality there is no such thing as the world. There is, of course, but I mean for all practical purposes. When I say practical I mean poetic and wonderful. The world which everyone other than myself seems to have identified and accepted as The World is in reality a figment in a nightmare of an idiot. No one could possibly create anything more surrealistic and unbelievable than the world which everyone believes is real and is trying very hard to inhabit. The job of art, I say, is to make a world which can be inhabited.[8]

Self-integration is thus achieved through the transforming powers of the imagination. Again, Saroyan emphasizes the therapeutic purposes of artistic activity and its central role in creating a livable world. The "real world" as it is, presents an awful panorama of absurdity, which the artist must redeem through the creation of a visionary realm of *true* reality.

To many commentators, however, it often seemed as though Saroyan were actually substituting his private fantasies for the irresolvable complexities of the real world. According to Heinrich Straumann, his plays were "like dramatized fairy tales without plots. . . . The conflict between reality and imagination is solved by the absolute supremacy of the world of fantasy transforming everyday life into a succession of dream-like moments of kindness and joy."[9] Yet it is simply not the case that the "world of fantasy" achieves "absolute supremacy" in Saroyan's plays. Rather, the plays strike a delicate balance between imagination and reality, one realm always subtly impinging on the other. Far from replacing reality with pure imagination, Saroyan repeatedly depicts the two realms in a state of dynamic tension.

The "two theaters," imagination and reality, the inner world and the outer world, are represented symbolically in the actual scenic design of his drama. In play after play, the inward life and the surface life are dramatically juxtaposed. For example, the poor families of *My Heart's in the Highlands* and *The Beautiful People* are enclosed within the fragile shelter of their homes, where they seek to affirm the values of love and beauty. In *The Time of Your Life* lonely refugees from the world's unrest find a temporary home in Nick's Pacific Street Saloon, Restaurant, and Entertainment Palace. A restaurant-bar is also the scene of *Across the Board on Tomorrow Morning*; the waiter Thomas Piper tells us that "outside of this restaurant is the illusion of the world. Here, in this restaurant, is the illusion of our reality."[10] And *The Cave Dwellers* takes place in an abandoned theater, the symbolic cave that is also another makeshift home for Saroyan's restless wanderers.

These plays, then, are far from being "fairy tales." On the contrary, Saroyan sought to depict the difficult struggle of the sensitive individual yearning for a home in a constantly threatening, increasingly hostile universe. As he pointed out later in his career, the work of the years 1939–43 was a "clear declaration of distrust of the popular values of a culture near bankruptcy: I am here, but if you want to know the truth, my heart isn't, my heart is in the highlands."[11] The noisy chaos of a "culture near bankruptcy" is often heard rumbling at the periphery of Saroyan's delicately poised dramatic world.

The feeling of estrangement, of not being at home in the "uninhabitable" world, is a dominant theme throughout his plays. What he has said of himself is equally true of his searching characters: they are here, but their hearts are not. Like their counterparts in the short stories, they are searching for the rest and warmth of home. Although many commentators have correctly perceived Saroyan's joyful comic genius, few have acknowledged the centrality of this difficult quest for life's most profound mystery. Seeing the plays through the distorting lens of a single perspective, we fail to recognize the sensitive balance between affirmation and despair, light and darkness; we also fail to come to terms with the full, rich complexity of Saroyan's characters.

Reading or seeing the plays, we are less interested in the author's philosophical or aesthetic rationale than in his vivid and exuberant characters. It is logical that he would turn to the writing of drama: his stories overflowed with people, with talk, with *characters*, and his imagination was essentially dramatic from the outset. To write a play, he simply set his characters talking on the stage; it required little effort to move from one genre to the other. The story "The Man with the Heart in the Highlands" from *Three Times Three*, for example, was easily transformed into Saroyan's first major play, *My Heart's in the Highlands*.

Although the tones and moods of the two versions are quite different, the theme in both is again exile and estrangement. In the story's opening, we are introduced to the elderly misfit, Jaspar MacGregor, seen through the child-narrator's eyes.

> In 1914, when I was not quite six years old, an old man came down San Benito Avenue on his way to the old people's home playing a solo on a bugle and stopped in front of our house. I ran out of the yard and stood at the curb waiting for him to start playing again, but he wouldn't do it. I said, I sure would like to hear you play another tune, and he said, Young man, could you get a glass of water for an old man whose heart is not here, but in the highlands?[12]

We then meet the boy Johnny's father, a boisterous unpublished poet who remains unnamed. He tells his son to get Mr. MacGregor (who we soon learn is both musician and Shakespearean actor) a pitcher of water and then invites him to lunch. But the impoverished family has no food, and Johnny's father instructs the boy to get bread and cheese from the neighborhood grocer, Mr. Kosak. Johnny is reluctant to go, for he is weary of begging for credit from Mr. Kosak, but Mr. MacGregor and his father finally convince him.

Johnny and the grocer have a humorous conversation as the boy tries (finally successfully) to obtain groceries. He returns home, and the three eat together, as Johnny's grandmother "paced through the house, singing arias from Puccini" (p. 20). Mr. MacGregor then consents to play his bugle again, and a group of neighbors come to listen to "My Heart's in the Highlands, My Heart Is Not Here," which brings them to tears. After MacGregor has stayed with the family for a few weeks, a young man from the old people's home comes and asks him to live there because they "need a leading actor for our next production, Old People's Follies of 1914" (p. 22). MacGregor, who has told us before that he is "five thousand miles from home," then goes away, as Johnny, his father, and grandmother return to their destitute yet joyous lifestyle.

Although the plot, characters, and dialogue are substantially unchanged in the dramatic version, the play addresses the problems of alienation and spiritual hunger from a more serious perspective. The play's stage directions place greater emphasis on the isolation and poverty of the family's house: "An old white, broken-down, frame house with a front porch, on San Benito Avenue in Fresno, California. There are no other houses near by, only a desolation of bleak land and red sky."[13] In addition, the first scene opens with the lonely cry of a train whistle in the background. The setting thus evokes a mood of sadness, yearning, and tender melancholy which is largely absent in the story.

In the play, Johnny is nine years old instead of six, and his father has a name: Ben Alexander. The father has a much larger role in the play, reciting his poetry in a roaring voice: "Crippled and weeping, time stumbles through the lone lorn heart" (p. 28). We are also told that the family is Armenian, and Ben speaks with his mother in their native tongue at various points in the play. Although this detail may seem insignificant, it adds a deeper dimension to the theme of exile: we now respond to Mr. MacGregor's homelessness within the context of Armenian estrangement in America. Saroyan himself has drawn the parallel in *Obituaries*: "Jaspar MacGregor, or Kaspar der Krikor, it comes to the same thing, you know, and highlands are highlands, whether in Scotland or Armenia, whether traversed by Robert Burns in actual singing strides, or by myself in shouting laughing strides of spirit both in Scotland and in Armenia thousands of miles from the streets of Fresno."[14] Even Saroyan's Scotsmen are

Armenian; the highlands for which Mr. MacGregor yearns are thus symbolic of the highlands of Armenia, which linger in the memory of many exiles.

In the play, MacGregor's longing for home is defined in tragic terms. The difference in tone between story and play is immediately apparent in the dialogue between Johnny and his father as they discuss MacGregor's situation.

> JOHNNY: Do you think he'll ever get home again some day?
> JOHNNY'S FATHER: He's an old man, Johnny. He will.
> JOHNNY: You mean he'll take a train and a boat and get back
> where the highlands are?
> JOHNNY'S FATHER: Not that, Johnny. It's a little different
> from that. He'll *die.*
> JOHNNY: Is that the only way a man gets home?
> JOHNNY'S FATHER: That's the only way.
>
> (Pp. 65–66)

The implication that spiritual turmoil and the longing of the human heart can be stilled only through death is absent in the story, but becomes a powerful theme in the play. One of the great messages of Saroyan's drama is first sounded here: that we are not at home on Earth; that the lonely train whistle blowing in the night is the stifled cry of every living soul for an impossible consummation. As Johnny's father tells him, for MacGregor, as for Everyman, life is exile and home is death.

Death pervades the play. Johnny's mother and the parents of Henry the newspaper boy have passed away. Furthermore, the threat of World War II hovers over the play, and Ben Alexander rages against the triumph of death over life. Reading the newspaper, he agonizes: "Austria. Germany. France. England. Russia. Zeppelins. Submarines. Tanks. Machine guns. Bombs. (*Shaking his head*) They've gone crazy again" (p. 63). His anger and pained disbelief are diametrically opposed to the gentle eccentricity he exhibits in the story: "You frauds of the world. You wretched and ungodly. (*He stands and points a finger, as if across the world*) Go ahead. *Fire* your feeble guns. You won't kill *anything.* (*Quietly, smiling*) There will always be poets in the world (*Lightning flashes silently*)" (p. 71). The rejection of the forces of light and life is symbolized by the rejection of Ben Alexander's poems by the *Atlantic Monthly*; the voice of the poet is ignored, and he is left to wonder why people "destroy themselves running after things of death, and thrust aside all things of life? I can't understand it. There's no hope for *anybody*" (p. 70).

War, as we have seen earlier, represents the ultimate destruction of humanity's hope for spiritual wholeness and integration. Yet if the race is to survive, the quest for brotherhood must not be abandoned. That Saroyan saw *My Heart's in the Highlands* as yet another formulation of his central theme is clear from the play's preface: "The imperative requirement of our time is to restore faith to the mass and integrity to the individual. The integration of man is still far from realized." As the play progresses, it becomes clear that Ben Alexander and Jaspar MacGregor are brother poets who seek to "restore faith to the mass" of despairing humanity. If we ask, with Hölderlin, "What are poets for in a destitute time?" the answer the play gives is clear: poets exist to show mankind its hidden potential for achieving inner wholeness and creativity.[15]

Toward the end of the play, MacGregor recites an improvised version of the "Blow, winds, and crack your cheeks" soliloquy from *King Lear* after he has deeply moved the neighbors with his bugle music. His defiant recitation of poetry links him directly to Ben Alexander—he too is an artist in revolt against the modern age. Furthermore, the lyrical, ecstatic music he plays stands for the spiritual essence of experience and the timeless joy the heart seeks. Both his music and poetry celebrate the mysterious meaning at the core of life and affirm a love for humanity in all its tragic grandeur.

MacGregor's fear that he will be taken away to the convalescent home, however, continues to haunt him, and his rendition from Shakespeare is finally to be understood as a last defiant gesture (like Lear's) against fate. After giving the speech, MacGregor dies, thus fulfilling Ben Alexander's prophetic utterance. This is the most important departure from the story, for MacGregor is now transformed into a tragic hero whose death symbolizes the annihilation of poetry in the modern world. The play ends as Johnny and his father leave their house to a young couple—they are no longer able to afford the rent. As they go to the street, Johnny turns to his father and asks:

JOHNNY: Where the hell do we think we're going, Pa?
JOHNNY'S FATHER: Never mind, Johnny. You just follow *me*.
JOHNNY: I'm not mentioning any names, Pa, but something's
wrong somewhere.
(The music grows louder. They walk up the street)
(P. 104)

This is a strange and terrible realization for a nine-year-old boy, yet
moments of grievious doubt repeatedly paralyze characters in Saroyan's plays. *Talking to You* ends with the young boy Paul hypnotically
asking the reason for the world's chaos: "What's the matter? What's
the matter? I don't like it anywhere. What's the matter? What's the
matter with everybody? What's the matter everywhere?"[16] Like
Paul, Johnny is wounded by the unyielding pain afflicting the entire
world; he is also confused at MacGregor's death and the senseless-
ness of his family's continuing poverty. Saroyan had written in the
play's preface that "in order to accomplish more than the trivial and
tentative, art must know deeply and intimately the grief, the despair,
and the frustration of its time. It must know the sources of these
things and the destinations of them."[17] Indeed, the characters in *My
Heart's in the Highlands* are fully acquainted with the grief of their
time.

Saroyan's second play also deals with the themes of estrangement
and homelessness. *The Time of Your Life*, however, confronted these
issues in a fresh and innovative manner. The author felt that "a new
kind of play impels or even demands a new kind of theatrical method and style"; he therefore extended the range of his dramatic technique through the use of that quintessentially American form of
theatrical expression—vaudeville.[18] He discovered in this native art
form the means to realize his vision of a drama which would celebrate play and spontaneity, yet also seriously grapple with the problems of contemporary existence.

In his stories, memoirs, and essays, Saroyan has often considered
the influence of vaudeville on his literary imagination. In "How and
Why to Be a Playwright," he unfavorably compares Ibsen's plays
(which he had read in his youth) to vaudeville.

I read these plays, and from not understanding them too well, enhanced or enlarged their greatness. But I didn't care to try to imitate the style. It was too cagey, crafty, and calculating. Vaudeville pleased me more, and seemed more real. It was easygoing and didn't try for too much and as a result very often achieved things Ibsen himself couldn't achieve. Vaudeville was American, too, which made a great difference.[19]

As we have seen earlier in connection with the short story, Saroyan also wished to bring ease into American drama. Because vaudeville eschewed the pretentious, it achieved an improvisatory freedom which transmitted the realities of American life without being ponderous.

Vaudeville also appealed powerfully to Saroyan because its structure corresponded exactly to his own conception of the nature of reality. Vaudeville's rapid shifting from scene to scene and its surreal amalgamation of songs, dances, gymnastics, cross-talk, and slapstick humor mirrored the chaotic juxtaposition of events in the real world. For Saroyan, reality was ever-changing, fluid, contradictory, absurd, miraculous, comic, and tragic—it was the gay and melancholy flux. Life, like vaudeville, was frenetic activity, unimpeded movement, the energy of pure being. In his plays, he sought to capture the flow of reality and life's eternal flux, unstopped by artificial intellectual constructs or formal constraints.

In the preface to the play *Subway Circus*, he explains that the circus (another form of vaudeville) is to be understood as a symbol which "most nearly approximates the simultaneity and disorder of events in the world." In the circus, as in the multiplicity of reality, "there is always more going on than any one human eye can perceive or enjoy."[20]

In *The Time of Your Life*, he attempts to translate the wild excitement and simultaneity of vaudeville and the circus into the world of the theater: he seeks to give the spectator a sense of the delightful con-fusion of multiple perceptions. Although the world and the vaudeville/circus seem separated, they are essentially one: "Living and the world and the circus are things that cannot be separated."[21]

Because the "super-actual" worlds of the circus and vaudeville celebrate the miraculous nature of reality, they become symbolic of man's potential to live life with a sense of wonder and faithful expectation.[22]

For Saroyan, then, vaudeville accurately mirrored the fact that reality is both chaotic and miraculous. It therefore reflected his feeling that in life one must "take everything earnestly and ludicrously at the same time."[23] Vaudeville made one laugh, yet beneath the comic mask lurked deeper and more tragic truths. Many of the acts in vaudeville seemed to portray the essential absurdity of the human condition: we see man as a tragic and pathetic creature caught in a web of meaningless events, in a tangle of conflicting realities. Here life seems to be, as Frank Ward O'Malley once observed, "just one damned thing after another." The causal links between events and actions are severed and life is depicted as a random series of unconnected experiences.

In many ways, then, vaudeville has deep affinities to the contemporary "theatre of the absurd," as Martin Esslin has carefully documented. Indeed, vaudeville often seemed to define the estranged condition of modern life more accurately than much "serious" drama. Esslin has pointed out that "the greatest performers of this genre reached heights of tragicomic pathos that left much of the contemporary legitimate theatre far behind."[24] According to Esslin, one of the greatest of these actors was Dan Leno, "whose patter sometimes contained passages of almost philosophical nonsense strongly reminiscent of the Theatre of the Absurd, when, for example, he asked, 'Ah, what is man? Wherefore does he why? Whence did he whence? Whither is he withering?'"[25] Indeed, Leno's dialogue here reminds us of the relentless parody of pretentious philosophical language in Beckett's *Waiting for Godot*, where man's efforts to enclose reality within intellectual constructs are exposed as absurd and laughable.

In many ways, then, vaudeville and the theater of the absurd were expressing the same truths through different means. Yet while Saroyan's affinity for vaudeville has been noted,[26] his profound sympathy for the writings of the absurdist dramatists has been infrequently acknowledged. He saw in their work a powerful depiction of the fierce struggle for coherence in a mad world: here the existential anguish of modern man's soul was laid bare. As he observed in 1958, "Beckett and Ionesco are not mad. They have discovered the means by which to reveal, in acceptable and deeply moving terms, that the human race is mad, and that the world has been in an uncharted and unknown dimension of hopeless lunacy—if not criminality—for centuries and is now away off in this dimension."[27] This "madness" is actually a sign of sanity, for the writer "is also mad, measurably so, but saner than all others, with the best sanity, the only sanity worth bothering about—the living, creative, vulnerable, valorous, unintimidated, and arrogant sanity of a free man."[28] The tragicomic dramas of Beckett and Ionesco show that they have seen deeply into the nature of contemporary reality and have bravely confronted its lunacy.

Saroyan's passionate advocacy of the absurdists' "madness" reveals an aspect of his sensibility rarely commented upon. He saw that they too were dark comedians whose laughter had its roots in a painful inability to "adjust" to the world. Saroyan's own comic spirit has often been taken at face value, but it is clear that he saw the comedic impulse as a disguise masking a profound psychological imbalance. As he pointed out in the late memoir *Chance Meetings*,

> all comedians are people who really deeply consider the human experience not only a dirty trick perpetrated by a totally meaningless procedure of accidents, but an unbearable ordeal every day, which can be made tolerable only by mockery in one form or another. And the comedian's method is to notice that *the joke* is steadfast in everything, there is nothing in which the joke is not centered, including (or especially) in all of those things which are ordinarily, even to the comedians, plainly sacred.[29]

Comedy is a way to make existence bearable, to overcome the essential meaninglessness of daily life's terrible "ordeal." These are strong words, and they illuminate Saroyan's profound love for the comedians who populate both absurdist drama and vaudeville.

Saroyan saw his greatest play, *The Time of Your Life*, as an attempt to translate into dramatic terms his vision of life's painful comedy. Written in 1939, it anticipates the theater of the absurd in portraying the confusions and paradoxes of modern experience (*Waiting for Godot* appeared in 1952 and Ionesco's *La Cantatrice Chauve* in 1948). Here again he sought to capture the gay and melancholy flux of existence, to make reality endurable through the play of art. The San Francisco bar where the play takes place is home for a variety of misfits who huddle to brave the gathering onslaught of the war. He depicts a fragile world in the throes of apocalyptic transition; for him, the saloon was "almost the last place in which to *remember* a world about to go up in smoke" (emphasis added).[30] I stress "remember" here because *The Time of Your Life* is very much a play reflecting the end of an era; it attempts to preserve the memory of a moment in history, a moment of hopeful time poised precariously at the edge of apocalypse.

Saroyan has pointed out that "the shadow of impending war" broods over the entire play; indeed, a sense of danger is apparent at the very opening.[31] As the first scene begins, we see the play's central character, Joe ("a young loafer with money and a good heart"), buy some newspapers, glance at the terrible headlines, and throw them angrily away. Later, Harry, the aspiring dancer and comedian, does a brief vaudeville routine which includes the lines: "It may mean war. *War*. Germany. England. Russia. I don't know for sure" (p. 44). And in the fourth act, the nurse Elsie Mandelspiegel tells Dudley, her lover: "All right, Dudley. Of course. Come on. The time for the new pathetic war has come. Let's hurry, before they dress you, stand you in line, hand you a gun, and have you kill and be killed" (p. 135). The outer world presents a menacing threat to the peaceful world of the saloon where Saroyan's estranged characters struggle to affirm life over death.

Against the dissolution and death that pulse outside the doors of Nick's bar, Saroyan offers in the play's epigraph his affirmative message of faith.

> In the time of your life, live—so that in that good time there shall be no ugliness or death for yourself or for any life your life touches. Seek goodness everywhere, and when it is found, bring it out of its hiding-place and let it be free and unashamed. Place

in matter and in flesh the least of the values, for these are the things that hold death and must pass away. Discover in all things that which shines and is beyond corruption. Encourage virtue in whatever heart it may have been driven into secrecy and sorrow by the shame and terror of the world. Ignore the obvious, for it is unworthy of the clear eye and the kindly heart. Be the inferior of no man, nor of any man be the superior. Remember that every man is a variation of yourself. No man's guilt is not yours, nor is any man's innocence a thing apart. Despise evil and ungodliness, but not men of ungodliness or evil. These, understand. Have no shame in being kindly and gentle, but if the time comes in the time of your life to kill, kill and have no regret. In the time of your life, live—so that in that wondrous time you shall not add to the misery and sorrow of the world, but shall smile to the infinite delight and mystery of it. (P. 15)

Later in his career, Saroyan repudiated the last section of this credo: "Within the Credo is one commandment I have never removed which nevertheless ought not to be there: about killing when it's time to kill. The flaw there is that if there can be a time to kill, then any time can be a time to kill. This unfortunate commandment rounds out the Credo, but it doesn't make any sense."[32] The epigraph as a whole, however, presents Saroyan's transcendentalist message of life's exhilarating possibilities, the self exfoliating out into "infinite delight and mystery." Yet as we see in the play itself, these idealistic, "romantic" affirmations are difficult to maintain in the face of the world's perpetual chaos. In a sense, *The Time of Your Life* tests the viability of the credo, as reality relentlessly confronts ideality.

As we have seen, precisely this tension between reality and the promises of the imagination powers Saroyan's drama. In *The Time of Your Life*, this tension is represented by his characteristically divided sensibility: the affirmative romantic and the existential alien. The reason he can successfully combine these two modes is that they are philosophically interrelated. They are connected because the romantic strain usually leads into questioning of meaning, feelings of homelessness, and disintegration. To want the ultimate from life is to be often disappointed.

The Time of Your Life keeps the audience deftly suspended, shuttling back and forth between these two states of consciousness: on the one hand, self-integration and ecstasy seem real possibilities; on the other, life seems a tragic condition of exile. A continuous mood of *expectancy* is projected in the play; the characters often appear trapped in a timeless realm of unrealizable hopes and dreams. As in *Waiting for Godot* or O'Neill's *The Iceman Cometh*, they constantly wait for something to happen, but the expected fulfillment never arrives. Transcendence seems just out of reach.[33]

We can observe this divided psychic condition most clearly in Joe, Saroyan's wealthy *raisonneur*. From the opening of the play, he appears to be a passive existentialist, drinking heavily and observing life and the people in the bar from a great, uninvolved height. Joe's struggle for balance is unceasing, and he experiences time as an unbearable burden. Indeed, his drinking stems from his desire to escape the pain of meaningless waiting, of dead time. As he explains to an unhappy woman in the bar:

> JOE: . . . Now, why do I drink? (*Scientifically*) No. Why does *anybody* drink? (*Working it out*) Every day has twenty-four hours.
>
> MARY: (*Sadly, but brightly*): Yes, that's true.
>
> JOE: Twenty-four hours. Out of the twenty-four hours at *least* twenty-three and a half are—my God, I don't know why—dull, dead, boring, empty, and murderous. Minutes on the clock, *not time of living*. It doesn't make any difference who you are or what you do, twenty-three and a half hours of the twenty-four are spent *waiting*.
>
> (Pp. 74–75)

This obsession with time is typical of much absurdist drama. As Richard N. Coe has observed: "The *avant-garde* theatre has grown to be, almost by definition, timeless: a drama of broken watches. Beckett's tramps, Pinter's caretaker, Adamov's employee (*La Parodie*), no less than Ionesco's Béranger, live in a world where all the

clocks have stopped—and are deeply, almost pathologically, discon-
certed by the fact."[34] Alcohol transforms Joe's experience of time
and eases his sense of spiritual vacuity. The slow, meaningless
movement of time drives him to the evasion of drinking: he wants
to live in the time of this life, and we hear verbal echoes of the play's
epigraph in his speech.[35]

The relationship between time and the struggle for true being is a
central philosophical concern of the play. The use of the word *time*
in the title alerts us to its double literal and metaphorical significance: the *time* of your life. It is also noteworthy that the horse that
Joe's factotum Tom wants to bet on (and which wins the race) is
named "Precious Time." Through these suggestive details, as well
as through the explicit commentary of Joe on the problem of time, it
is evident that Saroyan seeks to show that the world of "reality"
must be transcended—his characters must release themselves from
the shackles of time in order to achieve authentic being. Time
should be experienced as a vital, eternal, fluid dimension of life,
rather than as a constricting, static, sterile realm of death.

The author's ideas about time are directly related to his vision of
the self, for he sees its quest for integration as a dynamic, ongoing
process of growth and transformation. In act 2, Joe remarks: "Living
is an art. It's not bookkeeping. It takes a lot of rehearsing for a man
to get to be himself" (p. 112). The dramatic metaphor ("rehearsing")
is beautifully suggestive, for it implies that attaining true selfhood
requires the same qualities expected of an actor preparing a part in a
play: identity is temporarily achieved through acting, through artistic performance. The play here is the drama of life, and "getting to
be themselves" is exactly what Joe and his fellow actors are trying
to do against great odds. "Rehearsing" also implies a stage, support-
ing actors, and a temporary cessation of responsibility—contingen-
cies which the bar setting supplies. What early critics saw as the
play's "formlessness" was actually this very attempt to catch the
elusiveness of becoming, of the world of the self in metamorphosis.
Joe wants people to live their lives as works of art—without forcing,
without bookkeeping, without violating the inchoate, mysterious,
pulsing, and unpredictable energies of existence.

Later in his career, Saroyan continued his speculations on life as performance: "Actors require audiences, but in the nature of things it is not possible for an audience not to exist for everybody, for there is little difference between performing for the everlasting witness and performing for one's self. It is in fact much the same thing. In short, we are watched, and being watched we are helpless not to perform in one manner or another."[36]

Like Jean-Paul Sartre, Saroyan sees man as "project" rather than as a static, defined "object." Man creates himself and his meaning in the very act of living, in the quality of his "performance." "Acting" and *acting* in the world are twin poles of the same search for identity: both "stages" reveal the drama of self-realization in progress. Indeed, it is no accident that the daring young man on the flying trapeze was also a *performer* involved in a difficult yet absolutely necessary balancing act.

As the play progresses, Joe emerges as a kind of master of ceremonies who philosophizes and comments on the action of the play, while remaining essentially passive. Joe becomes a spectator of existence, the author has remarked, because he "didn't want to hurt people. He was so determined not to, he sat all the time. But even then, he discovered that he hurt them. To sit wasn't it, either, so he got up and left the saloon and the curtain came down and the play ended."[37] Indeed, Joe sees himself as a student of life who has "been trying for three years to find out if it's possible to live what I think is a civilized life. I mean a life that can't hurt any other life" (p. 77). Joe thus attempts to live according to this philosophy of noninterference and detachment because he fully realizes that true being requires a great deal of "rehearsing."

The melodramatic and simple plot of *The Time of Your Life* ultimately does not actually involve Joe's direct participation. The story revolves around the young man Tom's developing love for the prostitute Kitty Duval. Joe sits in the bar and drinks, sends Tom on various errands (to buy toys, for example), and encourages the couple's relationship. The only major action Joe performs occurs when he drives Tom and Kitty to the beach later in the play. Yet the outside world intrudes on the young lovers in the form of Blick, a vice-squad officer who threatens to arrest Kitty. Kit Carson, an "old Indian fighter" and teller of tall tales, intervenes at the end and kills Blick with a revolver. Tom and Kitty then escape to San Diego, and Joe quietly leaves the bar.

Around the main action of the play hovers a host of vivid characters whose energies and eccentricities bring the bar to life. After Joe appears on the scene, we quickly meet a melancholy and philosophical Arab; a black piano-player named Wesley; Harry, the young, aspiring dancer and vaudevillian; Kit Carson, a legendary old-timer; Willy, the Assyrian pinball enthusiast; a pair of absurd lovers; Krupp, a waterfront policeman; McCarthy, an intellectual longshoreman; Nick, the bar's compassionate Italian owner; Kitty Duval, a prostitute of Polish ancestry with the traditional heart of gold; and Blick, the vice-squad cop who is the incarnation of evil. The saloon is a microcosm of American society, where many different nationalities are represented, and the stage directions define the atmosphere as

> one of warm, natural, American ease; every man innocent and good; each doing what he believes he should do, or what he must do. There is deep American naiveté and faith in the behavior of each person. No one is competing with anyone else. No one hates anyone else. Every man is living, and letting live. Each man is following his destiny as he feels it should be followed; or is abandoning it as he feels it must, by now, be abandoned; or forgetting it for the moment as he feels he should forget it. Although everyone is dead serious, there is unmistakable smiling and humor in the scene; a sense of the human body and spirit emerging from the world-imposed state of stress and fretfulness, fear and awkwardness, to the more natural state of casualness and grace. Each person belongs to the environment, in his own person, as himself. (P. 60)

The saloon's ambience is "deadly serious" (a phrase which foreshadows the final murder of Blick), yet there is also a pervasive sense of unburdened laughter, bonhomie, unpretentiousness, and spontaneity.

Saroyan wanted his plays to come "straight from the living reality of everyday humanity and its everyday experience."[38] The prostitute, the longshoreman, the cop, the comedian, the lonely foreigner, the bartender—these are Saroyan's "beautiful people." He was striv-

ing to create an authentically American theater which would faithfully reflect "the temper and texture of inner and outer American
life."[39] He wanted to send into play a spontaneous dramatic universe composed of *real* people.

> If you will go back in memory you will surely recall any num-
> ber of everyday people—office workers, janitors, messenger
> boys, waiters, and so on—who have amused and entertained
> you artlessly, much more than any actor on any stage, because
> they have not *tried*, because it was real and free, and because it
> called for no applause and no bowing. . . .
>   The fundamental defect of the theatre as art is that it is
> theatrical. It is inhuman, or anti-human. People in plays are not
> people, they are actors, and sometimes you even know them by
> name and fame.[40]

Saroyan wants to capture "that quality of beauty as it is in the
living, in the plainest of people."[41] He seeks to "humanize" the
theater by insisting on the art of artlessness, to allow his characters
the opportunity spontaneously to rehearse their lives on stage.[42]

As we have seen, the most "artless" American dramatic form was
vaudeville, and the motley cast of *The Time of Your Life* includes a
score of "everyday" people from the most "humble" and "common"
walks of life who call to mind the vitality of the characters in vaudeville. Mary McCarthy has gone so far as to say that

> almost every incident and character in it can be translated back
> into one of the old time acts. Kit Carson, the trapper, is W. C.
> Fields; the pinball machine that plays "America" and waves a
> flag when the jackpot is hit is out of Joe Cook; the toys Joe buys
> are a visual reminder of the juggling turn, and his money, de-
> riving from nowhere and ostentatiously displayed, makes you
> think of the magic act; the young man who keeps telephoning
> his girl is the comic monologist; Harry the hoofer is Jimmy
> Durante; the boy out of a job is the stooge; and Joe (or God)
> . . . has that slim, weary, sardonic, city-slicker look that was the
> very essence of the vaudeville artist. Even the serious part of the
> play, the soul-searing drama involving Kitty, the beautiful

prostitute, and the boy who wants to marry her, and Blick, takes
you back to those short problem melodramas starring a passée
actress that were occasionally interspersed with the regular
acts.[43]

The Time of Your Life, then, corresponds closely on the levels of
theme, style, characterization, and structure to vaudeville. Here is
the circus of reality instanced earlier—the joyous, overabundant
energy of characters who perform more acts (one quickly following
another) "than any one human eye can perceive or enjoy."

Yet as we have seen, vaudeville had a twin-edged incisiveness. On
the one hand, it provided the humor and grace to balance the tragic
side of Saroyan's sensibility, and on the other, it communicated a
bleak awareness of the absurdity of contemporary experience. We
can observe a strange conjunction of both qualities in a monologue
which Harry, the dancer-comedian, tries out on the bar's clientele.

> I'm up at Sharkey's on Turk Street. It's a quarter to nine,
> daylight saving. Wednesday, the eleventh. What I've got is a
> headache and a 1918 nickel. What I *want* is a cup of coffee. If I
> buy a cup of coffee with the nickel, I've got to walk home. I've
> got an eight-ball problem. George the Greek is shooting a game
> of snooker with Pedro the Filipino. *I'm in rags.* They're wearing
> thirty-five dollar suits, made to order. I haven't got a cigarette.
> They're smoking Bobby Burns panatelas. I'm thinking it over,
> like I always do. George the Greek is in a tough spot. If I buy a
> cup of coffee, I'll want another cup. What happens? My *ear*
> aches! My ear. George the Greek takes the cue. Chalks it.
> Studies the table. Touches the cue-ball delicately. Tick. What
> happens? He makes the three-ball! What do I do? I get confused.
> *I go out and buy a morning paper.* What I *want* is a cup of
> coffee, and a good used car. I go out and buy a morning paper.
> Thursday, the twelfth. Maybe the headline's about *me*. I take a
> quick look. *No. The headline is not about me.* It's about Hitler.
> Seven thousand miles away. I'm here. Who the hell is Hitler?
> Who's behind the eight-ball? I turn around. *Everybody's behind
> the eight-ball!* (Pp. 94–95)

The speech mirrors the quick disjunctions of the vaudeville routine; here is the monologist carrying on a solitary conversation with himself, moving rapidly from subject to subject through association of ideas rather than through logical, linear progression. McCarthy the longshoreman says, "It's the funniest thing I've ever heard. Or *seen*, for that matter," yet he does not laugh (p. 95). Although Harry tries valiantly to be a successful comedian, he is not funny—his material actually lies closer to tragedy than to comedy.

As in a similar routine of Harry's earlier in the play, this passage moves inexorably from the specific, personal plight of a young man unable to make decisions to the universal chaos of the oncoming war.[44] In concentrating continually on temporal details ("quarter to nine," the day of the week and date of the month, the "morning paper") Harry underscores the theme of time's static aimlessness. His own lack of purpose is symptomatic of the wretched conflict and uncertainty trumpeted by the daily newspaper headlines, and his obsession with time begins to seem a kind of countdown to apocalypse.

The correspondence between Harry's unhappiness and the world's agony is emphasized through a tight, echoing verbal structure. The pool-room material introduced at the beginning of the monologue recurs at the end, yet now it is transformed into an image communicating universal bondage and malaise: *"Everybody's behind the eight-ball!"* It is no wonder that McCarthy finds it difficult to laugh; indeed, we begin to sense that his assurance that the routine was hilarious is meant ironically. Finally, the only thing Harry's routine has in common with comedy is its formal patterning and style of delivery. As in Beckett's *Waiting for Godot*, the forms of communication have been emptied of meaning and all that remains is a style devoid of its original content.

The "American naiveté and faith" of these characters, then, are highly qualified by their deep skepticism and spiritual hunger. Harry is far from being at "ease"; in a very real sense, he is not at home in the world. This feeling of homelessness afflicts virtually every person in Nick's bar. At the opening of the play, the Arab mutters to himself a phrase which will recur hypnotically throughout: "No foundation. All the way down the line" (p. 20). Here is the stranger, the foreigner, the outsider, conveying the anguish of confronting cosmic disorder. The Arab is rootless man, forever lost in a universe devoid of meaning, forever cut off from the sources of true being and wholeness. He is not only the alien in America but stranger Man in the world. For the Arab, Saroyan's nihilistic philosopher, there is no foundation, no security in existence: the center will not hold.

The Arab's feeling of estrangement is shared by other characters who dream of connecting to some *home*, who hope desperately to find faith. Home becomes the symbol for a place of spiritual peace and significance which forever eludes the heart. Kitty Duval, the tenderhearted prostitute, is lost in her memories of home.

> I dream of home. Christ, I always dream of home. I've no *home*. I've no place. But I always dream of all of us together again. We had a farm in Ohio. There was nothing good about it. It was always sad. There was always trouble. But I always dream about it as if I could go back and Papa would be there and Mamma and Louie and my little brother Stephen and my sister Mary. I'm Polish. Duval! My name isn't Duval, it's Koranovsky. Katerina Koranovsky. We lost everything. The house, the farm, the trees, the horses, the cows, the chickens. Papa died. He was old. He was thirteen years older than Mamma. We moved to Chicago. We tried to work. We tried to stay together. Louie got in trouble. The fellows he was with killed him for something. I don't know what. Stephen ran away from home. Seventeen years old. I don't know where he is. Then Mamma died.
> *(Pause)*
> What's the dream? I dream of home. (Pp. 48–49)

When Nick wonders what attracts so many people to his saloon, he finally realizes that "maybe they can't feel at home anywhere else" (p. 51). Yet Kitty Duval still feels trapped in the past, uprooted, lonely, and unhappy in the San Francisco bar—at best it is a temporary "home."

The mood of fluid, sad memory which pervades the play is suggested not only by the characters' reveries but also by the music— "The Missouri Waltz" is heard at key points throughout. Music, more than any other art, gives the audience a sense of the timelessness of experience and of the retrievability of the past through memory. Melancholy revery, music, alcohol—all contribute to the creation of a tender atmosphere through which Saroyan's lost characters travel, suspended in time.

Finding a home, an "inhabitable world," is the deepest desire of the denizens of Nick's saloon. When Elsie Mandelspiegel asks her puerile lover Dudley how they can escape the world's pain, she speaks for all the estranged around her. Dudley assures her that they will be able to achieve love and security, but Elsie tells him, "All right. We'll try again. We'll go together to a room in a cheap hotel, and dream that the world is beautiful, and that living is full of love and greatness. But in the morning, can we forget debts, and duties, and the cost of ridiculous things?" (p. 134). For Saroyan, this melancholy awareness of the impenetrable isolation of each individual is rooted in the nature of things, for "the expectancy of the human heart is, as it should be, a mysterious thing, full of religious shyness, strange and lofty longing. Longing that is never fully satisfied."[45] Home, as we saw with Jaspar MacGregor, is a long way distant, and arriving there is an unrealizable dream.

Yet dreams are affirmed throughout the play, for life is impossible without their power to encourage and heal. As Joe remarks, "I believe dreams sooner than statistics," thus celebrating the superiority of the imagination over the "practical realists" (like Blick) who bring death and destruction to the world (p. 98). Joe, Harry, Elsie and Dudley, Kitty Duval—all are dreamers whose hearts are full of a profound spiritual yearning. For them, as for the other characters in Nick's bar, life is not "statistics," not a quantifiable entity. Rather, it is an ever-changing and evolving energy which has the potential to be transformed and affirmed through love and imagination.

As the plot gathers momentum, the struggle between the worlds of imagination (dreams, intuition, the art of living) and reality (statistics, fact, death) intensifies. The pain and anguish of the bar's homeless denizens deeply affect Joe, and he becomes the most articulate interpreter of their desire to achieve wholeness. Yet Joe is fundamentally different from many of the other characters in the play who frenetically pursue a single activity or meaning in life— Dudley excitedly pursues Elsie, Willie is obsessed with winning at

pinball, Harry dreams of becoming a successful comic. Joe, as Saroyan's artist figure (or as Mary McCarthy suggests, his "God" symbol),
sums up and unites their confusions within his own self; their in-
tuitions are brought together in him.

He senses the contradiction at the heart of existence, and will not
be satisfied with a single, monolithic formulation of the significance
of reality. He says to McCarthy that "everything's right. Right and
wrong," and it is noteworthy that it is he who translates for Krupp
the depressed Arab's cryptic refrain, "No foundation. All the way
down the line. What. What-not. Nothing. I go walk and look at sky"
(pp. 89, 90).

> KRUPP: What? What-not? What's that mean?
> JOE: (*Slowly, thinking, remembering*) What? What-not?
>   That means this side, that side. Inhale, Exhale. What:
>   birth. What-not: death. The inevitable, the astounding,
>   the magnificent seed of growth and decay in all things.
>   Beginning, and end. That man, in his own way, is a
>   prophet. He is one who, with the help of *beer*, is able to
>   reach that state of deep understanding in which what
>   and what-not, the reasonable and the unreasonable, are
>   *one*.
>
>   (P. 90)

By accepting the duality of existence, the essential doubleness of
life's meaning, Joe arrives at an intuition of the unity underlying
seeming paradox: the gay and melancholy flux.

It is significant that Joe's style of delivery throughout the play is
offhand and mannered. He takes what he says seriously, but there is
an undercurrent of self-mockery which shows he is aware of his own
pose, his own act, as philosopher dispensing brilliant eternal veri-
ties. Joe tells Tom at the end of act 2: "Don't be silly. I don't understand things. I'm trying to understand them" (p. 117). Joe is careful
to disclaim any pretension to superior wisdom—he is hesitant to
acknowledge simple answers that would attempt to explain away
the complexities, the "what? what-not?" of his experience.

It is this irresolute aspect of Joe's personality which defines him
as a kind of modern antihero, a curious observer of life's irreducible

unknowability. The passivity that distinguishes his behavior can be seen in existential terms: his inability to act is rooted in the fear that he is powerless to alter the madness and absurdity of the world. Joe also knows that reality is not to be dominated, not to be understood; rather, it is to be experienced. When a woman in the bar asks him what his plans are, he answers: "Plans? I haven't got any. *I just get up*" (p. 73). This sentence might easily have been spoken by Meursault in Camus's *L'Etranger*: Joe is cool, uninvolved, dispassionate—in some sense looking through a window at life.[46] Yet this Zen-like detachment is projected because Joe is *so* involved, because he cares so deeply about the world's tragic fate.

It is the madness surrounding him which has paralyzed Joe's will. His inertness is a kind of shield against the insanity he senses beneath the superficialities of daily life, a way to balance himself psychologically. The other characters are also aware of the lunacy in themselves and the world, as we see when Krupp and Nick discuss their lives.

> KRUPP: I think we're all crazy. It came to me while I was on my way to Pier 27. All of a sudden it hit me like a ton of bricks. A thing like that never happened to me before. Here we are in this wonderful world, full of all the wonderful things—here we are—all of us, and look at us. Just look at us. We're crazy. We're nuts. We've got everything, but we feel lousy and dissatisfied just the same.
>
> (P. 137)

When Nick mentions the fact that the sad Arab is the "nicest guy in the world," Krupp responds "bitterly": "But crazy. Just like all the rest of us. Stark raving mad" (p. 141). Both Krupp and Joe are confounded at the failure of humanity to realize itself in "this wonderful world." They are convinced that spiritual anarchy has become universal, that man's inability to live life as miracle is the deepest and most inexcusable "madness."

The tensions in the play between imagination, between the "two theatres," culminate in Kit Carson's murder of Blick. Kit, all-American, Twainian folk hero, walks into the bar and tells Joe: "I shot a man once. In San Francisco. Shot him two times. In 1939, I think it was. In October. Fellow named Blick or Glick or something like that. Couldn't stand the way he talked to ladies. Went up to my room and got my old pearl-handled revolver and waited for him on Pacific Street. Saw him walking, and let him have it, two times. Had to throw the beautiful revolver into the Bay" (p. 193). Fantasy momentarily comes true—Kit's wild tall tales (which earlier in the play, significantly, Joe insisted he believed) are reality, for he has in fact killed Blick.

At this point the fragile world of the saloon has been irrevocably shattered: the madness and murder Krupp was so concerned about have infiltrated completely. The play leaves us delicately poised between what and what-not, between life and death, between affirmation and despair. The death of Blick, symbol of authority and the forces of repression, and the escape of Kitty and Tom resolve the plot "happily." Yet when Joe had learned earlier from the bartender that Blick had been killed, his response is illuminating; he drifts away, saying he does not know where he is going and will probably not return. Although Joe claims nothing is the matter, he is profoundly disturbed. When he steps from the bar into the night, he moves from the imagination to reality, from "home" to exile, from the theater to the world. It is a painful moment, and his sense of loss comes from the realization that neither Nick's Pacific Street Saloon, Restaurant, and Entertainment Palace nor the outside world is "inhabitable." Like so many works of modern literature, *The Time of Your Life* leaves its hero suspended between two worlds: one dying and the other powerless to be born.

CHAPTER 6

The Human Comedy

In 1941, after two active years on Broadway, Saroyan traveled to Hollywood to work on *The Human Comedy* for Metro-Goldwyn-Mayer. When the scenario was completed, it was made into a successful motion picture, and Saroyan soon adapted the story for his first novel.[1] This portrayal of small-town American life proved immensely consoling to a society in the throes of apocalypse. Saroyan's affirmation of love's power gave faith to millions ravaged by the suffering and death brought by World War II. As we have seen in *The Daring Young Man on the Flying Trapeze,* he had committed himself from the beginning of his career to celebrating the brotherhood of man, and in *The Human Comedy* he preaches a familiar sermon: love one another or you shall perish.

Although the novel centers around a specific family, the Macauleys, Saroyan's ultimate concern is with the family of humanity. Like the "families" in the plays, the Macauley family becomes symbolic of the unity of mankind (one thinks of the Alexanders in *My Heart's in the Highlands* or the outcasts who people *The Time of Your Life*). Typically, Saroyan's imagination moves progressively *outward*: from the individual self, to the family, to the entire world. While he had always shown an absolute allegiance to the individual, he also knew that the solely personal quest for wholeness meant nothing unless humanity itself could be integrated.[2] As the telegraph operator Spangler says late in the novel, "The people of the world are like one man. If they hate one another, it is themselves they hate."[3] This sense of the deep relation of the individual to all of mankind is a central theme in *The Human Comedy*. With John Donne, Saroyan believed that every man's death diminishes me, for he envisions humanity as a vast, organic, interconnected body of sacred life.

This yearning for oneness, for unification of the self with the pulsing body of the world, is a dominant feature of Saroyan's literary personality. The urge to identify the self with the universe, the perpetual "universalizing" of experience, is a quality he shares with earlier American writers—Whitman in particular.[4] That we are all the same person underneath the superficial masks of daily social interaction is for him a palpable truth. The driving impulse behind his vision of life is the conviction that we are all tied together by the bonds of common humanity—within each human breast beats the same cosmic energy.

In *The Human Comedy* this correspondence between the individual and the universal condition of humanity is emphasized in the names Saroyan chose for his setting and characters. The novel takes place in Ithaca, California (that is, the San Joaquin Valley), and the three Macauley sons are named Marcus, Homer, and Ulysses. Immediately, then, the *Odyssey* is called to mind; Saroyan is writing allegorically. Ithaca is not merely one specific small town but every small town in the United States. Furthermore, each of the three boys is Everyman confronting bravely the struggle of existence. In being given classical names, they are taken out of the quotidian world and placed into the larger world of universal mythic experience.

Yet it is clear that an exact parallel between the *Odyssey* and *The Human Comedy* cannot be drawn—nor is one intended. Kate Macauley is not Penelope waiting for her husband to return (Matthew Macauley is dead), and Ulysses is a boy of four. Furthermore, we might expect the eldest son to be named Telemachus instead of Marcus, for he is the character who is in the army, away from home, seeking his way back to Ithaca. Unlike Joyce in *Ulysses*, Saroyan is not constructing a careful system of correspondences between contemporary reality and the world of ancient epic myth. Rather, he intends the reader to identify Ithaca and the Macauley family with the universal experience of humanity—not with specific events and characters in Homer's *Odyssey*.

In general terms, however, we might see a connection between the struggles of the *Odyssey*'s hero during his fantastic journey and the painful movement of Saroyan's characters from innocence to experience. Both the fourteen-year-old Homer and his four-year-old brother Ulysses have embarked on their own private and allegorical travels: their odyssey is the journey from boyhood to maturity. Although we briefly glimpse Marcus in his role as soldier in the army, the focus throughout the novel is on Homer's (and, to a much lesser extent, Ulysses') slow and arduous process of inner growth and development. By the end of the novel, Homer has made the difficult transition into manhood, wrestling with the Cyclops, Sirens, and Laestrygonians of reality.

From the very opening of the novel, Saroyan strives to set up a clear opposition between the worlds of innocence and experience. The first chapter opens not with the agonies and sufferings of Homer's maturity but with the pristine, visionary, uncorrupted, and lovely world of childhood.

> The little boy named Ulysses Macauley one day stood over the new gopher hole in the backyard of his house on Santa Clara Avenue in Ithaca, California. The gopher of this hole pushed up fresh moist dirt and peeked out at the boy, who was certainly a stranger but perhaps not an enemy. Before this miracle had been fully enjoyed by the boy, one of the birds of Ithaca flew into the old walnut tree in the backyard and after settling itself on a branch broke into rapture, moving the boy's fascination from the earth to the tree. Next, best of all, a freight train puffed and roared far away. The boy listened, and felt the earth beneath him tremble with the moving of the train. Then he broke into running, moving (it seemed to him) swifter than any life in the world. (Pp. 3–4)

This opening paragraph sets the "miraculous" mood, which Saroyan associates with childhood. The young Ulysses is all eyes, keenly perceptive, in full awe of experience. He symbolizes the state of consciousness celebrated by William Blake: his doors of perception are cleansed, hence everything appears to him as it is—infinite.

Ulysses is at one with Nature and himself, enjoying an un-self-conscious sense of unity with all creation. Subject and object, self and world, have not yet been separated from one another by the sorrow of time.

As the chapter continues, Ulysses sees an old black hobo singing "My Old Kentucky Home" on a passing freight train and waves to him. The hobo waves back, and the child is ecstatically happy that he has received a response. When Ulysses returns home, his mother is busy feeding the chickens, and the chapter ends with a final moment of visionary clarity and innocence, as Ulysses "came quickly and quietly and stood beside her, then went to the hen nest to look for eggs. He found one. He looked at it a moment, picked it up, brought it to his mother and very carefully handed it to her, by which he means what no man can guess and no child can remember to tell." (p. 5). Ulysses sees the natural as supernatural, the temporal as eternal, a simple egg as symbol of the secret glory of the universe.

This first chapter thus presents in microcosm an important aspect of Saroyan's narrative method. Each connection Ulysses (and, as we shall see, his brother Homer) makes with reality is full of mysterious meaning—meaning which cannot be translated into definite, literal, denotative terms. Each event—seeing the gopher and bird, waving to the hobo who is singing of returning home (as Marcus Macauley seeks to do), and taking the egg to his mother—is rich in implied, suggested, poetic, and intangible significance. Simple, everyday occurrences are infused with the infinite, with "rapture" and "fascination," and resonate with vague hints of transcendence. At these epiphanic moments, the world seems to yield up its mystery—a secret, hidden dimension of reality bursts suddenly into the field of consciousness.

The Human Comedy is full of such *meetings*; strange encounters of the self with some deep beauty at the heart of existence. Later in his career, Saroyan wrote an interesting gloss on this opening chapter which illuminates not only this specific passage but the other epiphanic passages in the novel as well. A young girl in an English class had written him asking, "What did Ulysses mean by handing his mother that egg?" Warning her at the outset that "a writer may

not know what something he has written means, although this
doesn't necessarily mean that it doesn't mean anything," Saroyan
wrote:

> Now, of course, little children don't know very many words,
> they're not very good at language, they don't know how to say
> what they feel and believe and know, or think they know, as the
> rest of us do. Having greeted the traveler, who was going home,
> far away, and having become filled with a mixture of gladness
> and solemnity, and a little loneliness, by the sight and sound
> and gesture of the traveler, and by his warmth and understand-
> ing and swift friendship, Ulysses may have felt that now, for
> sure, he would be rewarded with an egg, a new egg, the egg of
> the mixture, of having been seen by a total stranger, a big man
> with a big voice and a dark skin, of having been astonished by
> the man's swift acceptance of him, a small boy standing among
> weeds watching another train go by, of feeling suddenly a part of
> the traveler, a part of all travelers, of all strangers, of the whole
> human race. He may have felt that he would find the egg of
> many meanings, the egg perhaps of all meanings, the gathering
> together in one small white real thing that you could pick up
> with your hand and look at, a gathering together into a perfect
> form of all mute truth, the truth of the eye, which all creatures
> have, but children most of all. . . . And his mother was there,
> and of course every man's mother *is* his mother, a wonderful
> and astonishing gift, but his father *wasn't* there, his father was
> gone, perhaps he had gone as the traveler on the freight train
> had gone, and the boy may have felt a renewal of his longing to
> see his father because of his separation from the traveler. . . . I
> certainly didn't *say* what he meant. I said he meant all the
> things he couldn't say. I suppose I let it go at that because I
> imagined the reader would remember having done pretty much
> the same thing and would get the idea, and perhaps even by
> then *know* pretty much what Ulysses meant. It means any-
> thing, Ava. Anything means anything. You will decide for
> yourself what anything means. It's really up to you entirely.
> The more you can make something mean the better.[5]

The phrase "all mute truth" explains precisely what Saroyan is attempting to communicate throughout *The Human Comedy*—a sense of the indefinite, elusive, unsayable, mystic truths which are the life of the human soul and which infuse life with meaning. Yet he is careful to emphasize that Ulysses' experience should not be confined to any *particular* possible interpretation; rather, young Ava will see in the text what she is.

As the novel progresses, Ulysses is portrayed as a typical little boy who asks all the who, what, where, and why questions of childhood. Although in the above passage Saroyan seems to imply that Ulysses possesses an almost mystic gift for intuition and deep awareness, his other experiences are more mundane: getting caught in a trap at a sporting goods store, going to the public library, tagging along with some older boys as they attempt to steal from apricot trees. Not until late in the novel, during his confrontation with Mr. Mechano (a terrible symbol of mechanistic death), does Ulysses reach a true moment of crisis which pushes him against the ugly truths of adulthood. As we shall see, it is at this point that the implied connection between Ulysses' experience and his older brother Homer's growth toward maturity is made more explicit.

The relationship between the two brothers' developments, however, is emphasized from the beginning of the novel. When we first meet Homer Macauley, he is wearing an oversized telegraph messenger's coat (the detail is significant, for he has yet to grow into his role as adult) while riding his bicycle through the countryside. Like Ulysses, Homer is at one with his environment and full of joyous enthusiastic energy—he is an innocent. His wide-eyed receptivity to life is underscored when Spangler, Homer's boss at the telegraph office, asks him how he likes being a messenger. Homer replies, "I like it better than anything. You sure get to see a lot of different people. You sure get to go to a lot of different places" (p. 11). At this point, Homer's tone is wholly ingenuous, and although he is ten years older than Ulysses, he exhibits the same faith in the rightness of the world. However, Homer's optimistic attitude will change radically as the novel progresses and he moves gradually into young manhood.

If the two brothers have much in common, their deep differences are also emphasized early in the novel. At the end of the chapter, for example, an ominous note intrudes upon Homer's idyllic life in the San Joaquin Valley. We are told that "he stopped at the next corner to behold a long line of Army trucks full of soldiers roll by. He saluted the men, just as his brother Ulysses had waved to the engineer and the hoboes. A great many soldiers returned the messenger's salute. Why not? What did they know about anything?" (pp. 7–8). Here Saroyan explicitly underscores the similarity of the two brothers' experiences: Homer waves as did Ulysses. Yet there is a crucial difference: this small gesture has connected Homer to the outside world of death and destruction. Here, then, is another *meeting*, yet Homer does not feel at this moment an epiphanic disclosure of the world's beauty. Rather, this is a sudden intrusion of the world's complexity into the clear and hopeful realm of childhood: the war has been *perceived*.

The relationship between the town of Ithaca and the outside world is similar to the structure we see in Saroyan's plays. Ithaca (and, microcosmically, the Macauley family) represents an imaginative realm threatened by the chaos and death of outside "reality." The ugliness of the war is at once palpably close (Homer seeing the army trucks) and curiously remote. We *learn* about the war secondhand, as though it were a drama being played out beyond the sealed world of the small town. We see army trucks, three soldiers on leave court Homer's sister Bess and her girl friend Mary Arena, Marcus travels in a train far from home. Or we receive information about the conflict through letters from Marcus, through the newsreels at the local cinema, through telegram messages. The war is out *there*, yet it infects the lives of everyone in Ithaca. We are given a sense of the war's ominous closeness and remoteness when the three lonely soldiers visiting Ithaca are described as "leaping over one another at a swift, crazy game of leap-frog, pushing down the dark, immortal street nearer and nearer to the War" (p. 136). This is an apt description of the situation in *The Human Comedy*, for the war comes progressively closer to the inhabitants of Ithaca, crushing their spirits with the terrible news of death.

The war has a central impact upon Homer's growth into maturity, for it is the catalyzing force that forges his identity; as he fights the forces of disintegration and death, he attains a new dimension of awareness. Suffering is a necessity for all positive transformations of the self: a part of the self must cease to be for spiritual integration to take place. The war offers Homer a kind of purgation—throughout the novel he experiences many dark nights of the soul in his role as harbinger of death.

Homer's first confrontation with the war's insanity occurs in chapter 5. Homer takes a telegram to a poor Mexican woman, Rosa Sandoval, informing her of the death of her son. Mrs. Sandoval is incredulous, and offers Homer candy in the desperate hope that there has been some mistake: "You would not bring me a bad telegram. . . . You are a good boy—like my little Juanito when he was a little boy. . . . You are my boy too" (p. 26). Homer feels the woman's anguish deeply and undergoes his first "sickness," a sickness which recurs repeatedly as the novel progresses.

> He didn't know why, because he only felt wounded by the whole thing, but for some reason he was sickened through all his blood and thought he would need to vomit. He didn't *dislike* the woman or anybody else, but what was happening to her seemed so wrong and so full of ugliness that he was sick and didn't know if he ever wanted to go on living again. . . . He felt neither love nor hate but something very close to disgust, but at the same time he felt great compassion, not for the poor woman alone, but for all things and the ridiculous way of their enduring and dying. He saw her back in time, a beautiful young woman sitting beside the crib of her infant son. He saw her looking down at this amazing human thing, speechless and helpless and full of the world to come. He saw her rocking the crib and he heard her singing to the child. Now look at her, he said to himself.
>
> He was on his bicycle suddenly, riding swiftly down the dark street, tears coming out of his eyes and his mouth whispering young and crazy curses. When he got back to the telegraph office the tears had stopped, but everything else had started and he knew there would be no stopping them. (Pp. 27–28)

Homer's crying here is immensely significant, signaling the occurrence of an authentically purgative or "baptismal" experience. He begins to be conscious of his dual role as messenger of life and messenger of death; in the brief time since he began work he has greatly changed.[6]

The telegraph office itself becomes a powerful symbol of the alternating dance of love and destruction which rages in the human spirit. On the one hand, the quest for unity, brotherhood, and integration which is *The Human Comedy*'s central focus is reflected in this place where people receive and send messages, attempt to communicate, to touch, to connect. It is a matrix of humming and pulsating energy, an orchestra which plays the world's yearning music. As Spangler tells Homer: "Music all around you—real music—straight from the world—straight from the hearts of people. Hear those telegraph keys? Beautiful music" (p. 14). Homer himself wants to become a composer, an artist who unifies humanity through his art, and the entire book is permeated with music—the singing of popular and gospel songs, the playing of instruments.

Yet on the other hand, it is most often a tragic symphony which Homer hears emanating from the telegraph orchestra, and he feels a sense of personal responsibility for the grief his occupation causes: "It wasn't Homer's fault. His work was to deliver telegrams. Even so, it seemed to him that he was part of the whole mistake. He felt awkward and almost as if he *alone* were responsible for what happened" (p. 24). Homer has a growing sense that he is becoming entangled in the web of the world's tragedy, and his deep sensitivity to the suffering of Ithaca's families makes it impossible for him not to become personally involved in the collective fate of humanity: every man's death diminishes Homer Macauley.

Homer reflects carefully on his experience throughout the novel, subjecting his emotions to close scrutiny and analysis. After each delivery of a death message, he invariably discusses his pain with his mother. In chapter 7 he confides to her his growing sense of loneliness: "All of a sudden . . . I feel lonely—not like I ever felt before. Even when Papa died I didn't feel *this* way. . . . In two days, everything is different. I'm lonely and I don't know what I'm lonely for" (p. 34). Mrs. Macauley listens to her son with understanding and compassion, answering his troubled questions with wisdom and gentle sensitivity: "The loneliness you feel has come to you because you are no longer a child. But the whole world has always been full of that loneliness. The loneliness does not come from the War. The War did not make it. It was the loneliness that made the War. It was the despair in all things for no longer having in them the grace of God" (pp. 34–35). At the end of the chapter she tells Homer: "The world is full of frightened little children. Being frightened, they frighten each other. Try to understand. . . . Try to love everyone you meet" (pp. 35–36). Mrs. Macauley emerges as an important source of moral sustenance for her son, steering him patiently and lovingly through his spiritual crises.

From this point on, Homer's suffering becomes increasingly difficult for him to bear. The task of bringing the impersonal news of death into the homes of Ithaca appalls him, and his attitude toward his job as messenger changes radically. Now he feels physically and emotionally ill before delivering messages, and openly rebels against his fate. But he musters the courage to deliver yet another message, one which informs Claudia Beaufrere that her son Alan has been killed. Homer's inner conflict reaches a climax in "Death, Don't Go to Ithaca" (chapter 23), as the terror of his role as death-bringer invades his dream life. He dreams of trying to ward off Death from Ithaca, and when he fails, he sobs bitterly—Homer's grief continues unabated.

Yet this continual suffering, as I have suggested earlier, serves a profound spiritual purpose. The task of becoming a fully conscious, integrated human being is fraught with difficulties; yet only by immersing the soul in the world's complexity and chaos can the individual grow. Throughout his struggles, Homer is occupied with the serious business of achieving an identity. In a famous letter, John Keats described the process by which the fledgling innocent soul is turned from coal to diamond-hard identity—an explanation which illuminates Homer's experience and Saroyan's intention in the novel.

> Call the world if you Please "The vale of Soul-making". Then you will find out the use of the world (I am speaking now in the highest terms for human nature admitting it to be immortal

> which I will here take for granted for the purpose of showing a
> thought which has struck me concerning it) I say *'Soul-making'*
> Soul as distinguished from an Intelligence—There may be
> intelligences or sparks of divinity in millions—but they are not
> Souls till they acquire identities, till each one is personally
> itself. I[n]telligences are atoms of perception—they know and
> they see and they are pure, in short they are God—How then
> are Souls to be made? How then are these sparks which are God
> to have identity given them—so as ever to possess a bliss
> peculiar to each one's individual existence? How, but by the
> medium of a world like this?[7]

Identity, for Keats, is something to be sought, to be achieved, and
self-knowledge is gained through the cathartic process of suffering.
Each individual soul must contend with the world's unrest, must
forge a sense of selfhood through a titanic struggle.

> Do you not see how necessary a World of Pains and troubles is
> to school an Intelligence and make it a Soul? A Place where the
> heart must feel and suffer in a thousand diverse ways! . . . This
> appears to me a faint sketch of a system of Salvation which does
> not affront our reason and humanity—I am convinced that
> many difficulties which christians labour under would vanish
> before it—there is one which even now Strikes me—the Salva-
> tion of Children—In them the Spark or intelligence returns to
> God without any identity—it having had no time to learn of
> and be altered by the heart—or seat of the human Passions.
> [Keats's original spelling and punctuation preserved.][8]

Homer's "heart must feel and suffer in a thousand diverse ways"
so that he might possess an identity, his own individual selfhood.
Otherwise, he would remain a child and return "to God without any
identity." According to Keats's system, Ulysses would return to God
"pure" but with an uncreated Self—for he has not yet "made" his
own soul in the fiery crucible of experience.

Homer is aware that he is undergoing a profound inner transformation, and slowly embraces Keatsian purgation as a necessary and
even overdue process. As he tells the old telegraph operator Grogan

in chapter 19, "Yeah, I guess I've changed all right. I guess I've grown up. And I guess it was *time* for me to grow up. I didn't know *anything* until I got this job. Oh, I knew a lot of things, but I didn't know the half of it, and I guess I never will, either. . . . How can any man ever really get it all straight so that it comes out even and makes sense?" (pp. 140–41).

Grogan also accepts struggle as metamorphosis, comparing the war to a vast cosmic body "fighting off its diseases." The travails of the individual and the world are inseparable, as he tells Homer in strongly Keatsian terms: "The sick body and the sick spirit are always restored to health. They may take sick again, but they will always get better, and as each fresh disease comes and is driven off, the body and spirit strengthen until at last, they are powerful, as they were meant to be, cleansed of all decay, refined, gentler, nobler, and beyond corruption" (p. 129). Both the self and the body of the world thus achieve the "bliss" Keats holds out as the promise of suffering.

The long "schooling" of Homer's "intelligence" begins to be apparent in the way he copes with the problems confronting the fatherless Macauley family. The pivotal chapter, "Mr. Mechano" (chapter 31), shows Homer consoling Ulysses, who has been frightened by a machinelike man in a drugstore window selling a cure-all, "Dr. Bradford's Tonic." Mr. Mechano is described in monstrous terms: "He seemed inhuman and in fact he looked like nothing so much as an upright, unburied corpse still capable of moving" (p. 219). When Ulysses becomes terrified and runs away crying, it becomes clear that Mr. Mechano is intended as a symbol of Death. Ulysses has had *his* first brush with the reality of suffering and death. Homer embraces his sobbing brother and takes him home on his bicycle. In this scene, Homer shows a tender concern and strength, ministering in a fatherly manner to his brother's pain. The two brothers do not speak about the incident, but Homer senses that Ulysses has begun on his own spiritual odyssey.

When they return to the house, Homer again shows a newly found sense of his own powers and leadership capabilities when he tells his sister Bess that she should not try to find a job. He takes command of the situation, speaking authoritatively and confidently:

"Just because there happens to be a war in the world isn't a reason for everybody to go out of their heads. Just stay home where you belong and help Mama" (pp. 232–33). He also insists, "in an almost impatient" tone of voice, that the entire family go to church.

Significantly, Homer, asserting his will assuredly and lovingly, becomes angry for the first time in this chapter, and his family notices the metamorphosis: "He was so bossy, his sister Bess was almost proud of him, because never before had she seen him so concerned about *anything*" (p. 233). The chapter closes with Ulysses again finding an egg, and when Homer asks him what he has in his hand, he responds: " 'Egg,' Ulysses said as if the word were also the word for God" (p. 233). It is a wonderful ending, linking an important moment in Homer's psychological and spiritual development with the miraculous symbol of regeneration and birth. Homer has birthed himself into a new father role in the family, where previously he was still a son.

Homer's new role as sole provider and father figure is underscored by the letter he receives from Marcus two chapters later. Marcus tells him that he can have his possessions, and Homer senses that his older brother is preparing him to take over the leadership of the family should he die in the war. Homer weeps (significantly, for the last time), and in an important passage the pattern of his suffering is made explicit.

> While he was reading the letter the messenger sat down. He read very slowly, gulping many times, and becoming sick many times as he had been sick first in the house of the Mexican mother and then the night that he had cried while riding his bicycle around Ithaca after work. . . . "If my brother is killed in this stupid War . . . I shall spit at the world. I shall hate it forever. I won't be good. I shall be the worst of them all, the worst that ever lived."
>
> He stopped suddenly and tears came to his eyes. (P. 254)

Saroyan emphasizes the progression of Homer's experience, from the first message he delivered to the Mexican woman leading to his assumption of the role of the eldest brother and father. His sickness at this point is terribly intense, for he knows intuitively that Marcus will be killed.[9]

When the news of his brother's death arrives in chapter 38, Homer responds with anger and outrage rather than "sickness" and tears. He "spits at the world," as he said he would do if Marcus were killed, and his outrage is exacerbated by the death of old Grogan, who passed away as the death telegram reached the office. When Spangler arrives, the mood moves to deepest tragedy, as Ulysses' precious symbol of life and hope makes a final appearance.

> Spangler telegraphed the other operator to postpone any more telegrams for a while. He then got up and went to his desk and sat down, looking at nothing. His hand fell idly on the hardboiled egg which he kept for good luck. Without knowing what he was doing, he tapped the egg idly on the desk until the shell broke and then slowly he removed all the shell, and in a kind of desperate stupor, ate the egg. Suddenly he discovered the shell of the egg on the table and pushed it off into the wastebasket. (P. 281)

The destruction of the egg symbolizes the death of the miraculous: fragile life for Homer has suffered a sea change. As he tells Spangler, "The whole world is different now. All the people in the world are different now. Something good has gone out of them" (p. 284). The shell of the egg is now in the wastebasket; it is no longer a luminous gathering together of all mute truth.

Yet Homer finds that he cannot hate anyone, for there is no one to hate. Marcus's death has left him paralyzed, and he confides in Spangler: "I don't know who to hate. I keep trying to find out who it is, but I *can't* find out who it is. I just don't know. What's a man going to do? What can I do about it? What can I say? How does a man go on living? Who does he love?" (p. 282). Spangler counsels Homer in words that recall Mrs. Macauley's earlier advice: "Love is immortal and makes all things immortal. But hate dies every minute" (p. 284). Humanity, we are reminded, is one organism, and the immortality of life symbolized by the egg must be affirmed by the power of love. When Homer consents to play a game of horseshoes with Spangler, there is hope that he realizes the truth of Spangler's faith.

Although the focus thus far has been on Homer's troubling passage through "soul-making," it would be a distortion to see *The Human Comedy* as only a tragic account of his moral development. Indeed, many of the novel's episodes recall the world of *My Name Is Aram*. Like Aram, Homer runs track, is interested in body building, goes to the Presbyterian church, and is fully capable of outrageous spoofing at school, as "A Speech on the Human Nose" indicates. In addition, the pastoral world of Aram Garoghlanian is evoked in Ulysses' foray into the apricot orchard and in the novel's "miraculous" opening chapter. Ulysses is also similar to Aram in his boredom with religion (in "Here Is a Kiss" he is more concerned with the bald head of the man seated in front of him than with the sermon) and the ease with which he gets into trouble (the episode with the animal trap in the sporting goods store is exemplary).

The comic energy of *My Name Is Aram* also pervades many of the novel's episodes and serves to relieve the continual tension of Homer's crises. Indeed, we should remember that the book is called *The Human Comedy*, and not *The Human Tragedy*. For example, in "At the Parlor Lecture Club" the pretentiousness of a famous "lady world traveller," Rosalie Simms-Pibity, is deflated with great gusto. The "romance" of Spangler and Diana Steed (she continually calls the aloof Spangler "darling") is laughable, and appears to be Saroyan's concession to the exigencies of Hollywood movie making.

An important difference between the two books is that, although both Homer and Aram are fatherless, Aram turns to his innumerable colorful uncles for spiritual sustenance, while Homer relates primarily to his schoolteacher Miss Hicks, Spangler, Grogan, and of course his mother. Mrs. Macauley's role as dispenser of moral wisdom and bearer of values establishes her as a central affirmer of faith in the goodness of life. As she tells Homer, "If you don't believe, you're not alive. . . . It's faith that makes anything wonderful—not the thing itself" (p. 43). She possesses great inner strength and conviction, although her husband is dead and her eldest son is in the war. Living under straitened financial circumstances (the Macauleys are poor, as are all of Saroyan's affirmers of spiritual over material values), Mrs. Macauley yet displays an openhearted generosity and a deep-seated faith in the goodness of people. She tells Ulysses that he must remember "always to give, of everything you have. You must give foolishly even. You must be extravagant. You must give to all who come into your life. Then nothing and no one shall have the power to cheat you of anything, for if you give to a thief, he cannot steal from you, and he himself is then no longer a thief. And the more you give, the more you will have to give" (p. 22). As Edwin B. Burgum has observed, it is "the natural affection of human beings for one another" which renders endurable the ceaseless pathos of life in Saroyan's fictional universe.[10] Like the poor Alexander family in *My Heart's in the Highlands*, who give openly to the visiting Mr. MacGregor, Mrs. Macauley preaches Saroyan's message of tender-hearted kindness and love.

This emphasis on the innate goodness and innocence of all people surfaces throughout *The Human Comedy*. Although men are continually being murdered in the war, there are no evil characters in Saroyan's world. In "Let There Be Light" (chapter 22), Spangler gladly gives money to a young man who has held up the telegraph office (illustrating by example Mrs. Macauley's dictum quoted above) and tells him sympathetically: " 'Here's your money. Yes, *yours*—it *is* yours, if you've got to take a gun out to get it! I know how you feel because I've felt the same way. We've all felt the same way. The graveyards and penitentiaries are full of good American kids who've had bad luck and hard times. They're not criminals. Here,' he said gently, 'take this money. Go home'" (pp. 149–50). The two men then chat amiably, and it is revealed that the young man is well-read: his favorite author is William Blake. The skeptical reader may find it difficult to assent to this scene's verisimilitude. Young men who set out to rob usually do not end up discussing literature with their intended victims.

Yet Saroyan is usually successful in resisting the temptation to soften the brute realities of contemporary life through his all-accepting, generous, and hopeful imagination. As we have seen, Homer's growth is portrayed in "realistic" terms. At the end of the novel, however, Saroyan attempts to ameliorate the tragedy of Marcus's death by having Tobey George, an orphaned army buddy of his, take his place in the family. Although this resolution of the novel's tensions is foreshadowed through earlier references to the interrelatedness of all humanity (Homer "replaces" Mrs. Sandoval's son, the resemblance between Ulysses and his dead father Matthew is commented upon, "the people of the world are like one man"), it is still extremely difficult to see Tobey as a surrogate son.

For some commentators, this ending is an unacceptable way to deal with the war's tragic impact upon Americans, and it therefore lessened their opinion of the book as a whole. Philip Rahv considered *The Human Comedy* "escapist literature" and attributed its success to the fact that "people have been so frightened by the horrid events of recent years that they would like to be absolved of all responsibility, to see themselves as intrinsically innocent and naive."[11] For Rahv, the author's attempt to make us believe that "evil is unreal" flies in the face of reality and is ultimately an act of self-delusion.

Saroyan himself was not pleased with the ending of the novel, and he wrote in his autobiography about its unfortunate "lapses."

> There are some lapses in it which many readers like even more than they like the stuff that is at least a little better, and this doesn't please me. If the stuff that went off the level is taken for gospel, as it frequently is, it can do more harm than I want any of my writing ever to do. Now, you might say that the harm is harmless harm, but as for me, the hell with that. I didn't *mean* to go off the level, I meant the opposite. I meant to take a lot of everyday stuff and bring out the drama of it, but near the end of the book I went to work and wrote that it appears to be unavoidable sometimes for people to be killed in a war. I went even further, and tried to demonstrate that the murder of somebody in a war can be a thing of great meaning—to somebody or other, sometime or other. Bullshit—but I was in a hurry, the war was upon me, and I wanted to get this thing out of the way before it got me, which it did soon enough, and the hell with that, too. I fought the United States Army for three years, and I won. I'm sorry for every man who fought, and lost.[12]

This recanting is similar to Saroyan's earlier disavowal of the credo section of *The Time of Your Life* and displays the same impulse toward self-correction.

In a recent "revised edition," some of the novel's passages have been cut and the ending of the last chapter is significantly changed in accordance with the author's later perceptions. In the original last paragraph, Tobey George's entrance into the house as the Macauley's surrogate son is described as follows:

> Mary Arena began to sing now, and then Ulysses Macauley came out of the house and took the hand of the soldier. When the song ended, Mrs. Macauley and Bess and Mary came to the open door. The mother, standing, looking at her two remaining sons, one on each side of the stranger, the soldier who had known her son who was now dead, smiled and understood. She smiled at the *soldier*. Her smile was for him who was now himself her son. She smiled as if he were Marcus himself and the soldier and his two brothers moved toward the door, toward the warmth and light of home. (P. 291)

The revised version reads:

> Ulysses came out of the house and took the soldier by the hand. When the song ended, Mrs. Macauley and Bess and Mary Arena came to the open door. The mother stood and looked at her two sons, one on each side of the stranger, the soldier who had known her son who was now dead. Sick to death, she nevertheless smiled at the soldier, and said, "Won't you please come in and let us show you around the house?"[13]

In the new version, Saroyan has added "sick to death," which greatly alters the mood. Mrs. Macauley is no longer "understanding," and her smile is qualified by "nevertheless"—it now seems almost forced. Tobey George is no longer "him who was now himself her son"—the sentence has been deleted. Finally, the last phrase of the original has been changed from "toward the warmth and light of home" to the more neutral "let us show you around the house." *House* is a much less emotionally connotative word than *home*, and the words *warmth and light* have been excised. Saroyan has thus attempted to make the final scene significantly more taut, austere, and cool—it is far less "optimistic" than the original version.

The passages in Saroyan that go "off the level" may be seen as the result of his powerful and continual need to affirm the brotherhood of man. Because he recognizes no "enemies," the ending of *The Human Comedy* avoids blaming Marcus's death on some evil principle in the world. Rather, the orphaned Tobey George finds a family and the Macauleys, a son. The fact that Saroyan was dissatisfied with this solution later in his career indicates a desire to confront his own inability to accept the fact of meaningless death. As Budd Schulberg wrote, he had always been an individualist who believed "in the Christian or fairy-tale world of good people on all sides."[14] Although Saroyan adjusted his vision to accommodate the stark realities of the postwar world, he would never abandon the possibility of love triumphing over death—this was a "lapse" he would never quite be able to cure.

CHAPTER 7

Allegories for the Stage

Following the success of *The Time of Your Life*, Saroyan continued to write prolifically for the theater. Although his official presence on Broadway ended in 1943, he wrote and published plays to the end of his career.[1] Stylistically and generically, these plays display a great variety of approaches, ranging from the romantic comedy of *Love's Old Sweet Song* (1940) to the Beckettian sterilities of *Assassinations* (1979); from the joy and tenderness of *The Beautiful People* (1941) to the existential anguish of *The Cave Dwellers* (1958). Yet although the dramatic treatment of each play is unique, Saroyan's central obsession throughout remains man's exile in a miraculous and troubling world.

Indeed, he continued to construct his plays based on the dynamic principle of opposition outlined in chapter 5: the confrontation between imagination and reality, between dream and despair. Yet again he wages what e. e. cummings called "the eternal fight of selfhood against mobism, the immortal battle of beauty against ugliness." Saroyan fully agreed with cummings, who believed life must be lived poetically, and who wrote in *six nonlectures* that "poetry is being, not doing. . . . You've got to come out of the measurable doing universe into the immeasurable house of being."[2] According to Saroyan's plays, inhabiting the "house of being" is impossible when the true sources of revitalization, transformation, and creativity are ignored—love and imagination. The world of being is embedded in, located *within*, the so-called real world, and is affirmed by poets, children, artists—all those who can see magically with the inward eye.

Yet as we have seen, the achievement of psychological balance and imaginative freedom is no easy or simple matter in his dramatic universe. Both literally and symbolically, many of his characters remain *imprisoned*; alienated, estranged, and homeless, they are in constant conflict with the external world. The jailed young men of *Hello Out There* and *Jim Dandy*; the innocent victims subjected to wholesale murder in *The Slaughter of the Innocents*; the spiritual malaise and loneliness of Harry Mallory in *Across the Board on Tomorrow Morning*—in each play Saroyan sought to represent allegorically the magnificent struggle for coherence in a violent cosmos.

Saroyan himself defined his dramatic practice as allegorical in the preface to *Sam Ego's House*.

> I must point out that everything I write, everything I have ever written, is allegorical. This came to pass inevitably. One does not choose to write allegorically any more than one chooses to grow black hair on his head. The stories of Armenia, Kurdistan, Georgia, Persia, Syria, Arabia, Turkey and Israel are all allegorical, and apart from the fact that I heard these stories as a child, told to me by both of my grandmothers, by great aunts and great uncles, and by friends of the family, I myself am a product of Asia Minor, hence the allegorical and the real are closely related in my mind.
>   In fact all reality to me is allegorical.[3]

Saroyan's plays, like all his work, are parables, fables, allegories of man's estrangement from himself and the universe. Yet Saroyan continued to be a maverick in the *way* he depicted his allegorical truths. He broke from the drama of "social realism" and concentrated instead on translating into dramatic terms man's subjective, interior life of spiritual yearning, on portraying the infinite longing and aspiration of the human heart for what Wordsworth called "something far more deeply interfused." His plays do not dramatize "social problems"; rather, they probe repeatedly and directly the titanic struggle between faith and doubt in contemporary life.[4]

Across the Board on Tomorrow Morning, for example, is a one-act play which, like *The Time of Your Life*, takes place within the warm confines of a restaurant-bar—Callaghan's in New York. It is also, like the earlier plays, haunted by the chaos of World War II; as the author remarked, it is a sad play "because it is about reality now."[5] Indeed, it explores the pulverization, disintegration, and eventual disappearance of "reality" and its replacement by the void, by nothingness.

As the play opens, the waiter, Thomas Piper, informs the audience that it is seeing "an illusion of a restaurant-bar in New York City," thus emphasizing in Pirandellian terms the illusory nature of "reality" as well as the fictive quality of drama itself (p. 217). Like the stage manager in Wilder's *Our Town* or Tom Wingfield in Williams's *The Glass Menagerie*, Piper becomes an explainer, a middleman between the play and the audience, between the theatrical world and the "real" world. Like Joe in *The Time of Your Life*, Piper stresses the idea of life as dramatic performance, believing that "some of the people who come here sometimes are, in my opinion, characters out of fiction" (p. 232). So too the actor Jaspar MacGregor was a performer who recited poetry, and as we shall see, *The Cave Dwellers* is peopled by unemployed actors who take up residence in an abandoned theater.

Immediately following Piper's opening speech, the bar's awkward and nervous proprietor, John Callaghan, welcomes the audience to the saloon. Harry Mallory then comes on the scene, "a swift-moving young man of twenty-seven or so" (p. 221). He requests wine, changes his mind and orders Scotch, asks Piper if he has read the paper, orders a steak, drinks the Scotch and orders another, makes a phone call—all in rapid succession. Finally noticing the audience, he remarks, "People stink. I avoid them" (p. 224). Although Harry's brash behavior and persistent sarcasm reveal a deep contempt for "reality now," it is clear that his anger and misanthropy are actually the result of his profound concern for an imperiled humanity. His gruff manner is a mask hiding a deep vulnerability, loneliness, and sensitivity.

Harry's impulsiveness and brooding link him to both Joe and the Arab in *The Time of Your Life*—he sees no foundation to the world of the early nineteen forties. When he offers to bring Piper his supper (thus defiantly reversing their accustomed social roles), Piper tells him it is against the rules. Harry then responds vehemently:

"Rules? (*Pause, standing*) Let me tell you, there are no rules. Honor, none. Grace, none. Truth, none. Therefore, rules, none. Where in this configuration of error and crime which is contemporary history, may we find one rule in operation? (*Pause*) Nowhere" (p. 236). Harry exposes the absurdity of clinging to a petty "rule" which prevents clients from serving their waiters, when modern life presents a vast panorama of moral and spiritual lawlessness.

For Harry, the onrushing war is the final, incontrovertible evidence of a deranged humanity. Later in the play he remarks: "The world, we know, is amok. The realm of *all* reality, therefore, is now also amok. The world has always been uninhabitable" (p. 251). Contemporary experience has become an arena in which absurdity is the norm. Indeed, imminent collapse is inevitable unless there is a transformation of consciousness, unless humanity becomes human. As Mallory warns at the rhetorical climax of his speech, "This may be the last day of reality. We had better try to be human while there is time" (p. 252).

Mallory's warnings, however, ultimately prove to be of no avail, as "the illusion of our reality" is finally shattered. A young man arrives on the scene and says tomorrow's newspaper will reveal "that for over one thousand and nine hundred and forty-one years the world has been inhabited by the dead, not the living" (p. 262). It is at this point that the play shifts into a deeply anguished, surreal mode, revealing a stripped, bare, Beckettian universe: "Ever since midnight the dead have been truly the dead, and the unreal has been truly the unreal. There is nothing any more anywhere" (p. 263). Here is a dessicated, empty, dehumaned landscape—that world of absolute spiritual and emotional nothingness which Hemingway christened *nada*.

The outside world, exterior "reality," has disappeared—there is "no street, no cab, nothing" (p. 267). Time has also burst into timelessness; no new action will ever be completed, for there is no linear time. Rather, "the same things are going to be repeated . . . more or less endlessly, but outside of that everything is ended" (p. 267). It is now a frozen world where nothing is and nothing happens save eternal repetition—the ceaseless movement of the self-regarding consciousness, powerless to transform either the interior or exterior worlds, to effect any change in a now shattered "reality."

This cosmic dislocation and fragmentation, this triumph of nothingness, leave characters like the cab driver Fritz and the bartender Jim unaffected. Although "the glue that held the illusion together" (p. 268) has disappeared, they continue with business as usual.

> FRITZ: Well, give me another drink anyway. You may be right, you may be wrong. For all I care, you may be sober, you may be drunk. Whether I'm alive or whether I'm dead, all I want is a drink. If it's ended or if it's just begun, a Scotch and soda, please. Illusion or reality, no illusion or no reality, one drink more before I go.
>
> JIM: My own words.
> *(Drinks all around)*
> My very own sentiments.
>
> (P. 269)

The reactions of the two men illustrate their desire to shut out the chaos and turbulence of life outside the saloon. As Saroyan had observed in *Three Times Three*, "The masses aren't ready, I'm afraid, for the shock of genuine knowing, and not spiritually equipped to face the inward tragedy which occurs with genuine knowing."[6] "Genuine knowing" here is the awareness that reality has become unbearably fragmented and amorphous. Becoming fully human (the task Mallory has assigned to the bar's clientele) is beyond the capabilities of those who fear and therefore attempt to escape the dark confrontation with nothingness. As Geoffrey Hartman has observed, "Every increase in consciousness is accompanied by an increase in self-consciousness"; it is precisely self-consciousness which the bar's denizens lack.[7] While Harry had been experiencing the dark night of the soul which is a concomitant of spiritual evolution, the people around him remain dead-in-life.

The play, however, does not end in this completely negative mood. The possibility of rebirth, redemption, and spiritual regeneration occurs when we learn that the young man who had given the disturbing news of reality's death is actually Harry Mallory's son (the boy's mother was the woman Mallory had been calling throughout the play). Mallory's son, as he tells us, "entered the world just as the illusion broke, consequently I was here all the time the illusion was unbroken, as well as all the time thereafter" (p. 270). Because he was born at the moment of time's disintegration, his being exists in timelessness, in eternity—hence he has become a young man instantaneously.

Harry now informs the bar's clientele that things have returned to normal—the disappearance of reality was "an improvement in optics, which was, perhaps fortunately, temporary" (p. 272). Fritz asks, "We're right back where we started from?" and Harry responds: "Nobly, and with that delicate balance of despair and delight which glues all unrelated things into the continuity and architecture which are the fable and fantasy of this world and life" (pp. 273–74). Mallory's son now leaves the bar to return to his correct place in time as an infant, while Jim and Fritz discuss the horse races—they behave as they always have, wrapped up in daily events as though nothing of consequence had occurred.

Across the Board on Tomorrow Morning finally attempts to reunite the forces of life and death in a "delicate balance of despair and delight." Although the people in the bar are blind to the "improvement of optics" which has caused the sudden slowing down of time into eternity and rendered palpable the chaos and darkness of the world about them, they are not rejected by Mallory. He understands them, and is himself heroically striving to maintain his balance in a nightmarish world. Indeed, at the end of the play he invokes the mother of his son and her lovely freckles, thus balancing despair with the possibility of love.

Across the Board on Tomorrow Morning, like many of Saroyan's plays written during this period, reflects the darker side of his imagination. Focusing on the individual anguished spirit of Harry Mallory, it conveys a surrealistic vision of the modern condition. *The Beautiful People*, on the other hand, is closer in spirit to *My Heart's in the Highlands;* here the author depicts a poignant family situation defined by the pathos and yearning of the human heart. The emphasis in this case is on the impoverished and poetic Webster family, rather than on the individual estranged person. The theme is again the confrontation between faith and doubt, imagination and reality; but here a mood of fantasy and tender melancholy reigns.

The play opens with the fifteen-year-old Owen Webster playing "Wonderful One" on the piano (we also hear this music being played on the cornet off-stage and learn it is his brother Harold in New York performing). The omnipresence of music throughout the play signals Saroyan's mood of sweet remembering, of time's suspension, of elusive truth, and affirms the warmth of human community. Owen flips a coin, sings "Row, Row, Row Your Boat," and looks at the *Saturday Evening Post*. Harmony Blueblossom, an elderly lady, comes to the door and asks for Jonah Webster, Owen's father. The two have an amusing, fantastic conversation, and Owen preaches his passionate gospel of freedom and spontaneity. He is against the idea of work, believing that "if nobody worked, nothing would collapse. Everybody would look around, take it easy, find out what they *want* to do, and then *do* it. Then it wouldn't be work, it would be living, which is what we're supposed to be doing around here, I guess."[8] Owen's vivid imagination, verve, optimism, and reverence for mystery are immediately delightful; he radiates a healthy contempt for convention and conformity. Loafing and meditating, he expresses an uninhibited love of life; he is a dreamer inhabiting his solitary kingdom of the imagination.

Owen's creativity marks him as an artistic searcher after being. A neophyte poet, he writes one-word books ("Tree") and has great awe for the sacred powers of language. Each new poem celebrates a new discovery, uncovers a new beauty in the world. Owen's immersion (even at age fifteen) in the wonder of childhood, his lack of repression, his insistence on "play" (as we have seen Saroyan define it in chapter 5), are all described by Freud as typical of the artistic imagination. As Norman O. Brown has observed:

> Our normal orderly responsible selves, dominated by the reality-principle, are sustained by a constant expenditure in psychic energy devoted to the maintenance of the repression of our fundamental desires. Art, by overcoming the inhibition and activating the playful primary process, which is intrinsically easier and more enjoyable than the procedures of normal re-

sponsible thought, on both counts effects a saving in psychic expenditure and provides relief from the pressures of reason.

Art, if its object is to undo repressions, and if civilization is essentially repressive, is in this sense subversive of civilization.[9]

Owen is indeed one of the most "subversive" youths in modern drama, and it is understandable that he is thought strange by the more "responsible" and "normal" characters in *The Beautiful People*.

When he tells Miss Harmony Blueblossom about his sister Agnes and the troupe of mice she cares for, she responds upon leaving, "And thanks again for your delightful fairy-tale about the mice," which causes Owen to lament, "People don't believe anything anymore—not even old ladies" (p. 34). Owen sees life as miracle, and Miss Blueblossom's failure to believe his story shows a failure of faith because it reveals a lack of wonder—wonder, imagination, and curiosity make the impossible possible.

In the following scene, Owen's sister, "St. Agnes of the Mice," and his father, Jonah, are introduced. Jonah, like Joe in *The Time of Your Life* or Ben Alexander in *My Heart's in the Highlands*, is a heavy drinker whose speech is marked by eccentric, richly metaphorical-rhetorical phrases. He expresses his concern about Agnes's lost mouse by declaiming: "Spectacles and satellites, what's the tragedy? What's troubling this space? I feel commotion in the air, as though great and tender values were the object of some brutal assault" (p. 41). As Miss Blueblossom remarked earlier to Owen, Jonah has "a mind as wild as yours" (p. 33); like that of Owen, Jonah's joyous, uninhibited eccentricity sparks life in everyone around him.

Jonah then discusses with Agnes the boy with whom she has fallen in love. Agnes's experience of love has caused her to perceive life afresh, as she describes to her father a recent epiphany: "I began to see! I didn't used to *see*. The street cars going by had people in them suddenly. There have always been people in street cars, but now they were beautiful people. I never saw people that way before" (p. 52). Like her father and brother, she deeply desires that people live completely, creatively, miraculously. "I can't believe to live—to *really* live—is foolish or impossible. (*In soft voice*) Is it impossible, Father?" (p. 54). Jonah and his two children establish the play's mood of lyric expectancy, of tenderness, love, and openhearted generosity.

Yet as in all of Saroyan's plays, the outside world poses a threat to the harmonious family united in peace and love. Soon, William Prim, an insurance man, arrives on the scene to tell Jonah that his company has discovered that the pension checks that had supported the Webster family were addressed to a dead person—thus the checks will be discontinued. Like David F. Windmore of *Love's Old Sweet Song*, Prim, an emissary from the orderly, rational, and efficient business world, seems to invade the fantastic enclosed universe of the Websters. Jonah takes the news calmly, and when Agnes offers Prim a glass of wine, he refuses. Blick, in *The Time of Your Life*, reacted similarly, refusing a drink because he had "responsibilities" as head of the vice squad. Prim must keep his "reason" as the representative of logic, fact, and business. Because alcohol is symbolic of the loss of restraint, order, and inhibition, it is shunned by the "authorities," the enforcers of the "law."

When not done as escapism, drinking is an embrace with the primal unity of creation, an uninhibited refusal of limitations. It is, after all, the spirit of Robert Burns which presides over *The Beautiful People*, the poet who celebrated the "cup of kindness" which Jonah shares with his friend Dan Hillboy in act 2 (p. 80). Jonah also quotes Burns's "To a Mouse" later in the play: "Wee sleekit, tim'rous beastie" (p. 63). Prim, however, is unresponsive to this Burnsian, lyrical, and tender inner world which the Webster family inhabits.

Prim is an uptight outsider whose name perfectly exemplifies his character. After Owen finishes writing another one-word book ("Mouse") and his father questions him, Prim's reaction to their exchange is revelatory.

JONAH: Pole star and pyramid, when are you going to write a
        book with *two* words?
OWEN: When I *know* two of 'em.
        (*Writing on a large tablet*)
        I've got to find out about nouns before I move to verbs.

You've got to be careful about verbs, otherwise you'll
get things all mixed up—even worse than they are
already. *Is. That's* a verb. I've got to be careful when I
use a word like that.
          (*Pause, shaping the earth with hands*)
Is.

PRIM: Is what?

OWEN: (*Angrily and loudly*)
What do you mean, what? Is, that's all. *Is.*

                                        (Pp. 67–68)

The insurance man is dead to the boy's lyricism and his moving
evocation of the indestructible strength of being itself as represented by the proud, single, pure word—"Is." Prim, as Dan Hillboy
says later, is one of "the little vice-presidents who stumble and fall
in every parlor. The little men with the wonderful official docu-
ments" (p. 80). Yet Prim is ultimately a harmless and laughable
character, and proves enough affected by the generous humanity of
the Websters to promise a continuation of the pension checks.

In the play's final scene, Father Hogan of St. Anne's church comes
to the house. The priest informs Jonah that Owen has fallen into the
pipe organ, and Jonah explains that his son was looking for the
mouse that had fled from Agnes. The arrival of the priest allows
Jonah to express the play's central message—the religion of life:
"Every life in the world is a miracle, and it's a miracle every minute
each of us stays alive, and unless we know this, the experience of
living is cheated of the greater part of its wonder and beauty" (pp.
87–88). Jonah reaffirms the love-of-life motif that both of his children had expressed earlier in the play. His church, unlike the priest's,
is "the whole blooming universe" (p. 88). Here we see again Saroyan's Whitmanesque pantheism, the oneness of all created things
with the self—"from the mite to the whale" (p. 88).

The symbolism of the mice is further explained when Jonah tells
Father Hogan that Owen was looking not only for a mouse but "for
the *image* of the heart's shyest, most kindly smile. (*Pause, sol-
emnly*) The absence of their brother has taught them—and myself,
too—the preciousness of one another. One's son, one's daughter,

one's neighbor—and the stranger, brotherless and homeless" (p. 91). The lost mouse signifies the tender mystery of the human heart as well as Jonah's son Harold, away from the family in New York.

Owen now returns from the church, and William Prim and Harmony Blueblossom return as well. Suddenly the music of a cornet becomes discernible, and Agnes rushes into the house. As all the characters stand motionless and silent, Harold appears playing his instrument, followed by his homeless friend, Steve. Jonah, Dan, and Father Hogan then arrive from the neighborhood bar as the family of humanity is enclosed by the music of faith singing from Harold's cornet. The various strands of the plot are drawn together: Agnes is deeply in love, the lost son and brother Harold is found, Harmony finally meets Jonah—even Prim is enfolded by the circle of warmth radiating from the Webster family. He too, as Owen says, is a "good man" who is not to be excluded from Saroyan's "enchanted universe."[10] The homeless Steve is also to be taken as the arrival of the lost mouse, and the final evidence that the Webster family truly believes in "*all* the living" (p. 86). Their home, like the saloon in *The Time of Your Life* and the Macauley home in *The Human Comedy*, is the place of refuge for those who have no home —for Dan Hillboy, for Steve, and even for Prim.

Because everything turns out positively, *The Beautiful People* has been criticized for its lack of dramatic tension. Even the "villain" Prim turns out to be good-hearted. The play seemed more of a lyric, affirmative poem than a dramatic structure based on conventional notions of conflict and resolution. The author was not unaware of such criticism, and acknowledged the play's "defects" (p. 4).[11] Yet *The Beautiful People* is a moving experience on stage, and ranks with *The Time of Your Life* and *My Heart's in the Highlands* among the author's early plays.

Saroyan's next major play, *Jim Dandy: Fat Man in a Famine* (1947), continues his exploration of faith versus doubt, spiritual death and rebirth through imagination.[12] A sprawling, dramatic symphony, an evocative tapestry through which is woven a rich pattern of symbolism and theme, *Jim Dandy* is a pageant or spectacle, not a play— rather than elaborate an orderly plot, it conjures a dreamlike mood. The play speaks in complex symbols, magically transforming reality through allegorical implication, *suggesting* the hidden realm of inner spiritual being.

Jim Dandy is set "in all or part of a transparent egg shell which is broken and open along one side. Inside the shell are miserable and majestic ruins."[13] The egg represents the womb where humanity is struggling to be born, and the ruins are labeled "The Public Library" —a place containing the precious remains of a rotting culture. Here an assemblage of typically Saroyanesque misfits gathers. Among others we meet Jock Arimathea, "a wild little man in a zoot suit"; the hugely overweight Jim Dandy; Jim Smither, a young convict; Johnny and Molly, two abandoned children; Fishkin, a skeptic; Flora, a proper librarian; Tommy Singh, a soldier; Jack Adams, an old poet; the Maharajah, a magician; Gibbon, an apelike creature.

These characters again present Saroyan's persistent themes: the innocence of man, as symbolized by the wrongly jailed Jim Smither; Jim Dandy's quest for "the blessed word" of love (p. 77); the movement from death to life, as represented by Jack Adams's death-rebirth at the end of the play and made explicit by his final words: "We're born at last!" (p. 125); Johnny's diagnosis of "reality now": "Youth in ruins; science and crime in partnership; the management of the affairs of men left to imbeciles, impostors, knaves and maniacs; mankind a sickly suicide writing his foolish farewell note; and the poet standing around with his mouth open" (p. 45); and, finally, Gibbon's efforts to transform himself from ape to man, to achieve fuller consciousness—an allegory of humanity's desire for spiritual truth and plenitude (it is evident that Saroyan had Shakespeare's *The Tempest* in mind while composing the play, for the relationship between the Maharajah and Gibbon is analogous to that of Prospero and Caliban).

Yet again, Saroyan's hypothetical world is not the everyday, work-a-day world; it is a place of continual becoming, of loveliness, of miracle, of the heart's truth. Even the doubter Fishkin is won over to affirmation as the play ends celebrating "His Majesty man!" (p. 127): "Somebody sing! Somebody dance! For Fishkin is born at last, and this time he's glad he's here! This world's no orphanage, no asylum for the mad, no hospital for the sick, no penitentiary for the criminal. This world's home and we are lucky tenants of the house. Fishkin is born! Somebody sing!" (p. 124). Fishkin has realized the play's existential message that he has entered life "to *act* my part, to *create* my role, to be whomsoever I should choose to be" (p. 123). The movement from death to rebirth initiated at the opening of *Jim Dandy* is now complete.[14]

Saroyan's last major published play, *The Cave Dwellers* (1958), is leaner, more tightly constructed than *Jim Dandy*. The dominant symbol here is the cave-theater, refuge of a humanity which "is still as fearfully sick as it was when it began."[15] According to his introduction to the play, "*The Cave Dwellers* happens on the stage of an abandoned theatre because all buildings are caves, and because the theatre is the cave at its best—the last arena in which *all is always possible.* In the caves of the government and the church, for instance, all has long since stopped being possible, in favor of a pattern of formal repetition, which some of us find only amusing and monotonous, by turns" (pp. 13–14). The institutionalized forms that religion and authority assume are meaningless, inadequate for the modern age: art alone—the theater—has the power to minister to man's deepest spiritual needs. The artist's ability to allegorize humanity's estrangement and still submerged divinity through drama is his greatest claim to supremacy.

As in earlier plays, life as performance is a dominant theme. The characters are unemployed actors—symbols of a humanity without a purpose, a role, a meaningful drama to enact.[16] Yet as in *Jim Dandy*, the play is dedicated to "His Majesty man." For, as Nona Balakian has observed, "two of the characters have given themselves royal titles, King and Queen (parts for which they were once well known), and represent human beings waiting to come to their rightful inheritance—the kingdom of Earth."[17]

Indeed, the condition of waiting, which we saw adumbrated in earlier plays, is a prominent theme throughout *The Cave Dwellers*. As the Queen says to the King: "Nothing happens! It's the story of our lives" (p. 49). The persistent complaint of Saroyan's spiritual vagabonds, his motley groups of troubled refugees, surfaces here again. The recurring feeling mapped in *The Cave Dwellers* is one of strangeness—the difficulty of achieving being in a universe of *nada*. As the runaway girl in the play suggests, "We all feel—*strange.* As if something were happening *everywhere*, not here alone" (p. 59).

None of the play's characters fits into the conventional structures of society. Although Fishkin had finally affirmed man's place in the cosmos, there is less certainty expressed by the King: "We *don't* belong here. It's not our place. It's a cave. What are we doing in a cave? We're angels. What are we doing in bodies? (*Pause*) For some reason, we're trying our best, helplessly, to pretend that we *are* in them, that we *belong* in them, and that we *are* here, and that we belong here" (p. 106). Mortally coiled, the King's anguished speech reflects an awareness of his angelic nature trapped within a human body. Living in a cave, in a state of spiritual exile, is not man's true estate. As ever in Saroyan's plays, the cave-world is uninhabitable by those richest in spiritual intensity and self-consciousness.

The connection between the cave and all other arenas of human activity and imprisonment is made explicit at the end of the play by the King: "Farewell, then—womb, cave, hiding place, home, church, world, theatre—a fond and loving farewell" (p. 120).[18] These are all matrices or arenas of human life which must be abandoned for humanity to enter into grace, into oneness, into belonging. Even the theater must finally be left behind. Yet, as the King says, the farewell is also a welcome, a new beginning—a movement from the womb of spiritual development and soul-making to a new and unknown mode of being.

It is perhaps not fortuitous that this farewell signaled (as Prospero's does for Shakespeare in *The Tempest*) Saroyan's actual farewell to the theater—he published no major plays after *The Cave Dwellers*.[19] World and theater were inextricably bound together in his imagination, and drama was the perfect vehicle for expressing his highly individualistic, original, and theatrical personality. It is arguable, in fact, that the plays constitute his highest achievement and are his greatest contribution to American literature.

CHAPTER 8

The Men of Your People Are Fathers

D. H. Lawrence once wrote that "one sheds one's sicknesses in books—repeats and presents again one's emotions to be master of them." This dictum applies exactly to the four major novels Saroyan published between 1951 and 1964: *Rock Wagram* (1951), *The Laughing Matter* (1953), *Boys and Girls Together* (1963), and *One Day in the Afternoon of the World* (1964).[1] Each novel represents the same psychodrama being played out, the same sicknesses being shed, as Saroyan repeatedly explores the troubled years of his marriage and its aftermath. That such a large part of his career was devoted to an examination of domestic difficulties illustrates the obsessive power of his need for love and family.

These thinly disguised transcriptions of Saroyan's own life might be termed the "fatherhood novels," for they are linked thematically through the author's concern with founding a family.[2] The Armenian-American protagonists in each of these novels are all searching (or have already found) a wife and children. In recounting the story of his own marriage, divorce, remarriage, and final separation, he has emphasized the yearning for a sense of human community, for close family relationships.[3] Edward Krickel has correctly pointed out that sex and love in Saroyan's novels are not ends in themselves, but rather "lead to family and the honorable roles of parent and grandparent, in short the traditional view. Children are the glory of the relationship."[4] In the novels, as in the plays and short stories, the family symbolizes the family of humanity in microcosm and localizes the desire for universal brotherhood which marked Saroyan's vision from the beginning of his career. The Webster family in *The Beautiful People*, the Macauleys in *The Human Comedy*, the Alexanders in *My Heart's in the Highlands*, and the Garoghlanians in *My Name Is Aram*—all were his imaginary fictional families before he sought to become a father himself and realize his dreams.

It might be argued that this profound concern with family and fatherhood can be traced to the death of his father when Saroyan was three years old. Indeed, there may be a kind of wish fulfillment at work in the many portraits of eccentric, lyrical, and happy families which dominate his early writings. These fantastic fathers preside over peaceful, kind, and loving families where imagination is enthroned as the highest virtue. This is true in some of his later work as well. The father Ralph Gallop of "The Poet at Home" is a whimsical, idealistic dreamer and free spirit. Having had no stable family life himself, Saroyan set out to create a world of loving fathers, mothers, grandparents, cousins, sisters, and brothers. An orphan in reality, he sought the love, warmth, and closeness he had missed within his imagination—through creating his generous-hearted characters.

Furthermore, Saroyan's quest for a father was internalized: *he* had to become a father in order to become his *own* father. The almost mystical significance he attaches to this quest is readily apparent throughout his writings. In *Here Comes, There Goes, You Know Who* he wrote: "Until sons find out how to become fathers, how to become both sons and fathers, the human race cannot have a father, it must go on having substitutes, and it has had them long enough. And it isn't that God isn't a good substitute. . . . But having God is too easy an excuse for sons not to become fathers when it is time to become fathers, or at least to try, and to go on trying."[5] Son and father are metaphysically connected in his imagination. In many ways, the fatherhood novels are spiritual communings with his own unknown, dead, Armenian poet-father; they are the anguished record of the process by which the Son attempts to become the Father.

Becoming a father is of course a central rite of passage within the Armenian-American community, insuring the continuation of the race and simultaneously affirming ancient traditions. It is significant that in *The Laughing Matter* Evan Nazarenus is told by his wife that "the men of your people are fathers."[6] To be an Armenian adult man is to be a father. In addition, the primacy of family relationships among the "mad Armenians" is a characteristic which Saroyan emphasizes throughout his work. After all, for the uprooted aliens in America, strangers in a strange land, it is the family which provides an anchor and stability in an otherwise tough and forbidding environment.

Yet most important, the fact that these middle-aged fathers are Armenian signals the appearance of Saroyan's central theme throughout the novels: estrangement, alienation, and a dominating sense of the "foreignness" of human experience. Following World War II and the failure of his marriage, he began to withdraw into the past, into the "dark, brooding world of Armenian ancestors."[7] The postwar America which men like Arak Vagramian of *Rock Wagram* and Evan Nazarenus confront has been defined by Isaac Rosenfeld as a "world of strangers and loose ends in which there is no real human contact."[8] We are again reminded of the Arab in *The Time of Your Life*—a foreigner whose sense of disconnection is profound and ineradicable.

The dark mood of despair which pervades the novels is presaged by two pieces in *The Assyrian and Other Stories* (1949).[9] Paul Scott, in the volume's title story, is a fifty-year-old Assyrian (read Armenian) who is vacationing in Lisbon. There, attempting to recover from the pain of his third divorce, he remains haunted by a sense of death, failure, and lovelessness. In "The Cocktail Party," Andrew Loring (despite the Anglo-Saxon name, yet another of the author's self-portraits) gives voice to the weariness of a middle-aged writer who feels a profound diminution of his creative powers: " 'Exuberance did the trick,' he thought, 'but now it doesn't, or maybe I haven't got any more of it. It did the trick for Thomas Wolfe as long as he lived, and for a lot of others, too, but exuberance seems to stop when a man gets past his middle thirties, or the man himself stops.' "[10] A sense of play and of humor is largely absent in both men's lives.

Indeed, there are relatively few passages in the novels which have the verve, spontaneity, drive, bounce, and ecstasy of the early prose.

Commentators began to speak of a "new Saroyan" whose works had become "strange battlegrounds" on which a divided psyche warred incessantly.[11] The characters in these novels lack what his earlier heroes often possessed in abundance—the gift of imagination and a belief in the power and reality of love.

Of course love had always been Saroyan's great theme, and it is the failure of love which has caused his divorced men to be stricken with an overwhelming sense of futility and anguish. For the author, love is the only and ultimate meaning of life, for "everything good comes forward out of love."[12] The awareness of love's power both to create and to destroy is allegorized in the novelette *Tracy's Tiger* (1951). Just as *The Assyrian and Other Stories* introduced the theme of alienation and creative impotence, so *Tracy's Tiger* presaged the quest for love which dominates the fatherhood novels. Here young Thomas Tracy keeps a strong black panther on leash: a relationship which symbolizes the tensed power of love. Tracy's love for Laura Luthy is fraught with difficulties and betrayal, yet the lovers are united happily at the end and the Blakean tiger-panther is vindicated.

This sort of resolution does not occur in the four novels, for here Saroyan's deep struggles with his own psychic demons cannot be overcome through recourse to either the imagination or symbolism. *Rock Wagram* and *The Laughing Matter*, the most powerful and artistically coherent of the series, are permeated with "the haunting of death."[13]

Rock Wagram (an anglicized version of the hero's name, Arak Vagramian) follows the career of a thirty-three-year-old Armenian actor. It is divided into three large sections: (1) "The Father," (2) "The Mother," and (3) "The Son and the Daughter." Interspersed throughout the novel at regular intervals are passages in italics which expatiate upon Rock's painful quest for self-knowledge.

The novel charts the progress of Rock's quest—not only for a wife but "for the mother of my kids."[14] This quest is closely connected to his quest for identity; at the beginning of the novel he asks himself, "Who are you?" and it is clear that for him marriage and children are one way (perhaps *the* way) to find out. When his marriage finally fails, he is not placated by his success as an actor; indeed, he is beset by a propulsive restlessness.

Rock's marriage to Ann Ford (which results in two children, a son and a daughter) ultimately brings him no closer to the secret meaning that he believes life holds. His existential aloneness is ineradicable, and breaking out of the closed circle of selfhood into authentic communion with others is impossible.

> A man lives his life in ignorance. He lives his entire life alone, out of touch with a secret, an instantaneous thing forever longing to be in touch with the secret, which he believes is *in* his woman. But his woman is not his woman, and the secret is not in her. His son is not his son, and the secret is not in him. His daughter is not his daughter, and the secret is not in her. Each of these is *also* alone, and out of touch. (Pp. 183–84)

Although Rock sought salvation in love and family, neither has brought him to the hidden quick of his own being. Because he had expected so much from the experience of fatherhood, his sense of failure is deeply anguishing.

His inability to connect, his persistent feeling of being "out of touch," is diagnosed early in the novel by his Armenian grandmother, Lula. She realizes that he is at a crossroad in his life, that the early thirties are a troubling time of transition in a man's spiritual development. Indeed, Rock's struggle to move from the role of Son to that of Father occurs at the same age as Christ's crucifixion, and his grandmother analyzes his anguish in Christian metaphors: "It is a decent fight, a fight to be born, as the man says it is written. The thirty-third year is the year of dying, of madness, of being born, one or the other, or all together. As you have hungered for bread and thirsted for water, begin now to be born" (p. 76). His year of "madness" is a kind of inner crucifixion, a trial by fire which will leave him purified and ready to be born again.

This "madness," in some sense, is in his genes, in his blood—a dark inheritance from his Armenian ancestors. Lula points out that her husband, Manuk, also "was mad of course, but all great men are" (p. 74). As we saw with the grandmother in the story "The Living and the Dead," Lula reorients Rock to his racial past, to the suffering and intensity of the Armenian people. To a great extent, Rock's agony, an unavoidable concomitant of spiritual striving, is traceable to the tensed, mystical-Christian sensibilities of his ancestors. Yet at the same time, this psycho-spiritual imbalance is implicit in the experience of *all* humanity, as the passage which follows this scene indicates: "There is no experience that is without madness from the time a man is born to the time he dies, and the madness of every man is enormous" (pp. 77–78).

Perhaps the most moving scene of the novel occurs in relation to another of Rock's family—his dead father. In the offices of an Armenian newspaper in Fresno (the *Asbarez*), he confronts the spirit of his father, who committed suicide at age thirty-seven. Rock's father had been a poet, and he wanted his son to be one as well—"A man who reads, who writes, who lives in a proud, lonely world" (p. 106). The dominant impulse dramatized in this scene is Rock's desire to connect with his father, and, simultaneously, to his buried Armenian heritage. In the office, he and his cousin Haig drink "To the Armenians, whoever they are, and to their language, whose majesty we all know, lost as it may be forever" (p. 101).

Remembering the death of his lonely father in an alien land serves to deepen Rock's own estrangement and sense of failure as a father. The unhappiness of his past and the terror of the present (his mother is about to die an agonizing death) reverberate in Rock's soul, and his spiritual loneliness becomes increasingly difficult to bear. At the end of the scene in the offices of the *Asbarez*, he is haunted by the realization that "a man travels through a mournful dream seeking many things, but in the end they are all only one thing: the Word, and nothing in the lonely world is lonelier, for the name of the word is Love" (p. 103).

In his mind, the quest for love is a sacred search for unity of being, for "the Word," and its loss fills him with a sense of profound emptiness. Time weighs heavily upon him as he begins "to number the hours, days, months, and years of loneliness, of discontent, of boredom and anger, of desperation and despair" (p. 56). It is through union with his wife that he hoped to overcome this fragmentation and, through love, achieve the balance of true being. "His secret is *being*, and his being is most truly being when he falls upon her to be bitten and to bite, to hold fast, to kiss, to put in her all of his family, from long ago, all of his time, to have her grow their families together in a new man, to capture the unknown one, the one long gone, to bring him back to the grass and green of being" (p. 283). Yet his desire to be taken to "the grass and green of being" through the love of a woman and the creation of a family is not to be fulfilled.

At the end of the novel, as at the beginning, Rock is driving his car alone—this time to Mexico rather than to California. Like Joe at the end of *The Time of Your Life*, Rock goes solitary out into the night.

> He was on his way to Tia Juana when he saw the sun come up. He stopped the car on the side of the highway, got out, and watched the sun. He watched it until he could feel the heat coming from it. Then he got back into the car, turned it around, and began to drive back, altogether alone now, without wife, without son, without daughter, without home, without hope, but not yet altogether without humor, for he knew that he had driven all night to the sun, as if the sun might be nearer a little farther south, to see it come up once more, and wink, for a man *is* nonsense all his life, as he himself knows. (P. 301)

Arak Vagramian's quest for fatherhood has ended in failure, although his life is "not yet altogether without humor" as he heads alone toward the sun.

If Rock is still able to see his experience with a measure of equanimity, the same cannot be said of the characters in Saroyan's second fatherhood novel, *The Laughing Matter*. This novel, like *Rock Wagram*, is the record of marital unhappiness; yet it takes the reader much further into the hidden depths of the author's wounded psyche. In many ways, *The Laughing Matter* is the furthest Saroyan ever went in the exploration of complex psychological interactions and subtly intricate states of consciousness.

Unlike the prose of *Rock Wagram*, the writing of *The Laughing Matter* (the title is ironic, for the book gives us virtually unrelieved tragedy) is taut, stark, and clinically objective, while the dialogue is hollow, concentrated, and abrupt. Indeed, of all Saroyan's books, this novel reveals most powerfully the influence of Ernest Hemingway's style. James D. Hart's analysis of Hemingway's originality is equally true of the prose in *The Laughing Matter*: "Emotion is held at arm's length; only the bare happenings are recorded, and emphasis is obtained by understatement and spare dialogue."[15] An example of Hemingwayesque understatement can be seen at the opening of the novel when Saroyan refers to his main characters, Evan and Swan Nazarenus, as "the man" and "the woman." Thus distanced from the characters, the reader sees the Nazarenus family objectively as tragic actors in an O'Neill-like family psychodrama; yet simultaneously, this distancing also serves to bring us closer to the action.

The mark of Hemingway's sensibility can be seen in the characterization as well as in the style of the book. Forty-four-year-old Evan Nazarenus is an unsuccessful novelist who has an academic career as a professor at Stanford. In the stoic fashion typical of Hemingway's heroes, Evan struggles throughout *The Laughing Matter* with the overwhelming problems threatening his family life. His conversations with his wife are terse, and communication between them is profoundly difficult. Their dialogue leaves much unsaid; as in Hemingway, we are left to read between the lines the tension that underlies their relationship. Words have become metaphoric weapons in the war of marriage; their marriage is static, caught in a vicious circle of emotional combat from which they are unable to free themselves.

Finally, a last link to Hemingway is the aura of emotional and physical violence, decay, and death which pervades the novel. Indeed, there is more violence in *The Laughing Matter* than in any other Saroyan work except *The Slaughter of the Innocents*. The intense and stark narrative is kept in tight bounds and moves swiftly. The Nazarenus family is composed of four members—Evan, his wife Swan, Rex, or "Red" (the son), and Eva (the daughter). Swan has become pregnant by another man, and as the plot progresses, Evan's fury at this betrayal grows at a frightening pace. The action becomes increasingly violent: Evan shoots his brother Dade, Swan dies in an attempted abortion, and Evan himself is killed at the end of the novel in an automobile accident.

This terrible story unfolds with perfect predictability, since it is obvious from the beginning of the novel that Evan's marriage to Swan is doomed. Their marriage has become full of the "oppression" and "compulsoriness" that are the sure signs of an unsatisfactory relationship (p. 189). However, Evan is continually self-analytical in his efforts to understand the reasons for his domestic sufferings, and it is evident that he wants to preserve his family at practically any cost. He clearly agrees with his brother Dade that "the family is all there is. Fool with the family and you've finished everything" (p. 228).

Although Swan and Evan attempt heroically to make their marriage succeed, the prevailing condition of their relationship is one of emotional disequilibrium and inner fragmentation. The atmosphere is one of frustration, loneliness, and fragility, movingly conveyed when a weeping Swan speaks to her son after a marital battle. The narrator comments: "What was the matter? What was it, always? Why couldn't anything be the way it *ought* to be? Why was everything always strange, mysterious, dangerous, delicate, likely to break to pieces suddenly?" (pp. 37–38). The emotional life of the family is in a constant state of uncertainty and psychological tension, and the threat of true terror and violence breaking out is always a possibility.

Indeed, even the rare moments of peace Evan and Swan enjoy together are called into question: "Still, for a moment they would know well-being. They would know well-being is a lie. They would know it is desperate and sorrowful, but they would not bother about this. They would hold glasses and drink, speaking swiftly and easily and meaninglessly" (pp. 95–96). Evan is obsessed by the idea of life's meaninglessness and by the universality of *lying*. In fact, he says he has given up writing novels because "it is a trick" and cannot disguise or ameliorate the fundamental absurdity of existence (p. 98).

Elizabeth Bowen has aptly defined the novel's theme as "alienness, an incapacity for the familiar, a temperamental refusal of the normal."[16] Evan thrashes against his aloneness, appalled at the terrible gulf of silence which has grown between him and Swan. At one point in the novel, Evan says to her, "I did not know we were so estranged, so deeply unknown to one another" (p. 132). Neither he nor his wife has been able to locate a source of faith or significance exterior to themselves which might alleviate their confusion. They remain unknown to themselves, to each other, and to their children.

As is so often the case, there is an effort to compromise because of the children. Evan asks himself why he still loves his wife. "Was it not their believing it was a thing to prolong indefinitely, forever, with sons and daughters coming forward out of it, as Red and Eva

had come out of it? Wasn't *that* the thing that had made their love—
made *something*—definite and meaningful?" (p. 127). Yet the children are also caught up in the domestic tragedy; as Bowen has
pointed out, they "were born with hair-trigger nerves, to an inheritance of night-dark apprehensions."[17] They carry on in their own
psychological intensity the conflicts that have ravaged their parents'
marriage.

The estrangement of the Nazarenus family is also emphasized by
the setting of the novel in Fresno and Clovis—the heart of the community of Armenian exiles. Furthermore, Evan's own father, Petrus,
had come to America only to become "a sad old man in a silly little
cigar store in Paterson, New Jersey, living for his sons" (p. 73). Evan
fears that he too, like his father, will end up estranged and alone. He
is not, however, interested in absolute assimilation into American
society; he wants his children to speak Armenian, although he himself speaks very little of the language. In many ways, then, the
Armenian theme in the novel places Evan's estrangement within
the larger context of the alienness and foreignness of his people in
the valley.

Yet the San Joaquin Valley is also meant to symbolize a kind of
prelapsarian world—the continuing references to fig trees and vineyards suggest the Garden of Eden, with Evan and Swan as fallen
Adam and Eve. The last name "Nazarenus" (and the names of the
children, *Rex* and *Eva*) also suggests biblical allegory. It is clear,
moreover, that Evan wants to reenter Paradise, for he says he is tired
of life at the university and would like to live on a vineyard.

The valley, site of abundant trees, rivers, and sunshine, comes to
represent a world free of the tensions and psychological trauma that
has characterized Evan's domestic life. A family outing in the country is described in the clear, terse, visionary language of Hemingway
described above, with the emphasis placed on sensation—on taste,
smell, touch, sight—on the physical realities of the phenomenal
world.

> They wore light clothing. The windows of the car were open.
> The air they breathed was good. The man followed country
> roads as far as possible, driving slowly, stopping now and then
> to look at a vineyard, a tree, or an abandoned house. He got out

of the car once to take some ripe nectarines off a tree, and Red got out with him. The nectarines were a little hot, but they were juicy and sweet. He counted out three for each of them. When they came to the river at Piedra he drove along the riverside road until they found a green place, a cluster of three willows. There they sat on a blanket. (P. 156)

This sunlit, intense, lovely world is uninfected by guilt, suffering, and death; it is in fact the fertile Garden from which the Nazarenus family has been exiled.

Although these moments of harmony cannot restore the lost innocence of the family, Evan still clings to the desperate hope that his role as father might be preserved and the Nazarenus family be united in love: "Love is no lie. I want you to live. I want Red to live. I want Eva to live. And I want to live in each of you. There is no other place for me to go. I am in each of you. I *am* each of you. It is no lie. Shall we try?" (p. 167). Ultimately, however, there is nothing left to do or hope, and as in a Shakespearean tragedy, all the principal characters are dead or wounded (physically or emotionally) by the end of the novel.

Like all the fatherhood novels, *The Laughing Matter* records a mood of middle-aged weariness and an autumnal resignation to death. Unlike Rock, Evan is finally unable to keep the delicate balance between life and death, hope and despair. Evan's demise in an automobile wreck is merely the external manifestation of a powerful death wish which he was unable to overcome. As a character in *One Day in the Afternoon of the World* puts it, "If you *don't* love, you've got to die. You've only got to stop loving, and you start to die."[18] Evan had been dying throughout the novel, for the belief in love had died in him.

Although the fatherhood novels are the record of a personal tragedy, they achieve universality in their depiction of failed love—love which alone can bring plenitude of being. The unsuccessful quest for identity through love and family life leaves Saroyan's men solitary and stricken. Though these novels have been little discussed, both *Rock Wagram* and *The Laughing Matter* remain strong works portraying the spiritual crisis that accompanies the struggle for both literal and metaphysical fatherhood.

CHAPTER 9

The Way of Memory

Following the dissolution of his marriage, Saroyan turned increasingly to the exploration of his past through a series of autobiographies, memoirs, and journals. Although he continued to publish plays and fiction, autobiography became his main form of self-expression. This impulse reflects a shift in emphasis from art to life, from "doing" to "being," from the creation of works to the creation of self. He sought in memory the key to his identity, for a meaningful pattern underlying the chaos of experience. "I want to think about the things I may have forgotten. I want to have a go at them because I have an idea they will help make known how I became who I am."[1] Like Whitman, Thomas Wolfe, and Henry Miller, Saroyan was always after the Self; he obsessively focused on his own responses, emotions, experiences in search of the psychological matrices of his behavior and personality. The writings of his final phase, however, are not only an important source of biographical insights—they also represent some of his best prose.[2]

A recurring motif in these works is Saroyan's chronic sense of estrangement, or self-division. In *Here Comes, There Goes, You Know Who*, the method of his autobiographical search is explained.

> I have so far mainly considered the earliest times, not especially intending to do so, but falling into it, as it were, perhaps because when the nature of your work is to remember, you tend to start at or near the beginning, and then to go back again and again, expecting most likely to find out a little more

fully why you have become estranged, why you are one place
and the world another, as the Armenian saying is.[3]

The similarity of the approach to psychoanalysis is readily apparent:
Saroyan returns repeatedly to his earliest memories in an effort to
locate the beginnings of his "maladjustment," the radical disjunc-
tion of Self and World.

Saroyan's interest in self-discovery through autobiography can be
traced back to 1936, when he first wrote of his fascination with the
journal as a form of literature. In a piece in *Inhale and Exhale*,
"Poem, Story, Novel," he mentions the Swiss journal-writer Henri-
Fréderic Amiel.[4] Saroyan feels that in telling his own story, the tale
of his life, the memoirist is performing as nobly as the novelist.

> Amiel, I think, once wrote a novel. It took him the major
> portion of his lifetime to do it, and he wrote only of himself. . . .
> I would rather call what Amiel wrote a novel than anything else
> I have seen that is supposed to be a novel. Christ, I think, lived a
> novel; which is even nobler than to write one. Living a novel is
> like carving your language into stone, or it is like placing your
> language in the wind and in rain and in the sea and in storms
> and in the heart of man, and in the depths of the earth, and in
> the emptiness of the cosmos, and it is like having your language
> everywhere in the form of the only language, silence. It is cer-
> tainly easier to write a novel than it is to live one. Almost
> anyone can write a bad novel, but hardly anyone can live *even* a
> bad novel.[5]

For both writers, the ultimate purpose of life is to learn to live it
as a work of art. Saroyan conceives of the journal as a means to
affirm the unity of life and art, as a way of writing and living one's
life simultaneously. Amiel is a novelist not by virtue of the fact that
he wrote a form of literature which fits into the genre "novel";
rather, "Amiel wrote a novel by writing himself."[6]

Amiel supplied the epigraphs for the best of Saroyan's late writings, *Days of Life and Death and Escape to the Moon*. A journal
kept during 1967–68 in Paris and Fresno, the book is notable for its
severe, spare clarity, exactitude of observation, and forthrightness.

According to Saroyan, "The interior weather is really the only weather a man lives in," and the task of the journal-keeper is to explore this interior world—the essentially private realm of individual thoughts, moods, and feelings.[7] For Saroyan, "the human experience is personal, private, and in every instance unique. That which each man *knows* he alone knows, however nearly like the next man's knowing it may be" (p. 111). Writing a journal for Amiel was part of a serious and unflinching search for the truth about himself, and Saroyan believed "he had a whole philosophy of journal-keeping. It was the only form of writing he felt was honest, and the only form he was willing to write" (p. 23).

The real business of these books, then, is the struggle for self-definition, for identity. Saroyan is concerned throughout these late writings with the difficulty of truly knowing one's self. As he remarked in *Not Dying*: "We don't know who we are and we can't find out. We therefore agree on something or another that's convenient."[8] This ignorance of one's real self leads to a kind of despair; yet this sense of inner division can be healed through an affirmation of man's potential for authentic being. In *Sons Come and Go, Mothers Hang In Forever*, he thinks "about all of us and how always near to despair we really are, except for something else equally powerful in us, a kind of balance to the despair, a sense of life as a blindly joyous action, a totally unreasonable, unjustified and unjustifiable sense that the reality of *being* is the most desirable of alternatives."[9]

He also emphasizes in these works the solitary fight for "the reality of being" through the act of writing itself. Like Hemingway, he confronts existence directly and explores the writer's struggle to wrest from the fierce complexities of experience some measure of simple truth and pure consciousness. In *Not Dying*, he muses about "the arrogant loneliness of the writer at work, the old writer in the old fight, the lone man in the great contest with time and mystery" (p. 102). The similarity to Hemingway is made explicit when Saroyan remarks: "A man can be as strong as a bull and still be dying. I don't want this to become mystical or anything like that, but the fact is that every man is a bull and a matador in a mortal struggle in his own bull ring" (p. 202). The central fact of the writer's existence is his fight with himself, with the intractable medium of language, with actualizing potential creativity hidden within the self. In his last published book, *Obituaries*, Saroyan repeated the metaphor: "It's a fight all the way, waking and sleeping, reading and writing: it is a fierce fight and you lose every day and you need time to try again in the morning."[10]

The titles of these memoirs illustrate the fact that his struggle is not only with the intransigent self and the craft of writing; he is quite literally fighting off death itself. *Not Dying, Days of Life and Death and Escape to the Moon, Obituaries*—all show Saroyan in the process of taking leave of life. In *Obituaries* he observes: "Why do I write? Why am I writing this book? To save my life, to keep from dying, of course" (p. 132). The deaths of close friends and heroes are often reported: the late books became a kind of extended necrology. In *Days of Life and Death and Escape to the Moon*, we are told of the deaths of, among others, Magritte, Steinbeck, Paul Muni, and Upton Sinclair. He points out that "it isn't because I am in my sixty-first year that I take particular interest in the daily dead, some of whom I know, it's simply that noticing death is a fact, and indeed an act, of survival" (p. 91).

Yet there is also in these last writings a vibrant *joie de vivre*, a deep pleasure taken in the small details of daily living. Saroyan buys cheap second-hand books in a Paris shop, brings home basil plants to his apartment, delights in solitude and reading. He writes of casual long walks, visits to libraries, meetings with dear friends. Musing over the strange disjunctions of a long life, he remembers many people: family, writers, former teachers, childhood comrades.[11]

Saroyan's search in these last years was the search of his youth. He began as the daring young man filling out an "Application for Permission to Live," and he continued asking the same hard questions of existence to the end. His primary emphasis had always been on the quest for individual identity, purpose, and meaning—and ultimately he sought the brotherhood of man, the spiritual realization of all humanity. His work attempts to define man's state of spiritual exile and fragmentation, to record his anguished yearning for completion and inner fulfillment.

He does not seek to escape from reality and its harshness; on the contrary, he fully realizes that "we live in a real world, a hard world, a mean world, an anxious, lonely, frightened, and angry world."[12] But this state of affairs must be understood, accepted, transcended, through an affirmation of the miraculous nature of being itself. We must "never stop being amazed by human beings. By what passes for reality. By what is unquestionably religion in all things."[13] This "religion" is of course not to be identified with conventional Christianity, or indeed any orthodox theological system. Rather, Saroyan places his faith in the religion of life, in that force which ties all creation together into unity.

As we have seen, he affirms the pantheistic tradition of Whitman—a mystical, all-embracing acceptance of the universe. For him, as for Whitman, there is an unknown tremendous meaning in our experience, a metaphysical dimension to existence which is implicit in actual life as it might be lived. These meanings and values cannot be imposed by some external philosophical or religious system. Creating "constructs" is unnecessary and deadening for those who live life in the timeless moment, who are one with the interior realm of being and authentic selfhood. He thus celebrates characters who throw off restraints, who seek an uninhibited embrace with the world rather than a fearful rejection of it. He sides always with those who transform and revitalize their lives through an affirmation of freedom, imagination, love, play, and humor. Reality must be apprehended poetically, *as poetry*.

For Saroyan, the self is not static and rigid; it can never remain the same. Rather, it is, as he once observed, "an entity in continuous transition, a growing thing whose stages of growth always went unnoticed, a fluid and flawed thing."[14] Not to grow and change is to die, because, as William A. Gordon has observed, "life is a process in which man is constantly being born. The refusal to be born is the acceptance of death."[15] The shape of human experience is amorphous, diffuse, fluid, ever-changing, spontaneous, and unpredictable. Therefore, those who attempt through repression and conformism to deny the necessity of continual becoming and expansion are always outsiders in the Saroyan universe.

As we have seen, it is precisely Saroyan's antipathy toward authority, repression, and the fettering of the human spirit which made him such an influence on writers of the Beat Generation. Beginning his career in San Francisco ("I am of Frisco, the fog, the foghorns, the ocean, the hills, the sand dunes, the melancholy of the place, my beloved city"), meeting ground of the spiritual East and expansive West, Saroyan, writing of "beautiful people" and preaching love not war, was a flower-child of the thirties.[16] It is thus no accident that he was a literary godfather to such writers as Kerouac, J. D. Salinger, Brautigan—new voices who celebrated with humor the sweet sad song of the tender heart.

Saroyan's innovative, hip, casual, jazzy voice—his paratactic stacking-up of images in Whitmanesque catalogs—was a major influence on modern American prose style. Yet he also pioneered in his absurdist, fantastic plays, which introduced a kind of rambunctious, whimsical, surrealistic energy into conventional drama. His "absurdity," however, was in direct relation to his sorrow at observing the waste of the true, vital flame of life in the contemporary world. His artist figures—Joe, Jonah Webster, Ben Alexander—all feel within themselves the dying of the old order and the painful struggle to birth a new consciousness.

Yet Saroyan's stylistic and philosophical contributions to modern literature were often overlooked by commentators. Such writers as Philip Rahv, Diana Trilling, and Mark Schorer were often quite critical (if not contemptuous) of his actual achievement.[17] Such attacks may be traced back to a distrust of "romanticism" endemic in American academic criticism. Irving Babbitt's *Rousseau and Romanticism* explored the pitfalls of the romantic sensibility and upheld the classical virtues of conventional form, discipline, "good taste," and literary decorum. Saroyan's aesthetic was of course poles apart from such a critical stance, and it follows that writers in the Dionysian tradition were held in low esteem by this critical faction.

Saroyan, however, was in fact a rich, complex, sensitive, and original writer who saw at the beginning of his career that humanity was entering a new age, that the great struggle of twentieth-century man was to slough off the old consciousness and embrace a new world of psychic liberation. His early short stories focused on an America paralyzed by the Depression and recorded faithfully the spiritual hunger and injustices of the thirties. During the war years, his plays consistently reflected his pacifistic beliefs and affirmed the individual struggle against death and mobism. Following the war, his novels conveyed a mood of brooding, middle-aged melancholy, recording the disintegration of his family under the pressures of an unhappy marriage. And, finally, his works of autobiography, memoir and journal attempted to uncover the secret springs of his past. His literary development thus recalls that of other American writers, such as Henry Miller, who did excellent work early in their careers, sustained steady achievement through their middle years, and spent their last phase in reminiscence.

Saroyan's struggle throughout his career had been to achieve a state of balance, of harmony, between the warring opposites of life— a sense of well-being in life's gay and melancholy flux. As Erich Fromm defines it, well-being is "the ability to be creative, to be aware, and to respond; to be independent and fully active, and by this very fact to be one with the world. To be concerned with *being*, not with *having*; to experience joy in the very act of living and to consider living creatively as the only meaning of life."[18] Saroyan also celebrated vitality, the life force, and admired (with Blake and D. H. Lawrence) quickness, intensity, and energetic engagement with the experience of the moment. This, and only this, is creative living and points the way toward oneness with self and world.

Finally, for Saroyan, "the truly important things are intangible, deep in a man's miracle, and not available for computation or scientific disintegration for the purpose of examination."[19] He felt that literature, like music, must suggest the subtle, unseen, and mysterious significance of human experience, which remains forever elusive and hidden. His material was the unsayable, the things that lie beneath.

> I was never interested in the obvious, or in the details one takes for granted, and everybody seemed to be addicted to the obvious, being astonished by it, and forever harping about the details which I had long ago weighed, measured, and discarded as irrelevant and useless. If you can measure it, don't. If you can weigh it, it isn't worth the bother. It isn't what you're after. It isn't going to get it. My wisdom was visual and as swift as vision. I looked, I saw, I understood, and I felt, "That's that, where do we go from here?"[20]

Saroyan always knew what he was "after"—that nameless, awful, and beautiful mystery at the heart of life. His genius lay in his ability successfully to evoke and celebrate it through art.

NOTES

INTRODUCTION

1. Collier, "I'm the Same, but Different," pp. 3, 16.

2. Rahv, "William Saroyan: A Minority Report," pp. 371–77.

3. See Aaron, *Writers on the Left*, for comments on Saroyan's political disaffiliation. According to Aaron, Saroyan was "regarded by the sober-minded of the Left as flip and irreverent" (p. 307).

4. "Armenians," *New Encyclopaedia Brittanica: Micropaedia*; Ternon, *The Armenians: History of a Genocide*, pp. 254–60; and information supplied by Dickran Kouymjian.

5. Saroyan, *Here Comes, There Goes, You Know Who*, p. 177.

6. Ibid., pp. 114, 115. Saroyan published a number of memoirs after 1952; they are the best biographical sources.

7. Ibid., pp. 2–3.

8. Saroyan, *The Assyrian and Other Stories*, p. 17.

9. Saroyan, *The Time of Your Life*, p. 20. On the Arab as symbolic of Saroyan's Armenian sensibility, see Sourian, "Places Where I've Done Time," p. 20. Sourian points out that "behind [Saroyan's] flamboyant moustache there lurks a spirit as anciently and profoundly depressed as that of the Arab who mutters at regular intervals throughout one of his plays."

10. Saroyan, *The Bicycle Rider in Beverly Hills*, p. 104.

11. Saroyan, *Days of Life and Death and Escape to the Moon*, p. 36.

12. Stevens, *The Necessary Angel*, pp. 7, 36.

13. Saroyan, *Don't Go Away Mad and Two Other Plays*, p. xv.

14. Saroyan, *Three Plays*, pp. 6–7.

15. Saroyan, *Obituaries*, p. 324.

16. Arnold, *The Poems*, "Empedocles on Etna," act 2, scene 1, 1. 371. The terms "being," "self-realization," and "self-integration" are used interchangeably throughout my text. All are meant to suggest the quest for identity, for the unification and harmonization of life's warring opposites.

17. Axelrod, *Robert Lowell: Life and Art*, pp. 10–11.

18. Saroyan comments on Beckett's *Waiting for Godot* in the essay "Good Old Goody Goody Godot," included in *I Used to Believe I Had Forever, Now I'm Not So*

Sure: "It is an important play, perhaps one of the most important of all, of all time. Nothing happens, but somehow or other a great deal happens, and none of it is strange, unfamiliar, unbelievable, or superdramatic. All of it is simultaneously delightful and annoying, laughable and heart-breaking, ridiculous and tragic" (p. 102). Saroyan's connection to Beckett is examined in chapter 5.

19. Hoagland, "He Can't Forget He was Young Once," p. 9.
20. Shinn, "William Saroyan: Romantic Existentialist," pp. 185–94.
21. Fisher, "What Ever Happened to Saroyan?" p. 338.
22. Saroyan, *Razzle-Dazzle*, pp. vii–viii.
23. Saroyan, *My Heart's in the Highlands*, p. 104.

CHAPTER I

1. *A Native American* (1938) contained all but six of the pieces that would appear in *My Name Is Aram* (1940).
2. Saroyan, *The Assyrian and Other Stories*, p. xxiii.
3. Saroyan, *The Daring Young Man on the Flying Trapeze*, p. 22. Further references to this work appear in the text.
4. Saroyan, *Inhale and Exhale*, p. 78.
5. Geismar, *Writers in Crisis*, p. vii.
6. Kazin, *Starting Out in the Thirties*, p. 12.
7. Saroyan, *Peace, It's Wonderful*, dedication.
8. "The Daring Young Man on the Flying Trapeze" first appeared in *Story* magazine, February 1934. Saroyan was first published in the *Overland Monthly*, August 1928, "Preface to a Book Not Yet Written." His early publications appeared under the pseudonym "Sirak Goryan." Concerning Saroyan's relationship with *Story*, Warren French has written: "For seventeen years, through depression and war, Whit and Hallie Burnett provided through their magazine *Story* an outlet for works too unconventional for the slick magazines. Although most of the young writers they discovered have lapsed into obscurity, *Story* carried the first published short stories of such later celebrated writers as Norman Mailer, William Saroyan, Tennessee Williams, Truman Capote." See French, *J. D. Salinger*, p. 47.
9. See *The William Saroyan Reader*, dedication page: "To the writers who impelled me to write: Jack London, Guy de Maupassant, Charles Dickens, Anton Tchekov, Mark Twain, August Strindberg, Maxim Gorky, Ambrose Bierce, Leo Tolstoy, Molière, George Bernard Shaw, Walt Whitman, Henri-Frederic Amiel, Henrik Ibsen, Sherwood Anderson, and Solomon, the son of David, who wrote *The Book of Ecclesiastes*." A similar list of authors significant to Saroyan appears in *Razzle-Dazzle*, pp. 351–56.
10. Later in his career, Saroyan echoed these sentiments. He remarked that he "meant to revolutionize American writing" and that he sought to bring a sense of freedom into his own work. See "A Writer's Declaration," in *The Whole Voyald and Other Stories*, p. 11.

11. In *Obituaries*, Saroyan remarked that Anderson "was perhaps the most significant literary influence on the first half of this century" (p. 25).

12. Anderson, *Winesburg, Ohio*, intro. by Malcolm Cowley, p. 1.

13. Ibid., pp. 233–34.

14. Asselineau, *The Transcendentalist Constant in American Literature*, p. 135. Howard Floan has also pointed out that Saroyan learned from Anderson "to reveal the true nature of an individual's life, not through a developed sequence of events—Saroyan rarely gives us narrative in this linear sense—but by means of a sudden flash of recognition that comes through symbolic gesture, a dramatized moment in time that implies an entire life." See Floan, *William Saroyan*, p. 31.

15. Hart, *The Oxford Companion to American Literature*, p. 33.

16. In *Obituaries*, Saroyan writes: "Way back in 1933 I began to publish my kind of essay-story, and instantly this writing seemed acceptable as well as significant: 'Seventy Thousand Assyrians,' 'Myself Upon the Earth,' 'Fight Your Own War,' 'The Big Tree Coming,' 'Sleep in Unheavenly Peace,' and so on and so forth" (p. 254). Saroyan here defines the genre he began to explore in *The Daring Young Man*—a form halfway between the short story and the essay.

17. Whitman, *Complete Poetry and Selected Prose*, "Song of Myself," p. 68.

18. Whitman's conception of poetry is apposite here: "Human thought, poetry or melody, must leave dim escapes and outlets—must possess a certain fluid, aerial character, akin to space itself, obscure to those of little or no imagination, but indispensable to the highest purposes. Poetic style, when address'd to the Soul, is less definite form, outline, sculpture, and becomes vista, music, half-tints, and even less than half-tints" (ibid., "Preface, 1876," p. 440). Edmund Wilson responded to Saroyan's prose-poetry in a letter to John Dos Passos, 11 January 1935: "I've just read William Saroyan's book and was surprised, after what I had heard about it, that it should be so good. He has a curious kind of rarefied poetry, very precisely expressed, quite different from anybody else; though there is a certain amount of second-hand Hemingway and Anderson, I think he is good." See Wilson, *Letters on Literature and Politics: 1912–1972*, pp. 256–57. Saroyan himself remarked on the Whitmanesque style of *The Daring Young Man*: "Some of the other stories were jazz, pure and simple, but jazz in writing. Some were prose poems, something like Walt Whitman's broken prose, or poetic prose, but more in feeling than in the use of language." See *After Thirty Years*, p. 125.

19. They are, "The Daring Young Man," "Seventy Thousand Assyrians," "Among the Lost," "Myself upon the Earth," "Big Valley Vineyard," "A Cold Day," "Three Stories," "Fight Your Own War," and "The Shepherd's Daughter."

20. Miller, *Tropic of Cancer*, p. 1.

21. Later in his career, Saroyan expanded on this notion of the writer as nonconformist: "The writer is a spiritual anarchist, as in the depth of his soul every man is. He is discontented with everything and everybody. The writer is everybody's best friend and only true enemy—the good and great enemy. He neither walks with the multitude nor cheers with them. The writer is a rebel who never stops. He does not conform for the simple reason that there is nothing yet worth conforming to. When

there is something half worth conforming to he will not conform to that, either, or half conform to it." See "A Writer's Declaration," p. 14.

22. The hero of the story "The Assyrian" is also a disguised Armenian. When asked by a friend why he did not call the story "The Armenian," Saroyan replied: "It comes to the same thing. The Assyrians have always been close to us, and lately almost the same thing." He then goes on to extend the connection: "I probably goofed saying we were Assyrians, but not really, because in a sense everybody in the world is an Assyrian, a remnant of a once-mighty race, now all but extinct." See *Letters from 74 rue Taitbout*, pp. 40, 42.

CHAPTER 2

1. Saroyan, "The People, Yes and Then Again No," in *The Trouble with Tigers*, p. 164.

2. Saroyan, "Finlandia," in *Inhale and Exhale*, p. 431. Further references to this work appear in the text.

3. Saroyan, preface to *Opera, Opera* in *Razzle-Dazzle*, p. 124.

4. A few years after writing "Finlandia," Saroyan expanded on this conception of time: "Now, when a man wants to *make* time, to literally create it, what he goes to work and does is *destroy* it and get his energy strongly integrated in timelessness. He does not create a vacuum, he creates the only real kind of time there is for art and immortality: everlasting time. A creation of art is the Eternal, going on now. There is nothing to minutes, days, weeks, months, years and centuries excepting what is in energy operating *now*. That is the only human time we have" (ibid., p. 117).

5. Ibid., p. 124.

6. The writer "must put his inner force, and the inner force of all living and all energy, into the contest with non-existence. He simply must do so" (ibid., p. 118).

7. Saroyan, preface to *The Hungerers* in *Razzle-Dazzle*, p. 318.

8. Saroyan, "The Home of the Human Race," in *The Whole Voyald and Other Stories*, p. 15. Art is also "the putting of limits upon the limitless, and thereby holding something fast and making it seem constant, indestructible, unstoppable, unkillable, deathless." See "Why I Write" in *The William Saroyan Reader*, p. xii. Also cf. "art is life arranged"—experience is formless and inchoate until the artist has uncovered its order through his work. See "Psalms" in *Inhale and Exhale*, p. 377.

9. *Three Times Three* was published privately by four U.C.L.A. students (the Conference Press). Each of the nine pieces is prefaced by an introductory note which answers various questions concerning its composition. In his subsequent career, Saroyan would communicate with the public through this method. Many of his plays, for example, have a preface in which he explains his artistic methods and aims and attempts to answer criticism. Saroyan (like Norman Mailer later) was ever his own advocate. His notorious braggadocio is often to be found in these prefatory remarks. He was very conscious of creating a literary persona, a public self which accorded

with the demands and ambitions of his ego. He was, as he said, an introvert with the good sense to act like an extrovert.

10. Saroyan, "A Writer's Declaration," in *The Whole Voyald and Other Stories*, p. 12.

11. Saroyan, *After Thirty Years*, p. 38.

12. Kerouac has remarked: "As for Saroyan, yes I loved him as a teenager, he really got me out of the 19th century rut I was trying to study, not only his funny tone but his neat Armenian poetic I don't know what . . . he just got me." See interview with Kerouac in *Writers at Work*, p. 378. Compare, for example, this passage from Saroyan's *Adventures of Wesley Jackson* with the prose of *On the Road*: "I said so long to the boys, and we drove straight up into the sweet California sky, down the great San Joaquin valley to Bakersfield, and rolled right up in front of the Dreamland Ballroom. A couple of boys in zoot suits came prancing and romping with a couple of girls to say hello to Joe and ask him where he'd been. Joe took a girl in his arms and went to waltz with her but the music stopped" (p. 191).

13. Lipton, *The Holy Barbarians*, pp. 227, 228. Aram Saroyan has written of his father's prose as a fusion of poetry and jazz: "He was a young prose writer, that is, who did something characteristic of young poets. He wrote with a purity and profundity from the depths of his own nervous system, celebrating less in narrative than in sustained, jazzlike song what it was like to be young." See *Last Rites*, p. 62. Also see Bartlett, *The Beats*, for overview of the Beat Generation. For remarks on Saroyan, see William Everson's "Afterword: Dionysus and the Beat Generation and Four Letters on the Archetype," pp. 181–94.

14. Saroyan, introductory note to "Life and Letters" in *Three Times Three*, p. 89. Further references to this work appear in the text.

15. The phrase "the place of your reality" occurs in "Nine Million Years Ago" from *Inhale and Exhale*: "So rent a room and stretch out upon the bed and dream; and draw the shutters tight against the shapes and rhythms of the world; and sleep. In sleep alone shall you find the hidden universe: the place of your reality" (p. 198).

16. Beckett, *Proust*, pp. 46–47.

17. Joyce Carol Oates has observed that "movement is not upward or outward but, as always in Beckett, inward to a primary zero: the natural, preferred condition of the human consciousness." Where Beckett focuses inward upon the single human consciousness, however, Saroyan is typically out-reaching, expansive. Yet they share a similar conception of the artistic sensibility. See Oates, "Anarchy and Order in Beckett's Trilogy" in *New Heaven, New Earth*, pp. 86–87.

18. Saroyan, "The Sweet Singer of Omsk" in *Peace, It's Wonderful*, p. 157.

19. Saroyan, "Finlandia," p. 429.

20. Saroyan, "To the Producer," *Subway Circus* in *Razzle-Dazzle*, p. 464.

21. Saroyan, *Love, Here Is My Hat*, p. 14. Further references to this work appear in the text.

22. Ibid., see "A Family of Three," p. 136. The lighter side of love is represented by "Jim Pemberton and His Boy Trigger," which recounts the sexual escapades of a father

and his adolescent son (pp. 101–9). "You're Breaking My Heart" tells of the fisticuffs and banter that occur between Mike Corbett and his chauffeur, and his final reconciliation with his wife (pp. 81–96). The typical Hollywood love story is spoofed in "The Genius" (pp. 64–69). It would be a distortion to imply that all of Saroyan's love stories end in frustration.

23. Saroyan, "The Little Dog Laughed to See Such Sport" in *Inhale and Exhale*, p. 413.

24. Other stories in *Inhale and Exhale* dealing with the war include "The International Song of the Machine Gun," a grim parody of a machine-gun manual (pp. 274–80); "The War" records growing anti-German sentiment, and reiterates the author's antinationalistic stance (pp. 130–35); "The Japanese Are Coming" considers the threat of a Japanese invasion (pp. 334–41).

25. Saroyan, *Here Comes, There Goes, You Know Who*, p. 225.

CHAPTER 3

1. Saroyan, "The Death of Children" in *Inhale and Exhale*, p. 140.

2. Saroyan's awareness of the importance of his success as a writer to the Armenian-American community and his desire to affirm the connections between Armenian and American culture can be seen in an unpublished letter to Leon Serabian Herald, dated 7 November 1934: "The acceptance of my writing by American literature is significant to every Armenian in this country, and especially significant to those members of the younger generation who wish to make some contribution to American art. I am deeply interested in the growth of an Armenian-American art, because I believe the Armenian consciousness is a rich consciousness, deep-rooted, wise, and strong." From a letter titled "My Armenia" in the Humanities Research Center, University of Texas at Austin. Saroyan may be seen as the most recent writer in a long Armenian literary tradition which includes the folk epic cycle *David of Sassoun*, the historian Moses Khorenatsi, and the great mystic poet of Lake Van, Grigor Narekatsi. The themes of Armenian literature surface repeatedly in his writing: exile, homelessness, and even the subliminal influence of Armenian Christianity (through suffering, rebirth). For an excellent overview of Armenia's literary heritage, see Aram Raffi, "Armenia: Its Epics, Folk-Songs, and Medieval Poetry" in *Armenian Legends and Poems*, compiled and edited by Boyajian, pp. 125–91.

3. It is interesting that Saroyan uses the word *evasion* to describe the drinking of liquor; it is the same word used in "Quarter, Half, Three-Quarter, and Whole Notes" in the passage concerning the difficulty of achieving personal wholeness. It is an "evasion" which many of his characters resort to: among others, Joe of *The Time of Your Life*, Jonah Webster of *The Beautiful People*, and Grogan of *The Human Comedy*. Later in "The Living and the Dead," the effect of alcohol is described lyrically: "Drink expands the eye, enlarges the inward vision, elevates the ego. The eye perceives less and less the objects of this world and more and more the objects and patterns and rhythms of the other: the large and limitless and magnificent universe

of remembrance, the real and timeless earth of history, of man's legend in this place" (p. 57). Saroyan wrote later in his career about his own drinking, and his remarks illuminate the story: "I did not begin to drink in earnest until I was well over twenty-five. Until that time I had on a number of occasions had a jug of wine. I never liked getting things blurred. I liked getting them clear, and then clearer and clearer. Wine-drinking got them blurred, but whiskey-drinking, I discovered, got them clear, and then clearer and clearer. This is not inaccurate. Whiskey made inner and outer realities clearer to me—provided, of course, I didn't drink too much." See *The Bicycle Rider in Beverly Hills*, p. 114.

4. Introductory note to "The Living and the Dead," p. 33.

5. Wilson, *The Boys in the Back Room*, p. 28.

6. Ibid., p. 29. Saroyan has written that "the writing in my first three books, perhaps even in my fourth, was not revised. . . . It didn't take me too long to begin to try for art in my work. This doesn't mean I didn't try for it from the beginning; it means I tried harder. And it means I began to think about the reader. I began to acknowledge that I had a responsibility to him." See *After Thirty Years*, pp. 19–20.

7. Ibid., p. 37.

8. Saroyan, *The Time of Your Life*, p. 90.

9. Canby, "Armenian Picaresque."

CHAPTER 4

1. Saroyan, "The Writer on the Writing" in *The Assyrian*, p. xxvi. See also preface to *My Heart's in the Highlands*: "The child race is fresh, eager, interested, innocent, imaginative, healthy and full of faith, where the adult race, more often than not, is stale, spiritually debauched, unimaginative, unhealthy, and without faith" (p. 14).

2. Saroyan wrote three books specifically for children: *Me, The Tooth and My Father*, and *Horsey Gorsey and the Frog*.

3. Saroyan, *My Name Is Aram*, p. ix. Further references to this work appear in the text.

4. Saroyan, *The Bicycle Rider in Beverly Hills*. In speaking of his important memories of childhood, he singled out "the family story-tellers. They put me to roaring with laughter when I was very small, and I was fascinated with the marvelous style of each of them" (p. 149). Saroyan also published a volume of Armenian folktales entitled *Saroyan's Fables* (1941), seven of which had appeared earlier in *Peace, It's Wonderful* as "Little Moral Tales from the Old Country."

5. Cox, *Mark Twain: The Fate of Humor*, p. 147.

6. Twain, *The Adventures of Tom Sawyer*, p. 29.

7. Saroyan wrote in *Days of Life and Death*: "Lunacy runs straight down the middle of every branch of my family. We have nobody who is not some kind of nut" (p. 52). The Garoghlanian clan is based on Saroyan's own family.

8. Dobrée, p. 354.

9. Saroyan, "Poem, Story, Novel" in *Inhale and Exhale*, p. 288.

CHAPTER 5

1. Saroyan observed that Shaw was "probably the greatest influence of them all when an influence is most effective—when the man being influenced is nowhere near being solid in his own right" (p. 351). Shaw was also "health, wisdom, and comedy"—qualities which appealed greatly to the young author (p. 352). Shaw was, like Twain or H. L. Mencken, an individual voice, an exposer of hypocrisy. Saroyan had always "liked the men who were most like bad boys, having fun all the time, playing pranks, talking out of turn, acting up, making fun of fools and frauds, ridiculing the pompous and phoney, howling with laughter or sitting by after ruining the works and being dead-pan and innocent about the whole thing" (p. 353). Finally, he remarks: "If it matters which of the writing men I have felt close to, and by whom my writing has been influenced, that man has not been Ernest Hemingway, as Mr. Edmund Wilson seems to feel, but George Bernard Shaw" (p. 356). See preface to *Hello Out There* in *Razzle-Dazzle*.

2. Saroyan, "The Two Theaters" in *The Time of Your Life*, p. 209.

3. Ibid., p. 211. Saroyan also remarks: "One knows there is little consciousness so far in man" (p. 211).

4. Saroyan, "On Reality," in *The Time of Your Life*, pp. 243, 242.

5. Saroyan, preface to *Three Times Three*, p. 3.

6. Miller, *Sexus*, p. 213.

7. Ibid., p. 205. In another context, Miller has affirmed that there is no need for the artist to continue "immolating himself in his work" because "we do not think of sweat and tears in connection with the creation of the universe; we think of joy and light, and above all of play." See *Sunday after the War*, p. 156.

Saroyan's literary and personal connections with Miller are several. He became a member of the staff of the *Booster*, joining Anaïs Nin, Lawrence Durrell, and Miller. His work was published several times in the magazine, the first appearance being 8 October 1937 ("The Man with the Heart in the Highlands"). He also appeared with Miller and Hilaire Hiler in the volume *Why Abstract?* (1945). According to Jay Martin, Saroyan was one of the few writers with whom Miller could "discover a common ground" early in his career. (See Martin, *Always Merry and Bright*, p. 308; also pp. 328, 363, 455 for other Saroyan references).

Philosophically, as shown above, the two writers shared many of the same ideas, yet they were never comrades. In the essay "Anderson the Storyteller," Miller wrote: "Saroyan is today the most daring of all our storytellers, and yet I feel that he is timid. He is timid, I mean, judged by his own criteria. His evolution is not in the direction one would imagine. He took a big hurdle in the beginning, but he refuses to go on hurdling. He is running now, and his stride is pleasant and easy, but we had expected him to be a chamois and not a yearling." See *Stand Still like the Hummingbird*, p. 175.

8. Saroyan, note for first performance of "The Great American Goof," in *Razzle-Dazzle*, pp. 63–64.

9. Straumann, *American Literature in the Twentieth Century*, p. 201.

10. Saroyan, *Across the Board on Tomorrow Morning* in *The Beautiful People and Two Other Plays*, p. 256.

11. Saroyan, *The Time of Your Life and Other Plays*, paperback reprint, pp. 1–2.

12. Saroyan, *Three Times Three*, p. 11. Further references to this work appear in the text.

13. Saroyan, *My Heart's in the Highlands*, p. 27. Further references to this work appear in the text.

14. Saroyan, *Obituaries*, p. 285.

15. Saroyan wrote that "the artist is not a freak. He is simply the isolation and extension of those good qualities which are in all men. . . . All the elements of art were always there, waiting for a perception in one man to reveal these elements to all men." See *Why Abstract?* p. 32.

16. Saroyan, *Talking to You* in *Razzle-Dazzle*, p. 455.

17. Saroyan, introduction to *My Heart's*, p. 8.

18. Saroyan, introduction to *The Time of Your Life* (reprint), p. 4.

19. Saroyan, "How and Why to Be A Playwright" in *The Time of Your Life*, p. 206. In the same essay, he points out that "good vaudeville came to town along about when I was twelve or so. Orpheum Circuit vaudeville. I remember Trixie Friganza and Sophie Tucker and a lot of acts that were wonderful whose players I do not remember by name" (p. 205). Also see "The World and the Theatre" in *Inhale and Exhale*, which describes his vaudeville experiences at the Hippodrome Theatre; also see *Here Comes*, p. 43.

20. Saroyan, *Subway Circus: A Vaudeville*, in *Razzle-Dazzle*, p. 461. *Subway Circus* was the first work Saroyan wrote for the theater. Its ten sections attempt to represent "the world of one man at a time: the inner, the boundless, the ungeographical world of wakeful dream" (p. 464). It is his first experiment with fusing vaudeville and "serious" drama. In the first section, a teacher asks a boy questions which he refuses to answer.

At the end of the scene the roles are reversed as the boy asks: "Can you tell me why everything changes every minute and is always the same? . . . Can you tell me why I'm alone when I have a mother, a father, brothers, and the whole world full of people? Can you tell me who I am?" (p. 470). As the play progresses, the scenes shift to a cripple who becomes an acrobat; a clerk and his unrequited love for a stenographer; a small man who knocks down a Big Man and a Fat Lady; a group of rich society people who chat pretentiously of their travels; a slim young Negress and a dapper young Negro who banter on the African-Harlem Express; an accountant, peddler, and clerk on the New York Stock Exchange; a Drunkard, Whore, Student, and a sandwich man named God, who, along with several cripples, stand on a street corner and "on the back-drop is painted a portion of the city and something that should suggest religious infinity, limitlessness: the holy universe, endless, without beginning and without end" (p. 496). The play's final scene shows an Italian Fruit Peddler singing softly to himself "O Sole Mio" as the new day begins. Later, the author commented that the play was not only about the New York subway but also about "the concealed way, the inside way, the hidden truth, the hidden life, the hidden meaning of people, of passengers, not of the subway alone, but of time, riding to the end of the line." See *Places Where I've Done Time*, p. 80. The play shows Saroyan packing into the brief compass of ten scenes as many disparate elements as possible, with the intention of conveying the multiplicity of reality.

21. Ibid., p. 461.

22. See "Curtain: Or the Happy Ending" in *Razzle-Dazzle*. Art is a "superactual world [which] can allow no accident in things. At the same time it can permit no reality which at its core is not miraculous. The surprise of art is not shock, but wonder" (p. 505).

He was not alone in his search for new forms that would convey this sense of miracle and wonder. According to Linda W. Wagner, Saroyan's contemporary John Dos Passos also "emphasized the need for a return to entertaining forms of theater— circuses, vaudeville, burlesque, melodrama, because in those forms lay 'the real manners and modes of the theater. There is the extraordinary skill with which vaudeville performers put themselves over individually to the audience in the short time allotted to them, in the satire and construction you get occasionally in burlesque shows and musical comedies, in the brilliant acting and producing it takes to get across trick melodramas and mystery plays, raw material for anything anyone wants to make.'" See Wagner, *Dos Passos*, pp. 71–72.

23. Singer, "Saroyan at 57," p. 3.

24. Esslin, *The Theatre of the Absurd*, p. 235.

25. Ibid., p. 236.

26. McCarthy, "Saroyan: An Innocent on Broadway" in *Sights and Spectacles*, pp. 46–52. This piece is the best on vaudeville and Saroyan.

27. Saroyan, "Ionesco," pp. 26–27.

28. Saroyan, "A Writer's Declaration" in *The Whole Voyald and Other Stories*, p. 14.

29. Saroyan, *Chance Meetings*, pp. 49–50.

30. Saroyan, *The Time of Your Life* (reprint), pp. 2–3.

31. Saroyan, introduction to *Three Plays*, p. 1. Further references to this work appear in the text.

32. Saroyan, *The Time of Your Life* (reprint), p. 3.

33. *The Iceman Cometh* and *The Time of Your Life* are very similar plays. According to Arthur and Barbara Gelb, George Jean Nathan read the script of O'Neill's play and "suggested Eddie Dowling for the role of Hickey and O'Neill had gone to see Dowling's performance in Saroyan's *The Time of Your Life* in San Francisco in 1940" (see Gelb, *O'Neill*, p. 856).

34. Coe, *Ionesco*, p. 32.

35. The drinking in the play contributes greatly to its atmosphere, and indeed Saroyan strives to make the audience itself inebriated. Edmund Wilson commented that "the peculiar spell exerted by his play, *The Time of Your Life*, consisted in its sustaining the illusion of friendliness and muzzy elation and gentle sentimentality which a certain amount of beer or rye will bring on in a favorite bar. Saroyan takes you to the bar, and he creates for you there a world which is the way the world would

be if it conformed to the feelings instilled by drinks. In a word, he achieves the feat of making and keeping us boozy without the use of alcohol and purely by the stimulus of art." See Wilson, *The Boys in the Back Room*, p. 26.

36. Saroyan, introduction to *Don't Go Away Mad*, p. xii. Other comments on life as performance include: "We know it is not possible for any man to be altogether whole, so the only thing that can save him is style" (ibid., p. xi). Also: "Every man has one character to play, himself. That is no easy thing. Before a man can give a good performance of himself he must spend many years rehearsing. It takes the average man almost a whole lifetime to be able to learn to speak like himself, to walk like himself, and to laugh like himself. It takes many men many generations to be able to *be* themselves. And that of course may be part of the plan of the play: to give them time in which to rehearse, furnish them with the apparatus of themselves, turn them loose in the world, expose them to everything, and see if they will be able to perform themselves. If you get to be conscious, you've got to perform. One way or another, and no two ways about it." See "The Two Theaters," p. 210.

37. Saroyan, *Here Comes*, p. 42.

38. Saroyan, preface to *Razzle-Dazzle*, p. xvii.

39. Ibid., p. xxii. He showed great interest in creating a national theater which would perform versions of classic American literary works, such as *Leaves of Grass*, for popular audiences. Furthermore, for Saroyan vaudeville, baseball, and Walt Whitman were all part of the woof and weave of American consciousness, and he held them all to be equally important to the creation of a new art. He believed "American life is still a total stranger to American dramatic art." See preface to *My Heart's*, p. 17.

40. Saroyan, *Razzle-Dazzle*, p. xvii.

41. Saroyan, "The Two Theaters," p. 242.

42. This attitude toward drama is reminiscent of Maxim Gorky's who felt the characters in a play "must be *driven by their own inner impulses*, create the incidents and episodes—tragic or comic—and direct the course of the play, being permitted to act in harmony with their own contradictory natures, interests, and passions. The author, throughout, should act like a host at a party to which he has invited imaginary guests, without in any way interceding, no matter how one guest may worry or torment any other." See Gorky, *The Lower Depths*, edited with an introduction by Chwat, p. 18.

43. McCarthy, *Sights and Spectacles*, p. 50.

44. An earlier passage exhibits a close structural similarity to the later monologue, and shows that Saroyan's plays are more formally coherent than many commentators have supposed: "Now, I'm standing on the corner of Third and Market. I'm looking around. I'm figuring it out. There it is. Right in front of me. The whole city. The whole world. People going by. They're going somewhere. I don't know where, but they're going. I ain't going *anywhere*. Where the hell can you go? I'm figuring it out. All right, I'm a citizen. A fat guy bumps his stomach into the face of an old lady. They were in a hurry. Fat and old. *They bumped*. Boom. I don't know. It may mean war. *War*. Germany. England. Russia. I don't know for sure. . . . WAAAAAR" (pp. 43–44). Harry attempts to "figure it out," yet arrives finally at the realization that there is no

rationale, that both daily local events and the world situation are absurd. If the people on the street are going anywhere, it is to war: Harry *has* figured it out.

45. Saroyan, preface to *There's Something I Got to Tell You* in *Razzle-Dazzle*, p. 270.

46. According to Ihab Hassan, the absurd hero, "vicar of the Self in the new fiction, serves to mediate the contradictions of culture. His dominant aspect is that of the rebel-victim. He is an actor but also a sufferer. Almost always, he is an outsider, a demonic or sacrificial figure, anarchic, grotesque, innocent or clownish, wavering still between martyrdom and frenzied self-affirmation. Thus, the rebel-victim incarnates the eternal dialectic of the primary Yes and the everlasting No; and his function is to create those values whose absence in culture is the cause of his predicament and ours. His morality is largely existential, defined by his actions and even more by his passions, a self-made morality, full of ironies and ambiguities." See Hassan, *Contemporary American Literature: 1945–1972*, p. 25. Also see Galloway, *The Absurd Hero in American Fiction*.

CHAPTER 6

1. Floan, *William Saroyan*, p. 124. That this is a scenario-turned-novel is clear from the book's episodic structure. For response to the film, see Agee, *Agee on Film*, review of 20 March 1943, pp. 30–33.

2. Norman O. Brown has observed: "The goal of psychotherapy is psychic integration; but there is no integration of the separate individual. The individual is obtained by division; integration of the individual is a strictly self-contradictory enterprise, as becomes evident in the futile attempts of the therapists to define 'what we mean by mental health' in the individual person. The goal of 'individuation,' or of replacing the ego by the 'self,' deceitfully conceals the drastic break between the *principium individuationis* and the Dionysian, or drunken, principle of union, or communion, between man and man and between man and nature. The integration of the psyche is the integration of the human race, and the integration of the world with which we are inseparably connected. Only in one world can we be one." See Brown, *Love's Body*, pp. 86–87.

3. Saroyan, *The Human Comedy*, p. 283. Further references to this work appear in the text.

4. See Lawrence, *Studies in Classic American Literature* for a spirited critique of the "universalizing" aspect of Whitman: "Oh, Walter, Walter, what have you done with it? What have you done with yourself? With your own individual self? For it sounds as if it had all leaked out of you, leaked into the universe" (p. 173).

5. Saroyan, *Here Comes, There Goes, You Know Who*, pp. 235–37.

6. Another famous teenager in American fiction was often sickened by the insanity of the adult world: Holden Caulfield in J. D. Salinger's *The Catcher in the Rye*. Frederick L. Gwynn and Joseph L. Blotner have pointed out the "remarkable parallels between *The Catcher in the Rye* (1951) and William Saroyan's *The Human Comedy*

(1943), whose boy protagonist expresses something very close to Holden's fumbling conclusion: 'I don't know anybody to hate. Byfield knocked me down when I was running the low hurdles, but I can't hate *him*, even' (Stradlater and Maurice had knocked Holden down). There is an objectionable (for different reasons) boy named Ackley in each story, and there is a metrical and orthographical similarity between the names of the protagonists Holden Caulfield and Homer Macauley (and cf. 'Byfield'). Holden (aged 16) and Homer (who passes for 16) each has a sister and two brothers with one of the brothers dead or dying. At Pencey Prep, Holden gets into trouble in a history course studying the Egyptians; at Ithaca High School, Homer gets into trouble in a history course studying the Assyrians; and there is some curious nose-imagery in both sequences. The student comic at Pencey is named Edgar Marsalla; at Ithaca, Joe Terranova. Holden and Homer both undergo scenes with somebody else's mother and with prostitutes." See Gwynn and Blotner, *The Fiction of J. D. Salinger*, pp. 55–56. Stylistically, Homer and Holden both speak the same ingenuous, halting, tender, vulnerable language. According to Arthur and Barbara Gelb, during a weekend spent with Oona O'Neill and Charlie Chaplin, "Saroyan began talking about a book he was reading. It was J. D. Salinger's recently published first novel, *The Catcher in the Rye*, and Saroyan was full of enthusiasm for it. 'This kid is great,' he told Oona and Chaplin. 'He's got it!' " See Gelb, *O'Neill*, p. 851.

7. Keats, *Selected Letters*, p. 215.

8. Ibid., pp. 215–16.

9. This "linking" of Homer's purgative experiences also occurs when he visits the Bethel rooms (a bordello) in chapter 30: "For some reason which he couldn't quite understand, the messenger felt sick. It was the same kind of sickness he had felt in the house of the Mexican woman whose son had been killed in the War" (p. 217).

10. Burgum, "The Lonesome Young Man on the Flying Trapeze," p. 401.

11. Rahv, "William Saroyan: A Minority Report," p. 372.

12. Saroyan, *Here Comes*, p. 140.

13. Saroyan, *The Human Comedy*, revised version, p. 192.

14. Schulberg, "Saroyan: Ease and Unease on the Flying Trapeze," p. 90. For response to the novel see Kazin, "The Cymbolon," pp. 289–91, and Carpenter, "The Time of Saroyan's Life," pp. 88–96. Diana Trilling offers a critique of Saroyan's "sentimentalism" in the *Nation*, p. 698. She writes that "these are frightening and pious days, in which the more we recognize evil, the more we wish to be assured that virtue is at least as original as sin." In *Dear Baby* (1944), Saroyan "arrests the mature world at the child level—a comforting act of fantasy, but a debilitating one." Also see Smith, "Saroyan's War." Smith echoes the opinions of Rahv, Trilling, and Schulberg, considering Saroyan "a gifted teller of fairy tales, of parables, which have little relation to a world faced with continued revolution, starvation, and the threat of another war" (p. 8).

CHAPTER 7

1. Many of these plays were not offered to producers or publishers; the author frequently commented that Broadway was incapable of properly producing his plays. Much work remains to be done in collating and determining the publishability of work Saroyan withheld during his lifetime.

2. Cummings, *i: six nonlectures*, pp. 50, 24. Cummings was a writer Saroyan deeply admired. Both exalted (in true Romantic fashion) the value of the individual, original artist of genius; the quest for selfhood; and love, imagination, and childlike innocence. In a letter to Charles Norman, 27 August 1957, Saroyan wrote: "cummings is one of the truly great writers of our time for the reason that he is one of the truly great men of our time" (letter in Humanities Research Center, University of Texas at Austin; partially reprinted in Norman, *e. e. cummings: The Magic-maker*, p. 232). In a review of *six nonlectures*, Saroyan wrote: "What a book, what a poet, what a man, what a patriot, what a proud nation he is the first (and only?) citizen of—no, he didn't discover New Jersey, nuclear fission, or nucoa, just himself." See Saroyan, "There Ought to Be More," *Nation*, p. 178. Cummings has also provided an apt description of what Saroyan's plays attempt to communicate: "Ecstasy and anguish, being and becoming; the immortality of the creative imagination and the indomitability of the human spirit" (*six nonlectures*, p. 111).

3. Saroyan, preface to *Sam Ego's House*, p. 101.

4. In addition to the plays to be discussed in this chapter, seven other plays written during Saroyan's early dramatic period warrant brief mention: (1) *Love's Old Sweet Song* (1940)—a romantic comedy, a hymn to love, freedom, and spontaneity. For critical response, see Krutch, "Mr. Saroyan Again," p. 635; Young, *New Republic* 102 (3 June 1940): 760. (2) *Sweeney in the Trees* (1941)—a vaudevillelike foray into surrealism. Heinrich Straumann notes its similarity to "the experiments of the surrealists. It has no discernible action, no logic in its dialogue, no tangible connection between events, characters, and setting." See *American Literature in the Twentieth Century*, p. 202. Also see Nathan, "Saroyan: Whirling Dervish of Fresno," pp. 303–8. (3) *Hello Out There* (1942)—published, with the three plays discussed below, in *Razzle-Dazzle*, a collection of sixteen theater pieces of varying quality. The author wrote that they are not only "plays for the stage"; rather, "they could be suitable for every possible variation of playing: ballet, opera, circus, vaudeville, carnival, sideshow, burlesque, street-corner, radio, moving picture, church or parlor" (preface, p. x). *Hello Out There*, one of the author's finest plays, recounts the story of a young man falsely accused of rape who is held prisoner in a Texas jail; it powerfully explores the need for human contact, the terror of loneliness and isolation. His death at the end stands for the murder of innocence by a brutal world. See Krutch, "Play and No Play," p. 357. (4) *Talking to You* (1942)—Blackstone Boulevard, a black prizefighter, is murdered as he reaches out to help an enemy. See Burnham, "The Saroyan Theatre," pp. 471–72; Clurman, *Nation*, p. 460; Young, *New Republic* (31 August 1942), p. 257; Young, *New Republic* (12 October 1942), p. 466. (5) *Elmer and Lily: Notes for a Musical Revue* (1942)—like *Subway Circus*, the play shifts rapidly from one vaudeville routine to another. Its nine sections present a wide range of American characters:

a cop, an anarchist, a student and professor, six small children, a pair of lovers, among others. The author commented on the play in *Letters from 74 rue Taitbout*: "I also wrote an absurd play called *Elmer and Lily*, long before the Theatre of the Absurd came to be famous" (p. 110). (6) *The Ping-Pong Players* (1942)—another absurdist experiment. As a young man and woman bat a ping-pong ball to one another, their dialogue moves from the meaningless to the meaningful, mirroring the deft dance of the game. The play is also anthologized in Benedikt, *Theatre Experiment: An Anthology of American Plays*. Benedikt comments: "The comparison of the requirements of conventional existence with a meaningless ping-pong contest is curiously similar to the basic idea of a major 'Absurd' drama of some decades later: Arthur Adamov's *Ping-Pong*, whose final scene seems like a pessimist's paraphrase of the Saroyan work" (p. 29). (7) *Get Away Old Man*—explores the hostile relationship of Harry Bird, a young writer, and Patrick Hammer, a motion-picture mogul. The play unsuccessfully dramatizes the author's contention that "the shabbiness of the American film constitutes without a doubt the most appalling failure of an art form in the history of the world" (see preface to *A Special Announcement: A Radio Poem*, in *Razzle-Dazzle*, p. 183). The author's distaste for Hollywood can be traced back to comments in *The Trouble with Tigers*; see, for example, "The Legend-Makers." Also see comments on L. B. Mayer in *Letters from 74 rue Taitbout*, pp. 156–61, and in "One of the Great Mothers of the World" in *Sons Come and Go, Mothers Hang In Forever*, pp. 136–39.

5. Saroyan, note to *Across the Board on Tomorrow Morning*, in *The Beautiful People and Two Other Plays*, p. 214. Further references to this work appear in the text.

6. Saroyan, *Three Times Three*, p. 70.

7. Hartman, "Romanticism and 'Anti-Self-Consciousness,'" p. 47.

8. Saroyan, *The Beautiful People*, p. 13. Further references to this work appear in the text.

9. Brown, *Life against Death*, p. 63.

10. See Krutch, "God Is Love, or Why Worry?" pp. 537–38, for a fine review of the play. According to Krutch, Saroyan's "enchanted universe" is distinguished by the fact that "everything done in kindliness and good faith turns out for the best" (p. 537). Also see Vernon, "More on Saroyan," and Young, *New Republic* (12 May 1941), p. 664.

11. Later in his career, Saroyan responded to Eric Bentley's charge of "false optimism," a common criticism of *The Beautiful People* and his work in general: "I know the existence of it in my work is a serious fault. I seem to insist that people are good, that living is good, that decency is right, that good is not only achievable but inevitable—and there does not appear to be any justification for this. At least, not in the terms of my own work. In short, the idea is all right but I don't know how to put it over. This is criticism that I accept, for I know I have failed to put it over. It's worth putting over, it's worth trying to put over, it's necessary for me to try to put it over, but I just haven't learned how to do it yet." See preface to *Don't Go Away Mad and Two Other Plays*, p. 8.

12. The play was originally published as *Jim Dandy: A Play* (1941) and was revised

as *Jim Dandy: Fat Man in a Famine* (1947). This latter version begins Saroyan's second dramatic period; four plays from this phase are (1) *Don't Go Away Mad* (1949)—depicts characters waiting to die in a hospital. One of the patients, Georgie, expresses one of the play's themes—that the human race is dying from "starvation, homelessness, exhaustion, fear, anger, despair, nervousness, overwork, worry" (p. 33). The play is a prayer to God to "help us in our naked and blind loneliness" (p. 90). (2) *Sam Ego's House* (1949)—explores "the American dream: the dream of the national ego, of individual achievement, of material wealth, of social importance, of personal security" (p. 103). (3) *A Decent Birth, a Happy Funeral* (1949)—an antiwar play ending in spiritual rebirth. (The first three plays here are collected in *Don't Go Away Mad*.) (4) *The Slaughter of the Innocents* (1952)—a bleak depiction of the postwar world: "The whole world's haunted now. Haunted by the homeless dead, and haunted by the homeless living, too" (reprinted in *William Saroyan Reader*, p. 188). "Crookshank's Food and Drink" becomes a prison in which the innocent are judged guilty and summarily executed. Saroyan's later plays have fared poorly at the hands of many commentators. Gerald Weales has remarked: "There is still fine and funny invention in the late plays—the reading of the dictionary in *Don't Go Away Mad*, the moving of *Sam Ego's House*, the business with the mute milkman's son in *The Cave Dwellers*—but too often the eccentricity is demanding rather than endearing. More damning, all the late plays are weighed down with passages in which the characters philosophize pompously rather than amusingly, explain themselves instead of be themselves." See *American Drama since World War II*, pp. 95–96. Joseph Wood Krutch wrote: "That none of his subsequent plays have quite come off or achieved theatrical success may be due in part to a simple exhaustion of the vein but is probably due also to an increasing slackness in construction, and what seems to be the failure to move in any discernible direction. Mr. Saroyan's theory that one should write by simply letting one's self go may have been responsible for the spontaneity of the first two plays but is more certainly responsible for the diffuse meanderings of the others." See *American Drama since 1918*, pp. 323–24.

13. *Jim Dandy*, p. 3. Further references to this work appear in the text.

14. For additional commentary, see Balakian, *The Armenian-American Writer*, pp. 12–13, as well as "The World of William Saroyan" in *Critical Encounters: Literary Views and Reviews, 1953–1977*, pp. 162–76. See also Dolman, "Jim Dandy: Pioneer," pp. 71–75.

15. Introduction to *The Cave Dwellers*, p. 19. Further references to this work appear in the text. For review of the play, see Chapman, "Saroyan, Bless Him," pp. 25–26.

16. Also see "A Word on the Theatre in General," printed at the end of *The Cave Dwellers*: "Most people never suspect that they are in fact living an epic drama, or that they are characters in any number of small plays in an enormous one" (p. 184). He also remarks that politicians "are the leading actors in a play that has no playwright and no director" (p. 187).

17. Balakian, "The World of William Saroyan," p. 175.

18. Cf. *The Slaughter of the Innocents*: "There is no place to escape *to*, my dear

fellow. This is the world we live in. A home, restaurant, saloon, Court of Justice" (p. 208).

19. Saroyan published three dramatic volumes after 1958. (1) *Sam the Highest Jumper of Them All* (1961)—an improvisational antiwar comedy. See *Time*, "Back on the Trapeze," p. 47. (2) *Three New Dramatic Works: The Dogs, or the Paris Comedy; Chris Sick, or Happy New Year Anyway; Making Money, and Nineteen Other Very Short Plays* (1969)—contains twenty brief, experimental dramatic sketches, mostly with only two characters. It is likely that the author was referring to these plays when he wrote in a memoir: "Also, for twenty-one days I wrote a new short play every day, which is part of an exploration of drama I began ten or eleven years ago, a study of drama, especially in commonplace things." See *After Thirty Years*, p. 117. *The Paris Comedy* humorously explores the aftereffects of the author's divorce; George Hannaberry's son visits him and "a parody of boulevard comedy" ensues (Taylor, "The Imaginative Vision," p. 46). *Chris Sick* shows an ill Santa Claus who is "sick to death of the crazy human race" (p. 238). See Taylor, "The Imaginative Vision," pp. 46–47. (3) *Two Short Paris Summertime Plays of 1974: Assassinations and Jim, Sam and Anna* (1979)—two stark, funny, Beckettian plays on old age, senility, and sterility. *Assassinations* depicts an elderly, quarrelsome couple exchanging absurd banter against a backdrop of political assassination and turmoil; *Jim, Sam and Anna* concerns characters whose central need is alcohol; their conversation is obscene and cloacal. For commentary on Saroyan's unpublished plays, see Kouymjian, "Saroyan on the Armenians: *Haratch* and Other Unpublished Plays," pp. 3–13.

CHAPTER 8

1. *Mama I Love You* (1956) appeared originally in a shorter version in the *Saturday Evening Post*, and *Papa You're Crazy* (1957) was serialized in *Family Circle*. Both are light, playful novels dealing with marriage and family.

2. It might be argued that the fatherhood theme surfaces in embryonic form in *The Human Comedy* (1943) and *The Adventures of Wesley Jackson* (1946). As we have seen in *The Human Comedy*, the father of the Macauley family is dead, so Homer must grow toward symbolic fatherhood in his older brother Marcus's absence. In *The Adventures of Wesley Jackson*, the author's poorly received antiwar novel, the narrative follows a nineteen-year-old army private through love, marriage, and a child, but stops before dealing with the complexities of family life and Wesley's role as a father. For reaction to the novel, see Wilson, "William Saroyan and His Darling Old Providence," in *Classics and Commercials*, pp. 327–30, and Trilling, *Reviewing the Forties*, pp. 177–79.

3. Saroyan married Carol Marcus in 1943. They were divorced in 1949, remarried in 1951, and finally separated in 1952. The psychological dynamics of Saroyan's family life are the subject of his son Aram's book *Last Rites: The Death of William Saroyan* (1982). Aram provides an illuminating and moving account of Saroyan's inability to overcome the trauma of his early life and hence become a father himself.

Also see Gold, "A Twenty-Year Talk with Saroyan," in *A Walk on the West Side: California on the Brink*, for comments on Saroyan and his marriage novels, pp. 109–16.

4. Krickel, "Cozzens and Saroyan: A Look at Two Reputations," p. 292.

5. Saroyan, *Here Comes*, p. 270. At least two of Saroyan's contemporaries also thought deeply about the fatherhood question. Thomas Wolfe wrote: "The deepest search in life, it seemed to me, the thing that in one way or another was central to all living, was man's search for a father, not merely the father of his flesh, not merely the lost father of his youth, but the image of a strength and wisdom external to his need and superior to his hunger, to which the belief and power of his own life could be united." See *The Story of a Novel*, p. 39. And Henry Miller speculated: "Why is the Oedipal so dominant in Lawrence's work—not only in Lawrence but in so many men of genius, noticeably the moderns? Because it is the central theme in the artist's conflict with life, the root-pattern of his struggle to emancipate himself, to raise himself to fatherhood—that is, to restore the great religious motive of life. . . . This search for God and fatherhood is only the expression of the search for one's true self." See *The World of Lawrence*, pp. 133, 134.

6. Saroyan, *The Laughing Matter*, p. 164. Further references to this work appear in the text.

7. The phrase is Budd Schulberg's in "Saroyan: Ease and Unease on the Flying Trapeze," p. 91.

8. Rosenfeld, "On One Built for Two," p. 27.

9. See "The Assyrian" in *The Assyrian and Other Stories*, pp. 3–77. The story is clearly autobiographical; Saroyan has commented in *Letters from 74 rue Taitbout* concerning his trip to Lisbon in May 1949: "I was forty-one years old at the time, and in a bad way, having just left my wife, small son, and smaller daughter, for reasons that were grave enough to make my leaving imperative. I was in a state of spiritual shock. . . . I was suddenly without home, continuity, and meaning. I was without myself, my own ghost. I was not only lost, I was cut down. I was in fact dead" (pp. 28–29). For critical reaction to "The Assyrian," see Peden, "Saroyan with Trumpet and Tremolo," pp. 15–16.

10. "The Cocktail Party" in *The Assyrian*, p. 251. Andrew Loring is also afflicted with the alienation that plagues Saroyan's fathers: "No man knows himself. No man knows another," he says late in the story (p. 265).

11. See Fisher, "What Ever Happened to Saroyan?" p. 338.

12. *Papa You're Crazy*, pp. 63–64.

13. *Boys and Girls Together* (1963) and *One Day in the Afternoon of the World* (1964) are variations on the fatherhood theme. They repeat, without significantly enlarging, the author's earlier preoccupations. *Boys and Girls Together* is a taut, bare, emotionally violent book, which plunges the reader directly into the combative atmosphere of a failing marriage. *One Day in the Afternoon of the World* is retrospective, portraying a divorced and solitary Yep Moscatian in New York City, visiting his ex-wife and children and brooding about the past. For reaction to *One Day*, see Maurer, "Still a Good Trapeze Act," p. 16.

14. Saroyan, *Rock Wagram*, p. 14. Further references to this work appear in the text. Similar sentiments are expressed throughout the author's novels. In *Boys and Girls Together*, the protagonist "wanted the mother of his kids to be all right, so he was taking his time" choosing a wife (p. 73). In *Mama I Love You*, the children's mother tells them: "A family is everything. It always has been" (pp. 155–56). For the Armenian critical response to *Rock Wagram* and the fatherhood issue, see Sarkisian, "Rock Wagram: A Psycho-Social Character Study," pp. 61–68.

15. Hart, *The Oxford Companion to American Literature*, p. 365. Saroyan corresponded with Hemingway early in his career. The two writers' tense relationship is discussed in Baker, *Ernest Hemingway: A Life Story*; see pp. 268–69, 388–89, 442, 612–13. Saroyan himself wrote in *Sons Come and Go*: "In 1935 when Ernest Hemingway attacked me in that ever-fat magazine, *Esquire*, because in one of my earliest stories I had kidded him about his fascination with bull-fights, I wrote directly to him instead of replying in the pages of the magazine, for money, and free publicity for everybody. . . . As far as I was concerned, Ernest Hemingway was ever after a very literary (and sensitive) soul, not a fearless hero of the physical world" (pp. 17–18).

16. Bowen, "In Spite of the Words," p. 19.

17. Ibid.

18. *One Day in the Afternoon of the World*, p. 241. The remark is made by Yep Moscatian's Armenian friend Zak, whose vital, energetic approach to life is in stark contrast to Yep's middle-aged inertia.

CHAPTER 9

1. Saroyan, *The Bicycle Rider in Beverly Hills*, p. 28.

2. Ten volumes appeared over a twenty-seven-year period: *The Bicycle Rider in Beverly Hills* (1952); *Here Comes, There Goes, You Know Who* (1961); *Not Dying: An Autobiographical Interlude* (1963); *After Thirty Years: The Daring Young Man on the Flying Trapeze* (1964); *Letters from 74 rue Taitbout or Don't Go but if You Must Say Hello to Everybody* (1969); *Days of Life and Death and Escape to the Moon* (1970); *Places Where I've Done Time* (1972); *Sons Come and Go, Mothers Hang In Forever* (1976); *Chance Meetings* (1978); *Obituaries* (1979). Although I do not treat each of these books individually (formally, they are mostly spontaneous, associative recollections), excerpts from all appear as commentary throughout my text.

3. Saroyan, *Here Comes*, p. 197.

4. Amiel also appears in a list Saroyan composed for the dedication to *The William Saroyan Reader*: "To the writers who impelled me to write" (p. v).

5. Saroyan, *Inhale and Exhale*, "Poem, Story, Novel," pp. 289–90.

6. Ibid., p. 290.

7. Saroyan, *Days of Life and Death and Escape to the Moon*, p. 29. Further references to this work appear in the text.

8. Saroyan, *Not Dying*, p. 15. Further references to this work appear in the text.

9. Saroyan, *Sons Come and Go, Mothers Hang In Forever*, p. 207.

10. Saroyan, *Obituaries*, p. 153. Further references to this work appear in the text.

11. For critical reaction to the memoirs, see the following: *The Bicycle Rider*—Rosenfeld, "On One Built for Two," pp. 27–28; *Not Dying*—"Not Dying," *Times Literary Supplement*, 5 May 1966, p. 385; *Letters from 74 rue Taitbout*—Kherdian, "Middle Aged Man on the Flying Trapeze," p. 46; *Days of Life and Death*—Hoagland, "He Can't Forget He Was Young Once," p. 9, and Taylor, "The Imaginative Vision," p. 46; *Places Where I've Done Time*—Collier, "I'm the Same, but Different," pp. 3, 16, and Sourian, "Places Where I've Done Time," pp. 3, 14; *Obituaries*—Lingeman, "A Variety of Curtain Calls," pp. 7, 49.

12. Saroyan, *Chris Sick, or Happy New Year Anyway*, p. 200.

13. Saroyan, *Three Plays*, "The One Easy Lesson," p. 145.

14. Saroyan, *Here Comes*, p. 164. Cf. Tristan Tzara's definition of Dada: "Dada est une quantité de vie en transformation transparente et sans effort et giratoire." See Middleton, " 'Bolshevism in Art': Dada and Politics," in *Bolshevism in Art and Other Expository Essays*, p. 58. Saroyan was himself an American Surrealist-Dadaist in his emphasis on the fluidity and continual "giratory transformation[s]" of our inner selves.

15. Gordon, *The Mind and Art of Henry Miller*, p. 88.

16. Saroyan, "Greenland" in "Three Stories" from *The Daring Young Man on the Flying Trapeze*, p. 218.

17. For criticism of Saroyan's "stylistic irresponsibility," see Schorer, "Technique as Discovery," pp. 82–83.

18. Fromm, *Disobedience and Other Essays*, p. 14.

19. Saroyan, preface to *Opera, Opera* in *Razzle-Dazzle*, p. 118.

20. Saroyan, *Here Comes*, p. 166.

BIBLIOGRAPHY

MANUSCRIPT SOURCES

Austin, Texas. The Humanities Research Center. The William Saroyan Collection
contains a number of unpublished letters, the playscript of *An Imaginary
Character Named Saroyan*, galley proofs, and other miscellaneous items.

Fresno, California. Both the Fresno County Free Library and the library of California
State University, Fresno, contain extensive Saroyan holdings: his complete works,
translations into foreign languages, magazine and newspaper articles. Virtually
everything connected with the author's life and work can be found in these two
locations.

BOOKS AND ARTICLES BY WILLIAM SAROYAN

For a full list of Saroyan's publications up to 1964, see David Kherdian, *A
Bibliography of William Saroyan*. A complete Saroyan bibliography has not yet
been published.

Saroyan, William. *The Adventures of Wesley Jackson*. New York: Harcourt, Brace,
1946.

———. *After Thirty Years: The Daring Young Man on the Flying Trapeze*. New York:
Harcourt, Brace and World, 1964.

———. *The Assyrian and Other Stories*. New York: Harcourt, Brace, 1950.

———. *The Beautiful People and Two Other Plays*. New York: Harcourt, Brace,
1941.

———. *The Bicycle Rider in Beverly Hills*. New York: Scribner, 1952.

———. *Boys and Girls Together*. New York: Harcourt, Brace and World, 1963.

———. *Chance Meetings*. New York: Norton, 1978.

———. *The Daring Young Man on the Flying Trapeze*. New York: Random House,
1934.

———. *Days of Life and Death and Escape to the Moon*. New York: Dial, 1970.

———. *Dear Baby*. New York: Harcourt, Brace, 1944.

———. *Don't Go Away Mad and Two Other Plays: Sam Ego's House; A Decent
Birth, a Happy Funeral*. New York: Harcourt, Brace, 1949.

————. *Get Away Old Man*. New York: Harcourt, Brace, 1944.

————. *Here Comes, There Goes, You Know Who*. New York: Simon and Schuster, 1962.

————. *The Human Comedy*. New York: Harcourt, Brace, 1943.

————. *The Human Comedy*, newly revised by the author. New York: Dell, 1980 (paperback reprint).

————. *Inhale and Exhale*. New York: Random House, 1936.

————. "Ionesco." *Theatre Arts* 42 (July 1958): 26–27.

————. *I Used to Believe I Had Forever, Now I'm Not So Sure*. New York: Cowles, 1968.

————. *Jim Dandy: Fat Man in a Famine*. New York: Harcourt, Brace, 1947.

————. *The Laughing Matter*. New York: Doubleday, 1953.

————. *Letters from 74 rue Taitbout or Don't Go but if You Must Say Hello to Everybody*. New York: World Publishing, 1969.

————. *Little Children*. New York: Harcourt, Brace, 1937.

————. *Love, Here Is My Hat and Other Short Romances*. New York: Modern Age, 1938.

————. *Mama I Love You*. Boston: Little, Brown, 1956.

————. *Obituaries*. Berkeley: Creative Arts, 1979.

————. *One Day in the Afternoon of the World*. New York: Harcourt, Brace and World, 1964.

————. *Papa You're Crazy*. Boston: Little, Brown, 1957.

————. *Peace, It's Wonderful*. New York: Modern Age, 1939.

————. *Places Where I've Done Time*. New York: Dell, 1972.

————. *Razzle-Dazzle*. New York: Harcourt, Brace, 1942.

————. *Rock Wagram*. New York: Doubleday, 1951.

————. *Sam the Highest Jumper of Them All or the London Comedy*. London: Faber and Faber, 1961.

————. *Saroyan's Fables*. New York: Harcourt, Brace, 1941.

————. *The Slaughter of the Innocents*. Reprinted in *The William Saroyan Reader*, pp. 168–210.

————. *Sons Come and Go, Mothers Hang In Forever*. New York: McGraw-Hill, 1976.

————. "There Ought to Be More." *Nation* 178 (27 February 1954): 177–78.

————. *Three New Dramatic Works: The Dogs, or the Paris Comedy; Chris Sick, or Happy New Year Anyway; Making Money, and Nineteen Other Very Short Plays*. New York: Phaedra, 1969.

————. *Three Plays: My Heart's in the Highlands; The Time of Your Life; Love's Old Sweet Song*. New York: Harcourt, Brace, 1940.

————. *Three Times Three*. Los Angeles: Conference Press, 1936.

————. *The Time of Your Life*. New York: Harcourt, Brace, 1939.

————. *The Time of Your Life and Other Plays*. New York: Bantam, 1967 (paperback reprint).

———. *Tracy's Tiger*. New York: Doubleday, 1951.

———. *The Trouble with Tigers*. New York: Harcourt, Brace, 1938.

———. *Two Short Paris Summertime Plays of 1974: Assassinations and Jim, Sam and Anna*. California State University Northridge Libraries: Santa Susana Press, 1979.

———. *The Whole Voyald and Other Stories*. Boston: Little, Brown, 1956.

———. *Why Abstract?* Hilaire Hiler, Henry Miller, and William Saroyan. New York: New Directions, 1945.

———. *The William Saroyan Reader*. New York: Braziller, 1958.

BOOKS

Aaron, Daniel. *Writers on the Left*. New York: Oxford University Press, 1977.

Agee, James. *Agee on Film*. New York: McDowell, Obolensky, 1958.

Anderson, Sherwood. *Winesburg, Ohio*. Introduction by Malcolm Cowley. New York: Viking, 1960. Reprint, Harmondsworth: Penguin, 1976.

Arnold, Matthew. *The Poems*. Edited by Kenneth Allott. London: Longman's, 1965.

Asselineau, Roger. *The Transcendentalist Constant in American Literature*. New York: New York University Press, 1980.

Axelrod, Stephen Gould. *Robert Lowell: Life and Art*. Princeton: Princeton University Press, 1978.

Baker, Carlos. *Ernest Hemingway: A Life Story*. New York: Scribner, 1969.

Balakian, Nona. *The Armenian-American Writer*. New York: Armenian General Benevolent Union, 1958.

———. *Critical Encounters: Literary Views and Reviews, 1953–1977*. Indianapolis: Bobbs-Merrill, 1978.

Beckett, Samuel. *Proust*. New York: Grove Press, 1957.

———. *Waiting for Godot*. New York: Grove Press, 1954.

Benedikt, Michael, ed. *Theatre Experiment: An Anthology of American Plays*. New York: Doubleday, 1967.

Boyajian, Zabelle C., ed. *Armenian Legends and Poems*. New York: Columbia University Press, 1958.

Brown, Norman O. *Life against Death: The Psycho-Analytical Meaning of History*. Middletown: Wesleyan University Press, 1959.

———. *Love's Body*. New York: Vintage, 1968.

Coe, Richard N. *Eugene Ionesco*. New York: Grove Press, 1961.

Cox, James M. *Mark Twain: The Fate of Humor*. Princeton: Princeton University Press, 1966.

Cummings, E. E. *i: six nonlectures*. Cambridge: Harvard University Press, 1953.

Esslin, Martin. *The Theatre of the Absurd*. New York: Doubleday, 1961.

Floan, Howard. *William Saroyan*. New York: Twayne, 1966.

French, Warren. *J. D. Salinger*. New Haven: College and University Press, 1963.

Fromm, Erich. *Disobedience and Other Essays*. New York: Seabury, 1981.

Galloway, David. *The Absurd Hero in American Fiction*. Austin: University of Texas Press, 1966.

Geismar, Maxwell. *Writers in Crisis: The American Novel, 1925–1940*. New York: Hill and Wang, 1966.

Gelb, Arthur, and Gelb, Barbara. *O'Neill*. New York: Harper and Row, 1973.

Gold, Herbert. *A Walk on the West Side: California on the Brink*. New York: Arbor House, 1981.

Gordon, William A. *The Mind and Art of Henry Miller*. Baton Rouge: Louisiana State University Press, 1967.

Gorky, Maxim. *The Lower Depths*. Edited with an introduction by Jacques Chwat. New York: Avon, 1974.

Gwynn, Frederick L., and Blotner, Joseph L. *The Fiction of J. D. Salinger*. Pittsburgh: University of Pittsburgh Press, 1970.

Hart, James D. *The Oxford Companion to American Literature*. New York: Oxford University Press, 1965.

Hassan, Ihab. *Contemporary American Literature, 1945–1972: An Introduction*. New York: Ungar, 1973.

Kazin, Alfred. *Starting Out in the Thirties*. New York: Vintage, 1980.

Keats, John. *Selected Letters*. Edited by Lionel Trilling. New York: Farrar, Straus and Young, 1951.

Kerouac, Jack. *On the Road*. New York: Signet, 1957.

Kherdian, David. *A Bibliography of William Saroyan: 1934–1964*. San Francisco: Roger Beacham, 1965.

Krutch, Joseph Wood. *The American Drama since 1918*. New York: Braziller, 1957.

Lawrence, D. H. *Studies in Classic American Literature*. Reprint. Harmondsworth: Penguin Books, 1978.

Lipton, Lawrence. *The Holy Barbarians*. New York: Messner, 1959.

McCarthy, Mary. *Sights and Spectacles*. New York: Farrar, Straus and Cudahy, 1956.

Martin, Jay. *Always Merry and Bright: The Life of Henry Miller*. Harmondsworth: Penguin Books, 1980.

Middleton, Christopher. *Bolshevism in Art and Other Expository Essays*. Manchester: Carcanet New Press, 1978.

Miller, Henry. *Sexus*. New York: Grove Press, 1965.

————. *Stand Still like the Hummingbird*. New York: New Directions, 1962.

————. *Sunday after the War*. Norfolk: New Directions, 1944.

————. *Tropic of Cancer*. New York: Grove Press, 1961.

————. *The World of Lawrence: A Passionate Appreciation*. Edited with an introduction and notes by Evelyn J. Hinz and John J. Teunissen. Santa Barbara: Capra Press, 1980.

Norman, Charles. *e. e. cummings: The Magic-Maker*. Boston: Little, Brown, 1972.

Oates, Joyce Carol. *New Heaven, New Earth: The Visionary Experience in Literature*. New York: Fawcett, 1974.

O'Neill, Eugene. *The Iceman Cometh*. New York: Vintage, 1957.

Salinger, J. D. *The Catcher in the Rye*. New York: Little, Brown, 1951.

Saroyan, Aram. *Last Rites: The Death of William Saroyan*. New York: Morrow, 1982.

Stevens, Wallace. *The Necessary Angel: Essays on Reality and the Imagination*. New York: Vintage, 1951.

Straumann, Heinrich. *American Literature in the Twentieth Century*. New York: Harper and Row, 1965.

Ternon, Yves. *The Armenians: History of a Genocide*. Delmar, N.Y.: Caravan Books, 1981.

Trilling, Diana. *Reviewing the Forties*. New York: Harcourt, Brace Jovanovich, 1978.

Twain, Mark. *The Adventures of Tom Sawyer*. New York: Harper, 1923.

Wagner, Linda W. *Dos Passos: Artist as American*. Austin: University of Texas Press, 1979.

Weales, Gerald C. *American Drama since World War II*. New York: Harcourt, Brace and World, 1962.

Whitman, Walt. *Complete Poetry and Selected Prose*. Edited with an introduction and glossary by James E. Miller, Jr. Boston: Houghton Mifflin, 1959.

Wilson, Edmund. *The Boys in the Back Room: Notes on California Novelists*. San Francisco: Colt Press, 1941.

————. *Classics and Commercials*. New York: Farrar, Straus, 1950.

————. *Letters on Literature and Politics: 1912–1972*. Edited by Elena Wilson. New York: Farrar, Straus and Giroux, 1977.

Wolfe, Thomas. *Look Homeward, Angel*. New York: Scribner, 1929.

————. *The Story of a Novel*. New York: Scribner, 1936.

ARTICLES

"Back on the Trapeze." *Time*, 28 March 1960, p. 47.

Bowen, Elizabeth. "In Spite of the Words." *New Republic* 123 (9 March 1953): 18–19.

Burgum, Edwin B. "The Lonesome Young Man on the Flying Trapeze." *Virginia Quarterly Review* 20 (Summer 1944): 392–403.

Burnham, David. "The Saroyan Theatre." *Commonweal* 36 (4 November 1942): 471–72.

Canby, Henry Seidel. "Armenian Picaresque." *Saturday Review of Literature* 23 (28 December 1940): 5.

Carpenter, Frederic I. "The Time of Saroyan's Life." *Pacific Spectator* 1 (Winter 1947): 88–96.

Chapman, John. "Saroyan, Bless Him." *Theatre Arts* 42 (December 1958): 25–26.

Clurman, Harold. *Nation* 193 (2 December 1961): 460.

Collier, Peter. "I'm the Same, but Different." *New York Times Book Review*, 2 April 1972, pp. 3, 16.

Dobrée, Bonamy. *Spectator*, 28 March 1941, p. 354.

Dolman, John, Jr. "Jim Dandy: Pioneer." *Quarterly Journal of Speech* 30 (February 1944): 71–75.

Everson, William. "Dionysus and the Beat Generation and Four Letters on the Archetype." In *The Beats: Essays in Criticism*, edited by Lee Bartlett. Jefferson, N.C.: McFarland, 1981.

Fisher, William J. "What Ever Happened to Saroyan?" *College English* 16 (March 1955): 336–40.

Hartman, Geoffrey H. "Romanticism and 'Anti-Self-Consciousness.'" In *Romanticism and Consciousness*, edited by Harold Bloom. New York: Norton, 1970.

Hoagland, Edward. "He Can't Forget He Was Young Once." *Book World*, 5 July 1970, p. 9.

Kazin, Alfred. "The Cymbolon." *New Republic* 108 (1 March 1943): 289–91.

Kerouac, Jack. Interviewed by Ted Berrigan in *Writers at Work: The Paris Review Interviews, Fourth Series*, edited by George Plimpton. Harmondsworth: Penguin, 1977.

Kherdian, David. "Middle Aged Man on the Flying Trapeze." *Ararat* 10 (Summer 1969): 45–46.

Kouymjian, Dickran. "Saroyan on the Armenians: *Haratch* and Other Unpublished Plays." In *William Saroyan Festival Program*. Fresno, California State University, 1981.

Krickel, Edward. "Cozzens and Saroyan: A Look at Two Reputations." *Georgia Review* 24 (Fall 1970): 281–96.

Krutch, Joseph Wood. "God Is Love, or Why Worry?" *Nation* 152 (3 May 1941): 537–38.

―――. "Mr. Saroyan Again." *Nation* 150 (18 May 1940): 635.

―――. "Play and No Play." *Nation* 155 (10 October 1942): 357.

Lingeman, Richard R. "A Variety of Curtain Calls." *New York Times Book Review*, 20 May 1979, pp. 7, 49.

Maurer, Robert. "Still a Good Trapeze Act." *New York Herald Tribune, Book Week*, 21 June 1964, p. 16.

Nathan, George Jean. "Saroyan: Whirling Dervish of Fresno." *American Mercury* 51 (November 1940): 303–8.

"Not Dying: An Autobiographical Interlude." *Times Literary Supplement*, 5 May 1966, p. 385.

Peden, William. "Saroyan with Trumpet and Tremolo." *Saturday Review of Literature* 33 (4 February 1950): 15–16.

Rahv, Philip. "William Saroyan: A Minority Report." *American Mercury* 57 (September 1943): 371–77.

Rosenfeld, Isaac. "On One Built for Two." *New Republic* 127 (8 December 1952): 27–28.

Sarkisian, Levon. "Rock Wagram: A Psycho-Social Character Study." *Armenian Review* 11 (April 1959): 61–68.

Schorer, Mark. "Technique as Discovery." In *The Theory of the Novel*, edited by Philip Stevick. New York: Free Press, 1967.

Schulberg, Budd. "Saroyan: Ease and Unease on the Flying Trapeze." *Esquire*, October 1960, pp. 85–91.

Shinn, Thelma. "William Saroyan: Romantic Existentialist." *Modern Drama* 15 (September 1972): 185–94.

Singer, Felix. "Saroyan at 57: The Daring Young Man after the Fall." *Trace* 60 (Spring 1960): 2–5.

Smith, Harrison. "Saroyan's War." *Saturday Review of Literature* 29 (1 June 1946): 7–8.

Sourian, Peter. "Places Where I've Done Time." *New York Times Book Review*, 2 April 1972, pp. 3, 14.

Taylor, Robert. "The Imaginative Vision." *Ararat* 11 (Summer 1970): 46–47.

Trilling, Diana. *Nation* 159 (2 December 1944): 697.

Vernon, Granville. "More on Saroyan." *Commonweal* 35 (16 May 1941): 85–86.

Young, Stark. *New Republic* 102 (3 June 1940): 760.

———. *New Republic* 104 (12 May 1941): 664.

———. *New Republic* 107 (31 August 1942): 257.

———. *New Republic* 107 (12 October 1942): 466.

INDEX

Aaron, Daniel, 151 (n. 3)

Across the Board on Tomorrow Morning, 71, 75, 118–22

Adamov, Arthur, xi, 86, 165 (n. 4)

Adventures of Wesley Jackson, The, 12, 42, 155 (n. 12), 167 (n. 2)

After Thirty Years, 153 (n. 18), 157 (n. 6), 167 (n. 19)

Alcohol: in Saroyan's work, 52, 86–87, 121, 125, 160–61 (n. 35); attitude toward, 156–57 (n. 3)

Amiel, Henri-Frederic, 143–44, 152 (n. 9)

"Am I Your World?" 41

"Among the Lost," 23

Anderson, Sherwood, xi, 18–21, 37, 153 (nn. 11, 14, 18)

"Anderson the Storyteller." *See* Miller, Henry

"And Man," 19–20, 22

"Antranik of Armenia," 47–48

"Armenian and the Armenian, The," 48–49

Armenians: genocide, 4, 24–25, 47, 48, 49; immigration to California, 4–5; prejudice against, 5;oral tradition in literature, 33, 63, 157 (ch. 4, n. 4); Armenian theme in *My Heart's in the Highlands*, 77–78; Armenian and Near Eastern allegory, 118; fatherhood in Armenian community, 132–33; Armenian literary tradition and connection to American culture, 156 (n. 2); Armenian Christianity, 135–36, 156 (n. 2)

Arnold, Matthew, 8

Asbarez, The, 49, 136

Assassinations and Jim, Sam and Anna. See *Two Short Paris Summertime Plays of 1974*

Asselineau, Roger, 20

"Assyrian, The," 6, 133, 154 (n. 22), 168 (n. 9)

Assyrian and Other Stories, The, 133, 134, 168 (n. 9)

Atlantic Monthly, 62, 79

"At Sundown," 37–38

Axelrod, Stephen, 8

Babbitt, Irving, 147

"Baby," 31–33

Bach, J. S., 22

Balakian, Nona, 129

Balzac, Honoré de, 24

Beat Generation, 32–33, 146–47, 155 (nn. 12, 13)

Beautiful People, The, 7, 71, 75, 117, 122–27, 132, 156 (n. 3), 165 (n. 11)

Beckett, Samuel, xi, 9, 26, 35, 82, 83, 86, 92, 117, 120, 151 (n. 18), 155 (n. 17), 167 (n. 19)

Benedikt, Michael, 165 (n. 4)

Bentley, Eric, 165 (n. 11)

"Best and Worst People and Things of 1938, The," 45

Bicycle Rider in Beverly Hills, The, 156–57 (n. 3), 157 (n. 4)
"Big Valley Vineyard," 23
Blake, William, 22, 100, 113, 134, 148
Blotner, Joseph L., 162–63 (n. 6)
Booster, 158 (n. 7)
Bowen, Elizabeth, 139, 140
Boys and Girls Together, 131, 168 (n. 13), 169 (n. 14)
Boys in the Back Room, The (Wilson), 53, 160–61 (n. 35)
Brautigan, Richard, 147
Broadway, xi, 71–72, 98, 117, 164 (n. 1)
Brown, Norman O., 123–24, 162 (n. 2)
Burgum, Edwin B., 113
Burnett, Whit and Hallie, 152 (n. 8)
Burns, Robert, 77, 125; "To a Mouse," 125

Caldwell, Erskine, 18
Camus, Albert, 96
Canby, Henry Seidel, 55
Cantatrice Chauve, La, 84
Capote, Truman, 152 (n. 8)
Catcher in the Rye, The (Salinger), 162–63 (n. 6)
Cave Dwellers, The, 75, 117, 119, 129–30, 166 (nn. 12, 16)
Cézanne, Paul, 22
Chance Meetings, 83
Chaplin, Charlie, 16, 163 (n. 6)
Childhood: as theme in Saroyan's work, 26, 117, chap. 4 passim; child as visionary in *Human Comedy*, 100–101; in *Beautiful People*, 123–24; in marriage novels, 131, 139–40; 157 (n. 1)
Christianity, 108, 116, 146, 156 (n. 2). *See also* Jesus
"Citizens of the Third Grade," 44, 61–62
"Cocktail Party, The," 133, 168 (n. 10)
Coe, Richard N., 86
Collier, Peter, 3

"Common Prayer," 22–23
Communism, 14, 43, 50, 52
Cook, Joe, 90
"Countryman, How Do You Like America?" 54–56
Cowley, Malcolm, 14, 18
Cox, James, 63
Cummings, e. e., 14, 117, 164 (n. 2)
"Curtain: Happy Ending," 160 (n. 22)

Dadaism, 170 (n. 14)
Daring Young Man on the Flying Trapeze, The, 3, 12, 14, 18, 20, 22, 23, 24, 26, 28, 31, 53, 98, 153 (n. 18)
"Daring Young Man on the Flying Trapeze, The," 12–13, 15–17
David of Sassoun, 156 (n. 2)
Days of Life and Death and Escape to the Moon, 7, 143–44, 145, 157 (n. 7)
Dear Baby, 163 (n. 14)
"Death of Children, The," 49
Decent Birth, a Happy Funeral, A, 166 (n. 12)
Dobrée, Bonamy, 70
Donne, John, 99
Don't Go Away Mad, 165 (n. 11), 166 (n. 12)
Dos Passos, John, 14, 153 (n. 18), 160 (n. 22)
Dostoyevsky, Fyodor, 15, 16, 17
Dowling, Eddie, 160 (n. 33)
Durante, Jimmy, 90
Durrell, Lawrence, 158 (n. 7)

"Earth, Day, Night, Self, The," 20
Eliot, T. S., 3, 8, 17, 41
Elmer and Lily: Notes for a Musical Revue, 164–65 (n. 4)
Esquire, 169, (n. 15)
Esslin, Martin, 82
Etranger, L' (Camus), 96
"Everything," 44

Existentialism, 4, 9–10, 83, 117, 129, 135, 162 (n. 46); in *The Time of Your Life*, 85–86, 96

"Family of Three, A," 155 (n. 22)
Faulkner, William, 18
Fields, W. C., 90
"Finlandia," 29–30, 34
Fisher, William, 10
Fitzgerald, F. Scott, 14
"Five Ripe Pears," 59
Flaubert, Gustave, 17
Floan, Howard, 153 (n. 14)
French, Warren, 152 (n. 8)
Fresno, Ca., 5, 6, 14, 21, 23, 40, 47, 59, 77, 136, 140, 143
Freud, Sigmund, 123
Friganza, Trixie, 159 (n. 19)
Fromm, Erich, 148

Geismar, Maxwell, 13
"Genius, The," 156 (n. 22)
Get Away Old Man, 165 (n. 4)
Gide, André, 36
Glass Menagerie, The (Williams), 119
"Good Old Goody Goody Godot," 151 (n. 18)
Gordon, William A., 146
Gorky, Maxim, 161 (n. 42)
"Greatest Country in the World, The," 45
Gwynn, Frederick L., 162–63 (n. 6)

Hart, James D., 20–21, 137
Hartman, Geoffrey H., 121
Hassan, Ihab, 162 (n. 46)
Hello Out There, 118, 164 (n. 4)
Hemingway, Ernest, 14, 18, 120, 137–38, 140, 144, 153 (n. 18), 158 (n. 1), 169 (n. 15)
Henry, O., 18
Heraclitus, 33
Herald, Leo Serabian, 156 (n. 2)

Here Comes, There Goes, You Know Who, 5, 132, 142
Hiler, Hilaire, 158 (n. 7)
Hoagland, Edward, 9
Hölderlin, Friedrich, 79
Hollywood, 98, 112. *See also* Saroyan, William
"Home of the Human Race, The," 154 (n. 8)
Homer, 99
"How and Why to Be a Playwright," 80, 159 (n. 19)
Human Comedy, The, 3, 12, 26, 42, 60, 62, 127, 132, 156 (n. 3), 162 (n. 6), 167 (n. 2)
Hungerers, The, 30

Ibsen, Henrik, 80–81
Iceman Cometh, The (O'Neill), 86, 160 (n. 33)
Inhale and Exhale, 12, 13, 28, 29, 37, 42, 47, 59, 143
"International Harvester," 13
"International Song of the Machine Gun, The," 156 (n. 24)
Ionesco, Eugene, xi, 9, 83, 84, 86
I Used to Believe I Had Forever, 151 (n. 18)

James, Henry, 3, 8
"Japanese Are Coming, The," 156 (n. 24)
Jesus, 135, 143
Jim Dandy: Fat Man in a Famine, 118, 127–29
"Jim Pemberton and His Boy Trigger," 155–56 (n. 22)
"Journey and the Dream, The," 45–46
Joyce, James, 3, 99

Kazin, Alfred, 13–14
Keats, John, 107–9
Kerouac, Jack, 8, 33, 147, 155 (n. 12)
Khorenatsi, Moses, 156 (n. 2)

Krapp's Last Tape, 9
Krickel, Edward, 131
Krutch, Joseph Wood, 165 (n. 10), 166 (n. 12)

Last Rites (Aram Saroyan), 155 (n. 13), 167 (n. 3)
Laughing Matter, The, 131, 133, 134, 137–41
Lawrence, D. H., 9, 43, 54, 131, 148, 162 (n. 4), 168 (n. 5)
Leaves of Grass (Whitman), 8, 21, 161 (n. 39)
Leavis, F. R., 23
"Legend Makers, The," 165 (n. 4)
Leno, Dan, 82
Letters from 74 rue Taitbout, 154 (n. 22), 165 (n. 4), 168 (n. 9)
Lewis, Sinclair, 18
"Life and Letters," 34
Lipton, Lawrence, 33
Little Children, 12, 28, 54
"Little Dog Laughed to See Such Sport, The," 42, 156 (n. 23)
"Little Moral Tales from the Old Country," 157 (n. 4)
"Living and the Dead, The," 50–54, 135, 156–57 (n. 3)
Look Homeward, Angel (Wolfe), 22
Love, Here Is My Hat, 12, 28, 38, 41
Love's Old Sweet Song, 117, 125, 164 (n. 4)

McCarthy, Mary, 90–91, 95
Magritte, René, 145
Mailer, Norman, 152 (n. 8), 154 (n. 9)
Mama I Love You, 167 (n. 1), 169 (n. 14)
Mann, Thomas, 9
"Man with the Heart in the Highlands, The," 76–77, 158 (n. 7)
Marcus, Carol, 167 (n. 3)
Martin, Jay, 158 (n. 7)
Maupassant, Guy de, 17

Mayer, L. B., 165 (n. 4)
Mencken, H. L., 18, 26, 158 (n. 1)
Metro-Goldwyn-Mayer, 98
Miller, Henry, xi, 8, 9, 13, 18, 24, 54, 73–74, 142, 148, 158 (n. 7), 168 (n. 5); "Anderson the Storyteller," 158 (n. 7)
"Missouri Waltz, The," 93
"Monumental Arena, The," 45
Muni, Paul, 145
Music: importance of, in Saroyan's work, 29–30; in *The Time of Your Life*, 93–94; in *The Human Comedy*, 106; in *The Beautiful People*, 123
"My Armenia," 156 (n. 2)
My Heart's in the Highlands, xi, 11, 71, 75, 76–80, 98, 113, 122, 124, 127, 132, 157 (n. 1)
My Name Is Aram, 12, 50, 56, 57, 59, 62–70, 112, 132; "madness," 67; style, 68, 69–70. Stories: "The Summer of the Beautiful White Horse," 63, 64; "Nice Old-Fashioned Romance, A," 64; "The Circus," 64; "One of Our Future Poets, You Might Say," 64, 65; "The Presbyterian Choir Singers," 64; "The Pomegranate Trees," 64, 67; "The Three Swimmers and the Grocer from Yale," 65; "Locomotive 38, the Ojibway," 65–66, 68–69; "The Poor and Burning Arab," 67, 69–70; "The Journey to Hanford," 67; "The Fifty Yard Dash," 67–68; "A Word to Scoffers," 70
"Myself upon the Earth," 21–22, 23–24

Narekatsi, Grigor, 156 (n. 2)
Nathan, George Jean, 71, 160 (n. 33)
Necessary Angel, The, 7
New Bearings in English Poetry, 23
New Critics, 3
New York City, 119, 168 (n. 13)
Nietzsche, Friedrich, 13, 30, 73
Nin, Anaïs, 158 (n. 7)

"Nine Million Years Ago," 155 (n. 15)
"Noonday Dark Enfolding Texas,"
    41–42, 53
Not Dying, ix, 144, 145

Oates, Joyce Carol, 155 (n. 17)
Obituaries, x, 8, 77, 145, 153 (nn. 11, 16)
O'Brien, Edward J., 62
Odyssey, The, 99–100
"O. K. Baby, This Is the World," 44
O'Malley, Frank Ward, 82
One Day in the Afternoon of the World,
    131, 141, 168 (n. 13)
O'Neill, Eugene, 86, 138, 160 (n. 33)
O'Neill, Oona, 163 (n. 6)
"One of the Great Mothers of the World,"
    165 (n. 4)
"On Reality," 73
On the Road (Kerouac), 155 (n. 12)
Our Town (Wilder), 119
Overland Monthly, 152 (n. 8)

Papa You're Crazy, 167 (n. 1)
Parodie, La (Adamov), 86
Peace, It's Wonderful, 12, 14, 28, 36, 41,
    45, 56
"People, Yes and Then Again No, The,"
    44
Ping-Pong (Adamov), 165 (n. 4)
Ping-Pong Players, The, 165 (n. 4)
Pinter, Harold, 86
Pirandello, Luigi, 119
Places Where I've Done Time, 159–60
    (n. 20)
Play: concept of, in Saroyan's work,
    72–74
Poe, Edgar Allan, 18
"Poem, Story, Novel," 143
"Poet at Home, The," 132
"Poor Heart, The," 41
Proletarian writers, 3, 13–14
Proust, Marcel, 17
Proust (Beckett), 35

"Psalms," 154 (n. 8)
"Public Speech," 43

"Quarter, Half, Three-Quarter, and
    Whole Notes," 35

Rahv, Philip, 3, 8, 114, 147
Razzle-Dazzle, 29, 160 (n. 22), 164 (n. 4)
"Resurrection of a Life," 59–60
Rilke, Rainer Maria, 29
Rock Wagram, 131, 133, 134–37, 141
Romantic tradition, 9, 10, 33–34, 36,
    85–86, 147, 164 (n. 2)
Rosenfeld, Isaac, 133
Rousseau and Romanticism (Babbitt),
    147

Sacre du Printemps, Le (Stravinsky), 36
Salinger, J. D., 147, 162–63 (n. 6)
Sam Ego's House, 118, 166 (n. 12)
Sam the Highest Jumper of Them All, ix,
    167 (n. 19)
San Francisco, 16, 17, 23, 51, 84, 93, 97,
    147, 160 (n. 33)
San Joaquin Valley, 5, 54, 56, 59, 60, 62,
    66, 67, 99, 104, 140, 155 (n. 12)
Saroyan, Aram, 155 (n. 13), 167 (n. 3)
Saroyan, Armenak, 4
Saroyan, Takoohi, 4
Saroyan, William: unpublished work, x,
    164 (n. 1), 167 (n. 19); last years, x,
    143–45; critical reception of work,
    3–4, 9–10, 53, 157 (n. 6); charged with
    "false optimism" and "escapism,"
    3–4, 114, 127, 147, 163 (n. 14), 165
    (n. 11); birth and childhood, 5, 6, 14;
    self-division, "madness," 6–7, 83, 96,
    135–36, 142–43, 157 (n. 7); conception
    of art and artist, 7–8, 28, 29–37, 154
    (n. 8), 159 (n. 15), 160 (n. 22); and art
    and imagination, 7, 72–75; writing as
    therapy, 7, 131; as "redskin," 8–9,
    53–54; effect of Depression on, 12–14,

30, 31–32, 147; compared with writers of the thirties, 13–14; belief in brotherhood of man, 14, 25–26, 43, 44, 48, 79, 98–99, 116, 131, 145; and World War II, 14, 29, 31, 42–45, 78, 84, 91, 92, chap. 6 passim, 119, 133, 147–48; as prose-poet, 16, 22–23, 32–33, 153 (n. 18); freedom of style of, 18–20, 53; and epiphanic narrative, 20, 21, 101; writer as rebel, 24, 153–54 (n. 21); vaudeville, 31, 80–83, 89, 90–92, 159 (n. 19), 160 (n. 22), 161 (n. 39), 164 (n. 4); search for love, 21, 37–41, 134–36, 141; and American theater, 89–90, 161 (n. 39); vision of life as performance, 87–88, 119, 129, 161 (n. 36), 166 (n. 16); fatherhood, chap. 8 passim, 168 (n. 5); marriage and divorce, 131, 168 (n. 9); shift in style, 133; as journal keeper, 142–45; on "essay-story," 153 (n. 16); distaste for Hollywood, 165 (n. 4). See also Alcohol; Armenians; Beat Generation; Childhood; Existentialism; Music; Play; Surrealism; Theatre of the Absurd; Time

Saroyan's Fables, 157 (n. 4)
Sartre, Jean-Paul, 88
Saturday Evening Post, 69, 123
Sawyer, Tom 63, 64
Schorer, Mark, 147
Schulberg, Budd, 116
"Seventeen," 21, 40
"Seventy Thousand Assyrians," 18, 25–26
Shakespeare, William, 17, 79, 128, 130, 141
Shaw, George Bernard, xi, 72, 158 (n. 1)
"Shepherd's Daughter, The," 23, 50
Shinn, Thelma, 9
Sibelius, Jean, 29, 30, 31, 37
Sinclair, Upton, 145
six nonlectures (cummings), 117, 164 (n. 2)
Slaughter of the Innocents, The, 118, 138, 166 (n. 12), 166–67 (n. 18)

Smith, Harrison, 163 (n. 14)
Sons Come and Go, Mothers Hang In Forever, 144, 165 (n. 4), 169 (n. 15)
"Sophistication" (Anderson), 19
Sourian, Peter, 151 (n. 9)
Special Announcement: A Radio Poem, A, 165 (n. 4)
Steinbeck, John, 14, 18, 145
Stevens, Wallace, 7
Story Magazine, 152 (n. 1)
Straumann, Heinrich, 74, 164 (n. 4)
Stravinsky, Igor, 36
Subway Circus, 81, 159–60 (n. 20), 164 (n. 4)
Surrealism, xi, 16, 71, 74, 81, 120, 122, 147, 164 (n. 4), 170 (n. 14)
Sweeney in the Trees, 164 (n. 4)
"Sweet Singer of Omsk, The," 36

Talking to You, 80, 164 (n. 4)
Tate, Allen, 8
Tempest, The (Shakespeare), 128, 130
Theatre of the Absurd: connections with, xi, 82–84, 147, 165 (n. 4); time in, 86–87; Joe in *The Time of Your Life* as absurd hero, 95–96, 162 (n. 46)
"There Ought to Be More," 164 (n. 2)
Thoreau, Henry David, 8, 21
Three New Dramatic Works, 167 (n. 19)
Three Times Three, 12, 23, 28, 31, 34, 43, 50, 73, 76, 121, 154 (n. 9)
"Tiger, The," 44
Time: as concept in Saroyan's work, 34; in *The Time of Your Life*, 86–87, 92, 154 (n. 4)
Time of Your Life, The, xi, 4, 6, 34, 37, 54, 62, 71, 75, 80–97, 98, 115, 117, 118, 119, 124, 125, 127, 133, 137, 156 (n. 3), 160 (nn. 33, 35)
Tolstoy, Leo, 41
Tracy's Tiger, 134
"Trains, The," 38–40
Trilling, Diana, 147, 163 (n. 14)
Tropic of Cancer (Miller), 13, 24
Trouble with Tigers, The, 12, 28, 44, 61

Tucker, Sophie, 159 (n. 19)
Twain, Mark, 17, 63, 64, 96, 158 (n. 1)
Two Short Paris Summertime Plays of 1974: Assassinations and Jim, Sam and Anna, 117, 167 (n. 19)
"Two Theaters, The," 72, 161 (n. 36)
Tzara, Tristan, 170 (n. 14)

Ulysses (Joyce), 99

Wagner, Linda W., 160 (n. 22)
Waiting for Godot (Beckett), 82, 84, 86, 92, 151–52 (n. 18)
"War," 26
"War, The," 156 (n. 24)
"War and Peace," 40
War and Peace (Tolstoy), 41
"War in Spain, The," 45
"Warm, Quiet Valley of Home, The," 56
Weales, Gerald, 166 (n. 12)
Whitman, Walt, xi, 8, 9, 16, 21, 22, 33, 36, 53, 73, 99, 126, 142, 146, 147, 153 (n. 18), 161 (n. 39), 162 (n. 4)

Whole Voyald and Other Stories, The, 152 (n. 10), 154 (n. 8)
Why Abstract? 158 (n. 7), 159 (n. 15)
"Why I Write," 154 (n. 8)
Wilder, Thornton, 119
Williams, Tennessee, 119, 152 (n. 8)
Williams, William Carlos, 9
Wilson, Edmund, 14, 53, 153 (n. 18), 158 (n. 1), 160–61 (n. 35)
Winesburg, Ohio (Anderson), 18–21
Wolfe, Thomas, xi, 9, 18, 22, 39, 133, 142, 168 (n. 5)
"Word on the Theatre in General, A," 166 (n. 16)
Wordsworth, William, 61, 118
"World and the Theatre, The," 30–31
"Writer's Declaration, A," 152 (n. 10)

Yeats, William Butler, 40
"You're Breaking My Heart," 156 (n. 22)

Zen, 32, 96